**DO NOT REMOVE
CARDS FROM POCKET**

MOZAMBIQUE: A HISTORY

MOZAMBIQUE: A HISTORY

THOMAS H. HENRIKSEN

REX COLLINGS LONDON *with* DAVID PHILIP CAPE TOWN 1978

First published in Great Britain by Rex Collings Ltd
69 Marylebone High Street, London W1

© Thomas H. Henriksen 1978

ISBN 0860 360172

Typesetting by Malvern Typesetting Services
Printed in Great Britain by
The Camelot Press, Southampton

CONTENTS

PREFACE

The following pages represent a modest first attempt at a history of Mozambique from before the advent of the Portuguese until after its independence from Lisbon's colonialism. The study is not definitive. The period before 1900 is covered in a less detailed manner than the years afterwards. Emphasis in Part One has been placed on a general discussion of the invasions into Mozambique and their effects. An appendix gives an overview of some of Mozambique's larger ethnic groups. Part Two focuses on the recent past and in some respects the most neglected segment of Mozambican history.

For most of the first part I have relied on the efforts of others; the mistakes, however, are mine. One noteworthy addition to the literature which arrived too late for inclusion is Edward A. Alper's *Ivory and Slaves*. The second part presents some new material on the evolution of Mozambican nationalism and offers a discussion of the war for independence which led to the formation of the FRELIMO government.

Grateful thanks are due the Research Foundation of the State University of New York whose financial assistance facilitated my research. Many of those deserving mention will by necessity of space remain unsung here. But two require mention: Mrs Mary Turner who was tireless in tracking down information, and Mrs Hortense Graves who typed and retyped many of these pages.

My wife, Margaret Mary, who helped in a myriad of ways in the preparation as well as Heather and Mungo, made it all possible. Together they kept up my spirits on many a dark day.

Woods Mills, NY   T. H. H.

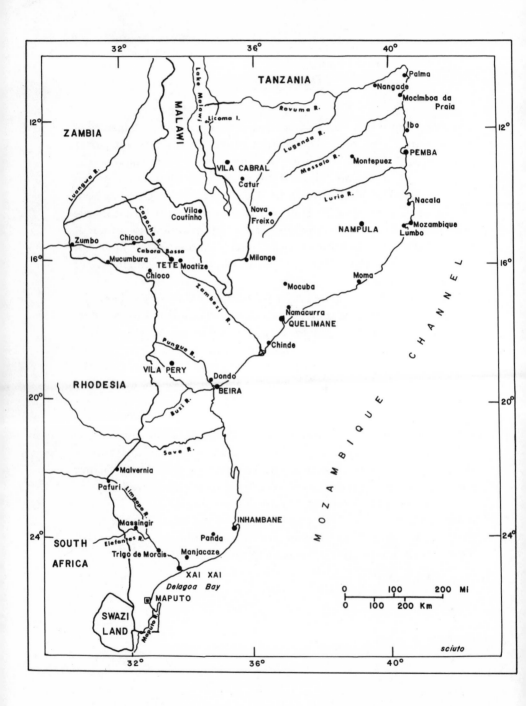

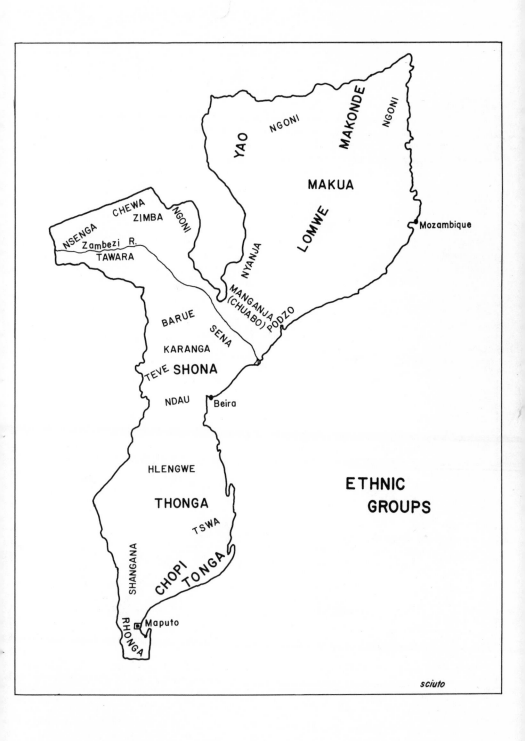

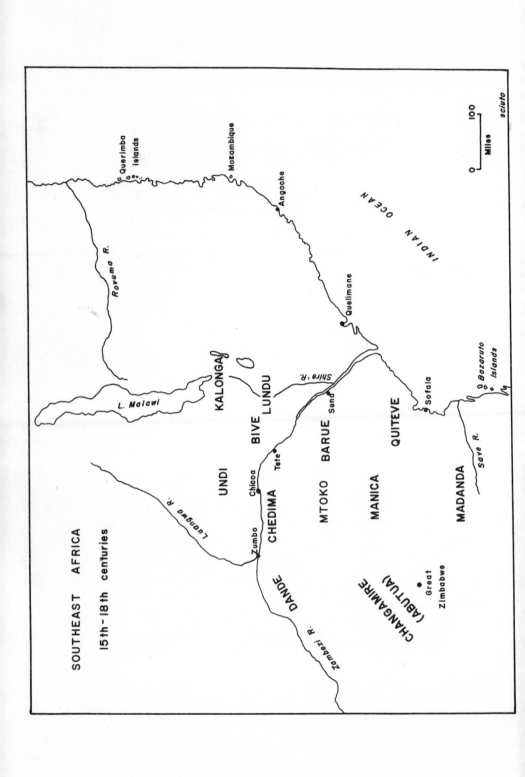

SOUTHEAST AFRICA

15th–18th centuries

Rovuma R.

Querimba Islands

Mozambique

Angoche

INDIAN OCEAN

Quelimane

L. Malawi

KALONGA

LUNDU

BIVE

Shire R.

Luangwa R.

UNDI

Chicoa

Tete

Zumbo

CHEDIMA

DANDE

Zambezi R.

MTOKO

BARUE

Send

Sofala

Bazaruto Islands

QUITEVE

MANICA

MADANDA

Save R.

CHANGAMIRE
(ABUTUA)

Great
Zimbabwe

0   100
Miles

sciuto

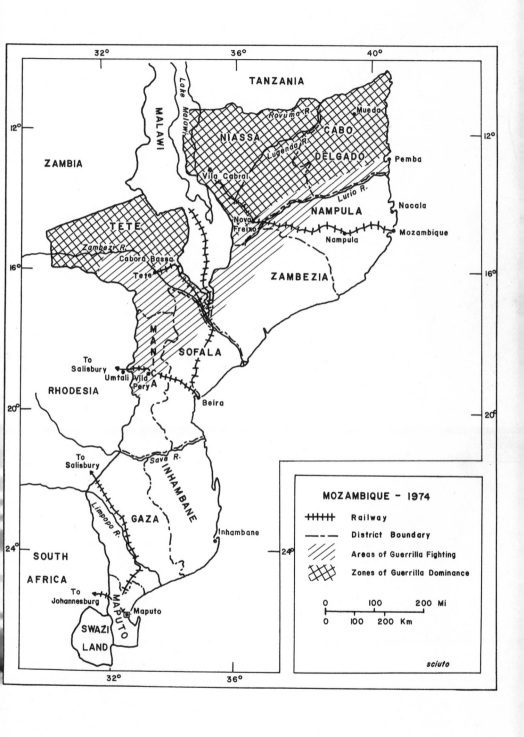

MOZAMBIQUE – 1974

┼┼┼┼┼	Railway
– · – · –	District Boundary
/////	Areas of Guerrilla Fighting
⧄⧄⧄	Zones of Guerrilla Dominance

0   100   200 Mi

0   100   200 Km

sciuto

PART ONE

Invasions and Empires

Over untold centuries the African continental block was uplifted from primordial seas and was eroded by relentless weathering to form an enormous complex of interior plateaus surrounded by coastal lowlands. On the tablelands ancient rains cut rivers that still course for thousands of miles before plunging over the continental edge and flowing through the low veld to the seas. The hot, humid coastline, although usually less well endowed with natural resources, first encountered seaborne foreigners and its rivers furthered commercial and military penetration beyond the shore.

Mozambique, a generally low-lying land on the Indian Ocean littoral, became one of the continent's earliest passageways between the high hinterland and the sea. Its rivers, particularly the Zambezi, sustained the trade of landlocked peoples with the outside world for over 500 years before the coming of the Europeans. In modern times, railways and roads across its territory have served the same purpose.

History placed Mozambique at least on the periphery of two of the world's important expansive movements. Bantu-speaking peoples had swept down east central Africa just before the Portuguese, the vanguard of European expansion, touched Mozambique on the way eastward. Their encounter acted to check each other's domination of this frontier land between African invader and Portuguese intruder. From prehistoric times no single African or foreign cultural, political, or economic influence ever rolled from land or sea to change suddenly or control all of Mozambique until the third decade of the twentieth century when Portugal established administrative posts in most areas. Yet the turbulence of contending groups was to make Mozambique one of the least peaceful regions of Africa and was to give it a legacy of war, slavery, misery, and turmoil that has lived on into the present. The first part of this work deals with aspects of the conflict between contending expansionist states. Deep in the core of Mozambique's history lie the twin facts that it is a gateway to the interior and that the inhabitants are the products of the cross-currents of its tumultuous past.

1

EARLY INHABITANTS AND EMPIRES

Mozambique's history began long before Vasco de Gama's ships cast anchor in the harbour of Mozambique Island in 1498. Human activity originated in the times of Africa's unrecorded beginnings, when history and myth mingled in easy harmony. Our knowledge of the early dwellers in Mozambique derives from a few scattered archaeological remains and the oral literature of later inhabitants. Here, as in much of Africa, the reconstruction of human history in the millennia prior to Portuguese contact and settlement is in an embryonic stage.

The aboriginal inhabitants of Mozambique were probably distant predecessors of today's Khoisan in south-western Africa.* In nomadic bands of a few dozen people, these Stone Age folk hunted and gathered food instead of herding and cultivating. Although only collecting fruits and eggs, snaring animals, and fashioning stone implements, they developed high artistic abilities. Some of the remarkable rock paintings of daily exploits and animals found in other parts of Africa and attributed to the San (Bushmen) have also been located in Mozambique. Without centralized organization, the roaming bands, of which the family was the basic unit, fell easy prey to more politically developed invaders. Small in stature and armed with wooden spears and arrows, they were subdued or fled southward under pressure of the Bantu-speaking newcomers.

Three or four groups of Iron Age agriculturists settled in Mozambique, displacing the ancestors of the Khoisan and co-existing with each other as many as 800 years before the Shona established themselves in east central Africa.* Pushed presumably by population pressures and ecological changes in the Sahara region, the initial Bantu migrations started from the savanna lands

---

* Khoisan is a composite term denoting both of the closely-related groups Khoikhoi (Hottentots) and San (Bushmen). The names Bushmen and Hottentot are considered not only unscientific but also pejorative to modern students of Stone Age people.

* See Appendix I for a discussion of the people of contemporary Mozambique.

near the present-day Nigeria-Cameroun frontier at about the time
of Christ's birth. Advance elements possibly reached the Indian
Ocean coast of Mozambique between AD 100 and 400. Before the
Karanga domination of the Zambezi River, the Zimba, Tawara,
Tonga, and Sena settled on its banks. They cultivated the soil and
made iron tools in furnaces with artificial draughts. As sedentary
agriculturists, the immigrants had evolved a more sophisticated
political and social organization than their Stone Age predecessors.
Each group was divided into independent chieftaincies which
weakened the political cohesion of the whole folk. Tonga and Sena
oral traditions recount that they were ruled by a *mambo*, or land
chief, who possessed important ritual powers and political functions
in his chieftaincy. But the Sena differed from the other riverine sub-
states in not having a royal clan, which suggests to one scholar that
the groups originated from 'a migration of unrelated peoples rather
than a movement of a conquering elite or homogeneous ethnic
group'.[1] In sum, the first Bantu immigrants lived in numerous,
small chieftaincies without establishing powerful centralized states.
Despite their disunity and weakness, they were never submerged by
the Karanga's military or cultural dominance.

The early Bantu inhabitants of Mozambique to the south of the
Zambezi first experienced the power of an organized military state
not from the Portuguese but from the Karanga, a sub-group of the
Shona people. At the end of the first millennium, the Karanga ventured into the present-day state of Rhodesia from Zaire as successors
to earlier Iron Age groups and built a court, Zimbabwe, 17 miles
south-east of the modern city of Fort Victoria. Judging by the
archaeological remains, they carried with them skills in cattle
breeding, hoe-agriculture, and metal work superior to but not al-
together different from those of their predecessors. Like many new
arrivals, they benefited from the cultural attainments of the indigenous inhabitants but went on to surpass them, to make distinct
contributions of their own. In political organization, religious con-
cepts, and stone masonry the Karanga represented an advanced
culture and in time dominated the original settlers.[2]

The site of Zimbabwe had served as the headquarters of previous
inhabitants but it was the Karanga who erected the huge stone
structures that are viewed with awe and admiration today.
Wrapped in frequent mists and rains from the Indian Ocean, the
hills are lushly green the whole year. In contrast to the surrounding

dry country, this spot seemed blessed for rain-making. Located on top of a hill and looking over its valley, the fortress-like structures baffled nineteenth-century European observers, who posited non-African creators of Zimbabwe and the smaller stone-works in other parts of central Africa. They concocted far-fetched explanations attributing the constructions to King Solomon, the Phoenicians, or others of the ancient Mediterranean world. These flights of poetic fancy that led some Europeans to surmise that Zimbabwe has a non-African origin have no basis in fact. Less biased scholars point to medieval Karanga stone masons.[3]

Made from unmortared granite and sandstone blocks, the citadel-like network of walls, walkways, and steps on the high ground has been called the 'acropolis' because to the first European observers it resembled the ancient Athenian construction. In certain ways, it resembles more closely the architecture of ancient Crete. Inside, the Karanga spirit mediums held sacred ceremonies to worship through their *mhondoro*-spirits to the supreme being of Mwari. In the valley below an 800-foot wall, 30 feet high and 15 thick, surrounds a conical tower and smaller stone encirclements. Termed the Great Enclosure, it housed the royal palace and perhaps the chambers of the wives and ministers of the court. The Karanga evolved a court with a complex hierarchy of officials and dignitaries who performed the functions of an organized state. Outside, the peasants lived in the traditional but more comfortable mud and wattle kraals; they farmed small plots, and raised cattle, pigs, and goats. But neither pastoral nor agricultural pursuits alone accounted for all the Karanga economic activity.

Mining and trade formed an important part of the Karanga economic system, but the wealth from long-distance trade only enriched the small oligarchy around the rulers. Profiting from the commercial and metallurgical skills of earlier residents, the Karanga organized trade and mining on an expanded scale. Ivory, long the staple commodity of east African trade with Muslim merchants, was hunted in larger quantities. In the Zimbabwe area there were rich deposits of gold, iron, and copper, which pre-Karanga peoples had begun to exploit. They fashioned tools and weapons from iron, and arm and leg bracelets from copper.

Relying on the earlier inhabitants to do the actual mining, the Karanga rulers increased their mining and trading operations in the pursuit of greater wealth.[4] João dos Santos, a Dominican who

spent over a decade at Sofala and on the Querimba Islands towards
the end of the sixteenth and early seventeenth centuries, left an
account of two mining methods in his *Ethiopia Oriental*. His
chronicle of African and Portuguese life is remarkably unmarred by
the usual Protuguese bombast so characteristic of reports then and
later. He wrote that one means of gold extraction was 'to make deep
holes and mines, from which they [Shona miners] dig into the earth
and along the veins which are known to them, and bring out the
gold, washing it in bowls'.[5] Most of the mines were less than 50 feet
deep but two that have been excavated reached 150 feet. As the
walls often caved in, this method of mining was dangerous but
widely used. Another way was to recover 'nuggets and pieces of
gold' from alluvial deposits in streams.

Under Karanga entrepreneurial acumen, the exchange of goods
widened. Inland Muslim merchants, who had traded on the
Mozambique coast since about AD 1000, increased their commerce
in the interior. In return for gold, copper, and ivory, they brought
by caravan to Zimbabwe considerable amounts of Asian cloth,
Indian beads, and even some Chinese procelain. As a result Zimbabwe's material culture flourished: the building of magnificent
stone-works took place; the artistic quality of its elegant pottery and
soapstone carvings improved; and the production of copper,
bronze, and gold ornaments increased. The power of the ruling
Karanga grew.

Before its military expansion into Mozambique, Karanga society
underwent other far-reaching changes. The Rozwi, a reigning
dynasty, ruled the Karanga polity by a more or less feudal system,
with vassal chiefs governing territorial fiefs and paying tribute and
homage to them. They were probably a group whose rise to power
was determined by their political shrewdness and control over ritual
functions. Rozwi leadership apparently faltered at the start of the
fifteenth century, and a particular group or family, the Mbire, re-
vitalized it or perhaps established a new Rozwi dynasty. The Mbire's
origins and methods of gaining dominance are shrouded in uncertainty. They may have been recent arrivals from Zaire or a
vigorous branch of the Rozwi themselves. What seems clear is that
under their rule the Karanga entered into a military expansionist
phase.

THE MWENE MUTAPA EMPIRE

The history of south central Africa is replete with the formation and collapse of major kingdoms dating from the fourteenth century. Among the most famous, because of the richness of Portuguese documentation, is the Mwene Mutapa empire. Like its sister states, it passed rapidly through periods of expansion and splendour to decline. It shared similar features with them: dependence on the ruler's personality for direction, succession disputes, rebellious provinces, and a desire for trade with ocean-going merchants. But unlike most kingdoms, its history cannot be disassociated from a long and intimate European connection. It was only about half a century before the Portuguese reached the south-eastern corner of Africa, that the Karanga began their expansion into central Mozambique.

Nyatsimba Mutota of the Mbire line launched before the middle of the fifteenth century a campaign of conquest to carve out a vast empire. Mutota marched at the head of a formidable army of Karanga warriors, who were called Korekore, or locusts, for the way they devoured the countryside. Because of the devastation wrought by his army, Mutota received the praise name of Mwene Mutapa, or master pillager. War was in the nature of human society; the Karanga, unlike the twentieth-century Portuguese, felt no need to justify their conquest. Power was the ultimate morality.

While Mutota pursued a policy of territorial acquisition in all directions of the compass, his sharpest thrust was north-eastwards and then down the Zambezi Valley into Mozambique. He extended Rozwi suzerainty to the mid-section of Mozambique's portion of the valley before his death in battle. His son Matope, spurred on by the same grand vision as his father, carried on the military expansion for thirty years more, from about 1450 to 1480. Matope, who assumed his father's praise name of Mwene Mutapa, moved his court, or *dzimbabwe*, northwards to about 60 miles south-east of the town of Zumbo on the Zambezi. He pushed Rozwi domination towards the Indian Ocean and southwards to the Save River to occupy or influence a large slice of what became Mozambique. Viewed as a peripheral region, the lower reaches of the Zambezi were ruled indirectly by the Karanga. It appears that only lands in Mozambique north of the Zambezi and south of the Save escaped the direct impact of the Mwene Mutapa's sway.[6]

Not until the Ngoni invasions of the 1830s did Mozambique again experience an intrusion of the same magnitude as the Karanga conquests. Most ethnic groups from the Zambezi to the Limpopo Rivers still preserve some traditions and oral accounts related to the Karanga empire. North of the Zambezi the country fell under the control of the Malawi kingdoms. In the south and along the coast, the small societies remained independent and distinct from each other, much as had their northern sister states before the Karanga arrival. But in the central zone of Mozambique the Mutapa's sovereignty was acknowledged shortly before Vasco de Gama's guns fired at Mozambique Island. For a brief period, the Mwene Mutapa empire arched high in a golden curve before descending to fragmentation. By the time the first Portuguese journeyed inland in the early years of the sixteenth century, the empire had undergone a secessionist crisis and a civil war, and had entered a period of disintegration.

As is usually the case with the rise or decline of early empires, the causes are not easily discernible from our distance. The reasons for the Rozwi's imperial policy have been usually diagnosed as the pressure of overpopulation and the critical shortage of salt. A further explanation is attributed to the behind-the-scenes intriguing of Muslim traders, whose numbers were exaggeratedly reported by fearful Portuguese to be 'more than ten thousand Moors'.[7] This argument holds that up-country Muslim merchants planted the idea of empire in the mind of the Mutapa so as to quicken their trade. That Muslim merchants profited from Rozwi campaigns by expanding trade networks and by selling cloth to the Mutapa for his army's pay and that Arab entrepôts at Sofala, Quelimane, and Sena escaped harm during the conquest are produced as evidence of Muslim persuasion.[8]

No doubt Muslim traders did benefit from the protective umbrella of the Rozwi empire. Muslim commercial activities spread into newly subjugated territory in the baggage trains of the Karanga army. Yet Mutota and Matope were unlikely to have been induced to conquer huge tracts at the instigation of avaricious merchants plotting at the court. It seems more likely, as Professor Alpers suggests, that Mutota and Matope, both of whom possessed outstanding military genius, were driven by vaulting ambition to subdue the surrounding peoples. The desire to widen trade with Muslim merchants along the Zambezi may have contributed to their expansionist designs. Their organizational abilities and martial deeds militate against an interpretation of passive natures triggered into action by the schemes of others.[9] Together they inaugurated one of the most significant Bantu states that endured for centuries, albeit in a weakened form, against African rivals and foreign intruders.

The Mwene Mutapa empire, as Arab and Portuguese called it, had been achieved by war and enforced surrender without battle. In reality, it was a loose confederation of states under Rozwi chiefs rather than a unified empire. At the apogee, it comprised several provinces. Mwene Mutapa's new *dzimbabwe* was located in Dande province of the empire in what is today northern Rhodesia, near the Kadzi River. South of Dande were the long-established provinces of Mbire, under the governorship of Togwa, and Guruhuswa province encircling the former court of Zimbabwe, which was handed over to Changa for his outstanding services to Matope. To the east in present-day Mozambique, south of the Zambezi and stretching right to the Indian Ocean, lay the newly subjugated provinces of Chidima, Manica, Barue, Quiteve, and Madanda, which were placed in control of Matope's sons, relatives, generals, counsellors, and favourites.[10] Variants existed among the Tonga and Tarawa on the Zambezi near the town of Tete, where the Mwene Mutapa left the traditional chiefly lineages in power as his governors. The appointed chiefs of several provinces became hereditary with the reluctance or inability of the central authority to remove them, and they or their descendants displayed independence. This far-flung empire defied cohesion. Its governance depended on the strength and political sagacity of the paramount *mambo,* for the empire contained many ingredients of fragmentation: an unwieldy size, poor communications, ambitious governors, ethnic and cultural diversity, an onerous tribute, and the blandishments and appeals from rival powers. Mutota and Matope were politically astute and sought means to check the centrifugal pulls, but their successors failed to halt the break-up.

Against the fissiparous pressures in the empire, the Rozwi pitted several centripetal buttresses and used various devices to keep it together. Some were symbolic; others were more substantive. One symbolic ritual to strengthen central authority was the annual re-kindling of local fires from the royal flame at the Mutapa's *dzimbabwe.* Each year provincial fires were extinguished, and vassal leaders sent messengers to return with a torch lighted from the royal flame as an expression of allegiance. On the death of the Mutapa, the new chief *mambo* also demanded that local fires be put out and relighted from his fire as a sign of fealty to him.

Religion played a predominant role in Shona society and in Rozwi attempts to integrate the diverse people of the empire. The Mutapa's hold on the loyalty of his subjects was in some respects more religious than secular. As the paramount *mambo*, he possessed the religious authority to communicate with the *mhondoro*-spirits, or ancestor-spirits, and the supreme deity Mwari on behalf of the community or to ask for rain. The fact that, the Mutapa became an ancestor-spirit when he died, enhanced his position while living. The royal *svikiro* mediums shared his powers of consulting the *mhondoro*-spirits and through them interceding with the supreme deity. As political and religious authority were closely bound in the Mwari cult, it was fortunate for the Mutapas that the *svikiro* mediums apparently acted in support of their rule.[11] The religious power of Mwari—worshipped by many Shona—is shown by the fact that, despite extensive contact with Muslims, Islam made no impact on them.

Blood being thicker than water, the Mutapas entrusted kinsmen or, when appropriate, loyal Rozwi vassals with provincial governorships. They in turn distributed authority to lesser *mambos* for administration and tax collection. The province chiefs were held responsible for the proper management of their territories and for tribute of cattle, slaves, gold or ivory to the Mutapa. Chiefs of significant regions were required to send a son once a year to the royal court with a present and affirmations of allegiance. These familial ambassadors, presumably duly impressed after a three-day wait, were ceremoniously welcomed to an audience with the Mutapa in a courtyard adjoining the royal enclosure. Portuguese accounts from the eighteenth century describe the elaborate protocol for communication between the ambassador and the Mutapa. The chief's son did not address the monarch directly, but rather spoke to the lowest member of the court who passed the message to the official next in rank. The message ascended to the highest noble who transmitted it to the Mutapa and waited for the reply which returned by the same indirect route. After his reception, the ambassador spent three more days in waiting before returning to his father with the usual gift of quality cloth from the

Mutapa. At times, the Mutapas held the sons of sub-chiefs as a ransom for their loyalty to the central government.

When danger threatened the empire, subordinate chiefs had to recruit warriors for the central authority as well as defend their own provinces from incursions. But lip-service to the court or religious practices failed to guarantee adherence to the Mutapa. The autonomy of the provinces helped to engender the conditions for successful secession from central control. Despite the ties of kinship, state ceremony, religious rituals, and a strong army, the Mwene Mutapa confederation faced challenges soon after the end of its phase of military expansion in the late fifteenth century.

The most serious and permanent threat to the new Rozwi empire arose shortly before the death of Matope in about 1480. Changa, the governor of Guruhuswa, took advantage of his isolation from the northern headquarters and of his firmly secured base and mineral wealth to consolidate an independent rule. To emphasize his separatism, Changa assumed the Muslim title 'Amir', perhaps cunningly bestowed on him by Muslim traders seeking to profit from his independence and a possible civil war.[12] With the death of Matope, the time seemed opportune for greater independence. A former shepherd, Changamire now openly established a separate kingdom, which was later known by the Portuguese as Abutua. Another dissident, Togwa, ruler of Mbire province, followed Changamire's example and detached his southern region from the Mutapa's domination.

Attempts to halt Changamire's secession in the south and west by Nyahuma, son and successor to Matope, resulted in civil war and the new Mutapa's death in battle. Changamire briefly held the dead Mutapa's *dzimbabwe* in about 1490. Usurping the throne, he ruled for about four years, until he was killed in battle and Nyahuma's son, Kakuyo Komunyaka, recovered the seat of empire.[13] The usurpation was ended but the balkanization of the empire continued apace.

The son of the first Changamire inherited his father's rebellious tendencies. Retaining control of the southern provinces, the new Changamire militarized his domain and successfully waged what Professor Abraham describes as a 'strenuous diplomatic campaign' to disengage partially the provinces of Quiteve and Madanda in eastern Mozambique from their loyalty to the Mutapa at the time of the advent of the Portuguese.[14] Not for 200 years would the

Changamires again overrun the Mwene Mutapa court but in the meantime they posed a military threat that weakened the older empire and made possible still more territorial defections. During the sixteenth century Manica and Barue broke away to enjoy virtual independence. These former provinces expanded their frontiers, engaged in hostilities, and suffered succession crises similar to those of the parent empire.

As elsewhere in Africa, internal rivalries and political decline often aided European penetration. Although their maritime supremacy waned in the sixteenth century, individual Portuguese seized the opportunities of deterioration in central Mozambique. Well acquainted through their own history with the political infighting of the tiny Iberian kingdoms, they exploited division and weakness to their utmost in order to supplant Muslim traders and to gain direct access to the fabled gold mines of east Africa.

NORTHERN EMPIRES

While the Mwene Mutapa empire broke up in the region south of the Zambezi, a series of three principal Malawi kingdoms made their appearance to the north of the river. Each Malawi kingdom underwent historical phases of military expansion, commercial consolidation, and political disintegration from the sixteenth to the early eighteenth centuries. These states originated from small groups of Malawi peoples who settled in the region to the south of Lake Malawi perhaps as early as the fourteenth century. Like the Shona, the Malawi invaders or immigrants prevailed over the inhabitants, but, unlike that of the Shona, very little of their pre-Portuguese history has been learned. Archaeological and oral evidence of the region remains to be gathered. Even Portuguese documentation is scantier than for Mwene Mutapa history. Lured toward the sources of gold on the Rhodesian plateau, the Portuguese fortune-hunters tended to neglect the Malawi states, which traded primarily in ivory, until gold was discovered in their lands.

The Malawi, or Maravi as the Portuguese called them, comprise in reality a number of ethnic groups, such as the Chewa, Nyanja, Chipeta, Zimba, Nsenga, and Nyassa. Malawi is a blanket term, for there are no people calling themselves by it. Small groups of people followed one upon the other from the Katanga (now Shaba) region of southern Zaire to the country north of Zambezi. This pattern of migration helps to explain the Malawi's diversity. Traditional accounts of the Chewa indicate that they left Katanga under the leadership of the first Kalonga, or great chief, probably in the late fifteenth or early sixteenth century.

The reasons for Kalonga's migration are obscure but seem to have been akin to those of the Shona. Personal ambition perhaps spurred the invasions, along with such contributing factors as the scarcity of land and more likely the desire for ivory and copper trade with the coast. Malawi chiefs in time controlled the ivory trade, exercising a near monopoly over ivory acquisition by demanding the ground tusk — the longest — of all elephants slain on their lands. As their authority diminished, subordinate and distant chiefs circumvented the laws and dealt directly with the Muslim traders.[15] Abundant elephant herds in the Zambezi Valley supplied a commodity in great demand in the Orient, where Indian ivory proved too brittle for the elaborate carvings of trinkets and especially bracelets worn in Hindu marriage ceremonies. African traders transported ivory to market towns where Muslim merchants shipped it down to Zambezi and then up the east African coast or directly across the Indian Ocean. The fact that the Malawi entered into active long-distance trade with Muslim traders supports the view that their expansion had a commercial impetus. But Kalonga's leadership must also be considered.

In the sixteenth century, while his kingdom was still in ascendancy, Kalonga's junior matrilineal kinsmen left the capital at Mankhoma on the lower shore of Lake Malawi to occupy the lowlands south of the lake. These expeditions initially increased Malawi domination but ultimately contributed to its disintegration with the secession of the provinces. To settle the Shire River, Kaphwiti and Lundu went down the valley. While Kaphwiti, the senior of the two commanders, established a headquarters on the western bank of the Shire on the same latitude as Lake Chilwa, Lundu marched into the lower Shire Valley, pushed eastward the Makua people, and had a greater influence on the Zambezi.[16] From his capital south of modern Chikwawa on the Shire's right bank, Lundu founded the Manganja kingdom, which extended to the coast along the northern bank of the Zambezi. The Malawi never established a permanent occupation on the coast among the

Makua- and Lomwe-speaking peoples but imposed chiefly dynasties who ruled them up to the nineteenth century. Manganja was for a time an integral part of the Malawi kingdom and a vital section in the long-distance ivory trade route from the deep interior to the coastal market towns of Quelimane and Mozambique Island. Aware of his power in Manganja, Lundu challenged the Kalonga's authority in the first years of the seventeenth century. Kalonga Muzura brought his disobedient province to heel with the help of the Portuguese, who also feared Lundu and had earlier received Muzura's aid in quelling a revolt against their puppet Mutapa. Although checked in its bid for independence, Manganja retained its autonomy until the middle of the next century when decay reduced it to a minor state.

Another offshoot of the Kalonga kingdom thrived for a time before experiencing a similar fate to that of its sister province. After the Kaphwiti and Lundu left Kalonga's capital, the Undi departed after a succession dispute to establish dominance to the west. The Undi, the chief of the Chewa, governed a large tract of land from a site south of the Zambian border in the Tete district of Mozambique near the Kapoche, an affluent of the Zambezi. He and his followers are reputed to have swept through the country of the 'little people without villages or gardens'[17] — the Khoisan.

The Undi's administrative organization differed from the Mwene Mutapa's bureaucracy by its absence of fixed military and political posts in the court and its reliance on councils and subordinates.[18] The Undi appointed close kinsmen as chiefs of large provinces and more distant relatives and deserving non-relatives to small territories within the provinces. Below the provincial and territorial chiefs ranked the village headmen. The important landed chiefs assumed the title of *mambo*, which denoted high standing in the Zambezi region. Each chief was held responsible in his chieftaincy for settling disputes, directing rain and harvest ceremonies, and defending the Undi's state. The *mambos* distributed land to loyal followers and collected tribute, some of which was passed upwards to reach the Undi. Payment of tribute, particularly in the form of ivory, was an act of fealty as well as revenue.

Royal councils of kinsmen and principal vassals advised the Undi on disputes and policy. Whereas the lack of specific cabinet posts may have reduced court intrigue, the heavy reliance on subordinate chiefs allowed for too much decentralization which ultimately sounded the death knell for the Undi kingdom. The Undi derived his powers from the prerogative to grant land, but once the land was awarded the loyalty of its recipient was not assured. The Undi had, of course, the theoretical right to take away what he had given, but a chief in revolt was unlikely to give up his land without the application of force, and the Undi lacked an army devoted to him alone.[19] Nor was his religious authority enough to check secession.[20]

Rebellious chiefs strained the Undi's fragile authority, while in the capital the paramount Chewa chief faced a spiritual-secular crisis. As in the Mwene Mutapa empire, the spiritual aspects of society were also of great political importance. Despite the belief that each Undi embodied the spirits of his predecessors, his powers of intercession were not as direct as those of Makewana, the influential rain-caller of reputed supernatural origin. Rain-callers derived their special powers from the ability to summon rain, to ensure good croops. Makewana's command over the natural elements detracted from the power of the Undi as sole mediator to the deities. Her subversive use of these spiritual powers, unlike that of the Mwene Mutapa mediums, did not reinforce the Undi's political position. With spiritual and secular forces of this magnitude arrayed against the Chewa kingdom, its dissolution seems understandable.[21]

Before its decline in the mid-1700s, the Malawi empire occupied a huge block of Mozambique territory north of the Zambezi which was bordered by that river in the south, the Luangwa River in the west, and the Indian Ocean in the east; it dominated the coastline from Mozambique Island in the north to the Zambezi estuary. Kalonga Muzura's conquest of Lundu's kingdom of Manganja in the early seventeenth century marked the high tide of the Malawi empire. Coastal Portuguese left accounts of Malawi attacks against them and their domination of the Makua and Lomwe. Little is known of why the Malawi state collapsed. The secession of subordinate states, competition from Yao traders, and the failure of Malawi religious systems to integrate the non-Malawi peoples have been suggested by one scholar to be the principle reasons for the decline.[22] To these could be added the activities of the Portuguese.

The Portuguese presence on the littoral perhaps exacerbated what are still ill-understood changes in the commercial and state structures of inland peoples as they struggled seawards to share or monopolize the newly arrived European commerce. Their desire for lucrative trade with Arab and European introduced the fresh yeast of political ferment, yielding tumult and change. Led by men craving for wealth, fame, or converts, the Portuguese advanced into the Mozambican hinterland. They were met not by cohesive states bent on unified resistance but by a hotchpotch of badly fragmented political units in various degrees of decline, some of them eager for a European alliance against covetous neighbours. It is little wonder then that even with slender resources the Portuguese secured a foothold on the lowland of south eastern Africa.

2

MUSLIM AND PORTUGUESE
SEABORNE EXPANSION

Vasco da Gama's bombardment of Mozambique Island two years
before the close of the fifteenth century initiated another, although
much less transforming, invasion of Mozambique. The Portuguese
strove primarily for mineral wealth from coastal bases to pay Indian
merchants for spices and wares; it was at the beginning a policy of
trade, not territorial domination. Their slender wedge of
penetration up the Zambezi Valley was driven by a commercial
impulse. Portugal's material and cultural superiority over the
African civilization of that time were insufficient to contribute
markedly to the life of the indigenous inhabitants in the way of
the Bantu-speaking newcomers. Portuguese accomplishments were
confined over the years to introducing manioc (cassava), Indian
corn (maize), tobacco and pineapple from Brazil, thus altering
African eating habits. Bantu migrations displaced the Stone Age
Khoisan and moved Mozambique towards an Iron Age civilization
with a more complex social and political organization as well as
greater technological and agricultural advances than had previously been made.

PORTUGAL'S SEA EMPIRE

Portugal's seaborne expansion began in 1415 with the capture of
the Muslim trans-Saharan terminus of Ceuta in Morocco. How
much strategic and economic forethought preceded the attack
across the Strait of Gibraltar is still open to question. True, seizure
of the north African coast denied it to another European power.
But it is generally acknowledged that a stronger impetus stemmed
from the Portuguese nobility's thirst for personal glory and from a
zealous crusading spirit against Islam. The Muslim occupation of
Portugal for centuries had instilled a deep hatred of Islam that had
a lasting influence on Portuguese thought and actions.

Subsequent military expeditions extended Portuguese occupation
from Tangier to Agadir on the Atlantic coast. This brought little

material advantage to the crown or to oceanic exploration, but the psychological impact was great. The spirit of the campaigns crystallized—perhaps ossified—Portuguese attitudes during the expansion and after. Participants in the Moroccan fighting took with them to the East a contempt for non-Christians and a sublime belief in the righteousness of military means to achieve their goals. Often the nobility trained in north Africa commanded ships bound for Mozambique and the Orient and captained official posts in the empire. Other social classes from Portugal ventured after material wealth or spiritual fulfilment in the growing empire but the military nobles stamped their outlook and prejudices on imperial formation and rule. They disdained work, believed in privileges for themselves and services from those considered beneath them and held themselves as being both the repository of Christian civilization and its bulwark in the tropics. The delusions to which these attitudes gave rise were passed on by chroniclers to influence future generations and to put Portuguese policy in Africa out of touch with modern, anti-colonial opinions for so long. However, a less deluded view of themselves might have made the Portuguese seafarers heed the superstitions of the age and quail before the hazards of ocean exploration in frail ships and thus stay at home.

One of the strongest advocates for the attack on Ceuta was Prince Henry, the son of Philippa, daughter of the duke of Lancaster, and John of Aviz. This half-English prince, eager for fame, geographical knowledge, and the progress of Christianity, kept up the land assault on Islam at the same time becoming the principal architect of Portugal's sea exploration. Retiring from the duties and intrigues of the court whenever possible to the ascetic seclusion of Sagres on the south coast of Portugal, Henry gathered about him Italians, Scandinavians, and Jews from the Mediterranean who possessed knowledge of navigation, shipbuilding, cartography, and the sea. Here he questioned his advisers, designed ships, and laid plans for the exploration of the western Atlantic. At that time the Atlantic was largely unknown; its fierce winds and heavy seas were an unwelcome contrast to the warm, placid waters of the Mediterranean. The southern limit of European geographical advance lay at Cape Bojador, now in the Spanish Sahara. Prince Henry the Navigator pushed his crews, despite fears and frequent setbacks, to round the Cape and to sail out into the western Atlantic to alight on strings of small islands. Catalan and Genoese sailors probably sighted some of the mid-Atlantic chains but the Portuguese landed on the Madeiras about 1419 and the Azores by 1439. Claims to them and settlements soon followed. In 1441, one of Prince Henry's captains seized from a west African beach the first batch of African people to be sent to Portugal as curiosities. Later, millions followed as slaves to the New World's mines and plantations in what became a deplorable international commercial system. By 1460, the year of Henry's death, captains sailing under the Portuguese colours had colonized the uninhabited Cape Verde Islands, some 300 miles off Dakar, and established small trading factories on the West African coast to gain slaves, *malagueta* pepper and gold.

Aware of threats to this profitable trade, the Portuguese Crown sought to guarantee its monopoly by granting commercial licences to a few favoured nobles and by securing papal recognition of its discoveries. A series of Bulls published over half a century gave the sanction of international statute to Portugal's holdings and to future acquisitions within specified zones. The Papacy in return obtained the crown's patronage of church establishments and missions in Portugal's African, Asian, and Brazilian territories. The Pope's decrees were strengthened by treaties with Castile — the earliest and strongest threat to Portuguese global hegemony. In the famous Treaty of Tordesillas (1494), Portugal and Castile divided the world between them at a point some 100 leagues west of the Cape Verde Islands.[1] Unwittingly, but fortunately for them, the Portuguese included in their sphere the yet to be 'discovered' land of Brazil, which was found quite by accident six years later.

These treaties and licences were regarded as mere paper hopes by the roving British, Dutch and French predators of succeeding years, but they revealed a yearning in the Portuguese soul for international recognition and justification of their activities. In modern times, Portugal similarly strove to legitimate its hold on tropical areas before the United Nations and the North Atlantic Treaty Organization.

Once begun, the voyages set off an evolution in imperial motives from a ferocious assault on Islam and a search for the legendary Prester John to include a lust for African gold and Oriental spices. The riches of Africa and the East excited men's avarice to a fever pitch, for European poverty was extreme and almost universally felt. Setting sail from the Tagus were men who genuinely sought souls for Christianity, still more who quested after worldly wealth, and a few who viewed the two motivations in discord.

After Henry's death, the crown continued the exploratory voyages and the increasingly valuable commerce in gold, spices, ivory, and human beings along the shoreline from Guinea to Angola. Trade with African rulers on the west coast was usually free of conflict.[2] Amiable and co-operative relations insured the flow of goods in Portuguese caravels—the partially lateened-rigged ships originally developed from Arab vessels by Mediterranean seamen to sail to windward. Just south of the Congo River, Captain Diogo Cão, at the farthest point reached in 1483, struck up one of the most remarkable relationships between Portugal and an African people. In contrast to subsequent Luso-African relations in Mozambique or indeed elsewhere on the continent, Portugal began an aid and diplomatic programme with the Kongo kingdom that was limited in scope but co-operative and useful in nature. John II sent and received ambassadors, dispatched skilled artisans and trained Africans in crafts, commissioned missionaries, and schooled converts in religious orders. He also supplied tools and military assistance, as well as shipping gifts, to win over the Manikongo, or king, and his court. Help in trekking to Prester John in the interior of the continent provided one motive; but it did not lessen the Portuguese preoccupation with the route to India nor check the São Tomé slavers who ruinously undermined the development venture.[3] The original idealism faded away. Similar assistance to an African people was not seen again for centuries and then only when continued neglect and oppression promised certain loss of the African territories. Regrettably, it furnished no inspiration for Portuguese activities in Mozambique.

Maritime reconnaissance for a route to the East went forward uninterrupted by commercial and diplomatic involvement on the west coast. By the last years of the fifteenth century, the quest for direct access to the source of Asian spices became of supreme importance to Portugal, to by-pass the Venetian and Genoese monopoly of the Mediterranean spice trade. The rounding of the Cape of Good Hope in 1488 by Bartholomeu Dias was a significant step towards that goal. Nearly ten years elapsed, however, before Vasco da Gama hoisted sail at Belém Tower for his epoch-making voyage to India in ships with crucifixes painted on the sails and plenty of gunpowder in the holds. The time was not wasted. In

1486, Pero de Covilhã journeyed at the King's request by way of the Mediterranean through the Middle East, the Persian Gulf, and India, and to the east coast of Africa, possibly as far south as Sofala. If the report is true, he was the first Portuguese to visit Mozambique. Covilhã never returned from his mission, spending the last thirty years of his life in Ethiopia, which was considered in 1490 to be Prester John's kingdom, a mythical Christian rampart against Islam.[4] Before he reached Ethiopia, he sent back from Cairo a report of his observations. The evidence of its arrival in Portugal is inconclusive, but anticipation of his findings may account in part for the delay of the da Gama voyage. Professor Charles R. Boxer, a distinguished historian of Portugal's expansion, suggested that da Gama used the ten-year interval to study the south Atlantic winds so as to avoid beating to windward along the entire length of the African shoreline. In contrast to previous voyages, Vasco da Gama and the future annual East-Indiamen fleets sailed far out into the Atlantic in order to run with the prevailing westerly winds past the Cape.[5]

Pressing north-eastwards after rounding the Cape, da Gama's three small vessels first touched Mozambique just north of Delagoa Bay.* The crews were greeted on the beach with such friendliness by the African people, who exchanged food for Portuguese cloth, that the mariners dubbed the spot Terra da Boa Gente ('land of the good people'). This propitious beginning was to be in sharp contrast to the course of African-Portuguese history in Mozambique.

On 2 March 1498, da Gama's ships anchored opposite Mozambique Island, which astonished the European mariners with its stone buildings, quays, and atmosphere of prosperity.[6] Facing the Indian Ocean, its earliest seaborne influences came from the East. Indonesian seagoers brushed south-eastern Africa during the first millennium primarily via Madagascar and left outrigger canoes, the xylophone, and the banana as traces of their influence. More recent and more pronounced was the Arab impact on the eastern seaboard. Commercial contacts preceded the settlements in the coastal towns of Mombasa, Malindi, and Kilwa, which were probably an outgrowth of the military and religious expansion of Islam. The Arabs introduced rectangular or square buildings, sugarcane, rice, coconuts, orange and lemon trees, the weaving of

---

*   The name derives from lagoa ('lagoon') and not as some writers imagined à Goa ('to Goa').

cotton, the dhow sailing craft, and their religion. That an estimated 900,000 Muslim Africans lived in the coastal zones of Cabo Delgado, Mozambique and Zambézia districts in 1967 underscores the impact and durability of Muslim influence.[7] Yet the Bantu base of the Swahili language and the persistence of African customs created a blending of Arab and African cultures that still exists.

Mozambique Island's market town, although poor in comparison with Muslim entrepôts further up the coast, nourished Portuguese hopes of great wealth, for fanciful tales of ships loaded with precious metals, gems, and spices found credulous listeners.* Da Gama gleaned valuable information on coastal trade from the merchants and obtained two pilots from the sheikh before a quarrel broke out between the islanders and the Portuguese. Dismissing the sheikh's conciliatory appeals for peace, da Gama, who was no diplomat, ordered his guns to open fire on the Muslims in what was the first sounding of European cannons on the peacock waters of the Indian Ocean. The Portuguese seafarers not only fired the first shots in Mozambique but also inaugurated Western domination of the East. After the bombardment of the town, da Gama's ships coasted in gentle breezes northwards and repeated their depredations on Mombasa before sailing to India from Malindi.[8] His voyage prepared the way for the argosies, the cargoes, and the dividends of Portugal's most gloriously remembered age.

In da Gama's wake followed other Portuguese captains and crews bent on eliminating the Muslim middlemen from the trade in Asian spices and luxuries. Military campaigns against Muslims in Morocco, superior ships, the most advanced cannons of the day, and strongly held religious convictions presupposed the elimination to be accompanied by violence and bloodshed. Portugal's lack of desirable goods for trade also made for a strategy of naval warfare to supplant Arab and Indian Muslim carriers in the Indian Ocean. Acquiring control of entrepôts and bases on the surrounding littoral of the Indian Ocean was a fundamental part of Portuguese policy. So, too, was the monopoly of the sources of ivory and gold from Mozambique that could be exchanged for the commodities of the formidable Indian land empires, not easily subjugated by Portuguese sea power. Hence strategists considered Mozambique to

---

*   The origin of the name Mozambique is uncertain, but it may derive from one Musa al Bique, a sheikh or prominent person on the island.

be of importance as a base in the empire and as a source of ivory and especially gold.

Befitting the scope of this bold strategy, the Portuguese accomplished it with astounding swiftness. Now by taps, now by blows, they hammered at their rivals until they were virtual masters of the Indian Ocean trade. For nearly a century after Francisco de Almeida's lopsided victory over a ragtag Egyptian-Gujarati fleet off Diu in 1509, Portugal's naval hegemony in the Indian Ocean remained unthreatened until the arrival of the Dutch. From India, they pushed eastward by sea to snatch trade as far away as Japan and to establish posts at Hughli in Bengal, Malacca in Malaya, and Macão in China. In the west, Brazil was added to the Portuguese empire, by the unexpected landfall of an India-bound fleet in 1500. Twenty-two years later the *Victoria*, in the service of Castile but commanded by the Portuguese Ferdinand Magellan before his death in the Philippines, completed the circumnavigation of the globe.

In the hundred years after the fall of Ceuta, Portugal linked by sea heretofore insular continents, monopolized the Asian spice trade, introduced for good or ill Western civilization into the East, and conquered a global seaborne empire. It was a sunburst of activity. It has been venerated in Portuguese literature and history as O Século Maravilhoso ('The Marvellous Century') and celebrated in Luís de Camões renowned epic poem, *Os Lusíadas*, which appeared in 1572. He sailed the Portuguese imagination to the outer edges of Mercator's projection. Although the Portuguese never again equalled their achievements in this age, they doggedly struggled to recreate the epoch's grand aura, notably by national exertions in the late nineteenth century and again during the 1960s and 1970s. The imperial vision was enshrined in Portuguese thought, and over the years it exerted an influence on the course of history and policy in Mozambique.

THE PORTUGUESE AND SOFALA

Just down the coast from the present-day port of Beira, the site of the original Sofala at low tide reveals little trace of its former importance to first Arab trade and then Portuguese commercial dreams. A storm at the beginning of this century carried out to sea the ruins of the Portuguese fort. Located on the feverish coastal marsh, Sofala owed its existence to the traffic in gold from the Rhodesian plateau. Gold drew merchants and traders from Arabia, Persia, and India. Their mixing with the Bantu-speaking peoples helped to create the distinctive Swahili civilization. Sofala at the time of the Portuguese coming was a microcosm of the Afro-Arab centres of Mombasa, Kilwa, and Malindi. Of the reported 10,000 men in Sofala's territory, about 800 were designated as Arabs by one early Portuguese observer.[9] Some Africans who came in contact with the Muslims of Arabia and India practised enough Islam to be considered Muslims themselves, while not entering into the typical Swahili culture and language of the east African coast. Nor did they have much Arab blood in their veins. These Muslims often worked as intermediaries for Arab merchants just as mulattos subsequently served Portuguese interests. Relations between Muslim traders and their African counterparts appear to have been pacific, but merchants were killed and robbed in lawless regions. The merchants were also subject to tolls and taxes imposed by African chiefs.

Sofala served as the primary port of Mozambique for the shipment of ivory and gold to the Indian Ocean market; but it was not the only point of exchange for African goods. The Arabs also set up entrepôts at Quelimane, Angoche, and Mozambique Island, and Muslim traders established several inland fairs. Information on these early market-places is regrettably scant. What is known of them derives almost totally from Portuguese sources of the sixteenth century and afterwards. Muslim traders apparently journeyed to the interior to be nearer the mines and to gather what otherwise was too small an amount of gold to warrant an individual's passage to the coast. Medieval Arab geographers chronicled the trade from Sofala and Muslim commercial travels to the hinterland. They recorded that Arab ships sailed up the Zambezi for some 300 miles. But what is known of Arab vessels and the river itself makes this assertion open to scepticism. Portuguese documents report that ships travelled up the river for about sixteen leagues (48 miles) to a point where a local Tonga chief exacted a toll for passage through his lands. Before reaching the Lupta Gorge, the traders transferred their cloth, beads, and ornaments to porters who carried them to the fairs.[10]

The exact number of fairs and the location of most of them is unknown. Markets were probably connected to the Limpopo, Save, and Zambezi rivers. Arab scholars noted fairs at Sena, Tete, Zumbo, and Zimbabwe, but many more Muslim fairs existed and formed the pattern for Portuguese trade. African chiefs welcomed them as sources of revenue, foreign commodities, information, and prestige.[11] Dating at least from Portuguese times, the fairs had one or more mud-walled structures that may have been enclosed by a tree-trunk stockade. In addition to the fairs, Muslims settled in small, widely scattered enclaves. They intermingled with the neighbouring populations, producing offspring and founding communities. Generally, the Muslims shied away from farming, although the early Portuguese left accounts of Muslim plantations using African slaves. In 1511 António da Saldanha estimated that there were 10,000 Muslims in what is now central Mozambique and eastern Rhodesia.[12] This was certainly an inflated figure, attributable either to the captain's fear of Islam or to a desire to spur his countrymen into action against the Muslim monopoly. Half a century later another estimate put the figure at only some twenty turban-wearing Muslims along the Zambezi, their principal trade route to the interior.[13]

The extensiveness of the trade system and its profits can be verified by the avarice it excited in the Portuguese and by the tenacity and resilience with which the Muslims resisted European incursions. Soon after reaching the Indian Ocean the Portuguese realized the need for African gold to purchase cloves, nutmeg, and pepper from Asia. Sea power could not wrest control of the precious spices from Asian merchants whose land interests were protected by powerful rulers, but the sea lanes were another matter, for the empires of Persia, Egypt, and Vijayanagar possessed no warships.[14]

Less than a decade after da Gama's first voyage to India, Portugal launched an assault to seize east African and Indian bases and displace Muslim carriers in the Indian Ocean. That the Portuguese formulated this plan so quickly has been offered as proof that Covilha's report from Cairo reached the King safely.[15] This seems possible, since the Portuguese were well informed about the commercial system of the Indian Ocean. But it is just as likely that Portuguese activities were an ambitious and warlike reflex to their transportation services begun in West Africa where they inserted themselves into African commerce. There, the Portuguese had acted as transporters of African trade, carrying Benin cloth and beads to the Ghanaian coast and labour to the Akan goldmines.[16]

On the eastern side of the continent, however, the Portuguese encountered an efficient and organized trading system with little need for the skills and ships of an interloper. To the Portuguese, trade and war became synonymous.

The implementation of Portugal's policy to dislodge its Muslim rivals was direct in approach and swift in coming. In 1505, Francisco de Almeida embarked with a fleet of over 20 ships to make the Indian Ocean a Portuguese lake. One of Almeida's instructions called for the seizure and fortification of Sofala and its use as a collection depot for gold.[17] The flagship of the six-vessel task force assigned to this task sank on the eve of the fleet's departure. This inauspicious beginning set the pattern for the Sofala venture.

When the ships reached Sofala, the crews cloaked their intentions behind displays of friendship and signs of commercial interest. The wily octogenarian sheikh, Yusuf, and Pero d'Anhaia, captain of the ships, made a bargain in which the Portuguese were to share in the gold trade in return for constructing a fort to protect both Portugese and Muslims from African chieftains. Lacking stones, the crews erected rows of palisades and filled them with sand to form a stockade. In the classic naïvete—now so widely acknowledged—of the West dealing with the East, the Portuguese held the belief that a fort and a show of force ensured access to the flow of gold. Once the wood and sand walls were completed, the contingent turned with energy to collecting gold and ravaging Muslim sailing *zambucos* along the coast. Their land and sea piracy dried up, if not totally choked, the stream of gold to Sofalan merchants.

Soon the trading factory helped to erode Muslim profits. The unhappy merchants plotted the destruction of the stockade and its inhabitants and pressed the aged sheikh to endorse the scheme. Fearing the fort's armament, the plotters bought the services of Mokondi, a nearby African chief, who swelled the attackers' numbers by over 1,000 men. With Yusuf's approval, they laid plans for a fire assault on the combustible palm-thatched huts in the fort. But the merchants were not alone in buying assistance from Africans, who they pejoratively called *cafre* ('unbelievers') after the Muslim manner. D'Anhaia had plied the sheikh's closest advisers with gifts to win them over to the Portuguese side. One of them, Akoti, an African, not only betrayed the plan but also reinforced the ranks of the 40 fever-plagued defenders. Akoti's motives are unknown; he may have hoped to enhance his own position, or he may have been genuinely at odds with the sheikh's policies. Whatever the reason, his help was decisive. With water buckets handy and about a hundred additional men, the garrison repulsed the attack. In a counter-assault the garrison laid waste the village and decapitated Yusuf. After three more days of fighting, the Muslim resistance dissolved.[18] Portugal had won in 1506 its first battle on the mainland of Mozambique. There were to be many more battles of much the same pattern, with a handful of Portuguese either dividing one section of the population against the other or insinuating themselves into an internal feud to gain their ends. It was a policy not only of success but also of necessity. This was one of the first occasions when Africans supported the Portuguese forces in Mozambique — a policy which in time was to lead to their own subjugation. As part of the Muslim surrender, d'Anhaia installed a compliant puppet as sheikh — a practice often repeated in the history of Mozambique.

Not all Portuguese-appointed rulers proved tractable, however. Sheikh Maulide of Sofala fled the restraints of his status and blockaded the settlement by land and sea in 1511. He gained African allies by the political marriages of his daughters, stopped communications with the settlement by land and sea, and prevailed upon Chief Mokondi to increase drastically the price of grain sold to the Portuguese. Against Maulide, the local officials mounted a surprise attack, sending 24 soldiers — over half the garrison — to bring him back dead or alive. He refused to return and was put to death. Maulide's actions encouraged the Muslims to blockade the Portuguese from Kilwa to Sofala the following year.[19] This was a fortaste of the Muslim resistance that in the seventeenth century forced the Portuguese to confine their settlements and activities on the east African coast to below Cape Delgado. Seeing their centuries-old trade taken over and their ships pirated by the Portuguese, the Muslims attempted at first to cut off the Franks (a term applied to all Europeans) from coastal food supplies. The food situation became perilous at times, but the real threat to Protugal's position in Sofala lay in the gold trade.

MOZAMBIQUE ISLAND

According to the king's instructions, gold gathered at Sofala was to be shipped to Mozambique Island, added to the gold locally collected, and placed on board the ships that sailed to India once a year. There it was used to purchase spices and luxury items for Europe. Some was spent in Portugal on cheap cloth, beads, manu-factured wares, and fire-arms to trade for more gold. The factor from Sofala would return from the island with a load of goods for another year's trading. Mozambique Island played a central role in the trading system of the Indian. [20]

The Portuguese occupied the Island in 1507, two years after landing at Sofala, and within a generation, along with Sena and slightly later Quelimane, it superseded the earlier settlement, which rapidly stagnated. On the route to India, the island station with its good harbour was intended by Almeida as a stopping-off place for sea-fatigued sailors. Its abundant coconuts provided relief from scurvy. The Portuguese built a dispensary, church, and warehouse, and in 1552 began to construct a stone fortress which was not completed until the end of the century. Long before it was finally fortified, the island was an essential link in the chain of outposts in the Estado da India ('State of India')—the Portuguese name for their trading posts and possessions from Sofala to Maco More accessible than Sofala's shallow harbour, outward-bound India-men preferred it in the stormy season. They could wait there for favourable winds and set out with the tail-end of the monsoon in September. The island was ruled by the viceroy of Goa, who governed Portugal's empire in the East, and its southerly position, away from resurgent Arab power of the seventeenth century, rendered it a secure and lasting stronghold. From Sofala to Malindi, the garrison and its small protecting fleet preyed on Muslim coastal shipping, seizing the cargoes and slaughtering the sailor-merchants.

The Makua people on the coast opposite Mozambique Island formed a redoubtable barrier to Portuguese expansion on the mainland. They defeated the Portuguese soundly in 1585, and their vassals did so again in 1753, when Lisbon was trying to establish a hold on the shore. [21] Mozambique Island, like its sister settlement to the south, traded for gold, ivory, and foodstuffs, but its gaze —un-like that of Sofala —was seaward. It was cut off from the mainland not only by sea and African resistance but also by its imperial mission.

Mozambique Island's strategic position was recognized, and Portugal retained it as a bastion of imperial communication and a refreshment station despite four severe buffetings from Dutch sieges. After the fall of Mombasa to the Arab state of Oman in 1698, the island fortress demarcated Portugal's northernmost boundary on the east African coast and guarded the colony against sea-going enemies.

With the decline and breakup of the Estado da India, the island housed Portugal's top government official in Mozambique. The colony's subordination to the Viceroy of Goa's rule lasted until 1752, when it was given a separate administration to increase efficiency and self-sufficiency. With headquarters on Mozambique Island it beckoned to a succession of Captains-General and Governors until 1834 and thereafter Governors-General who came to enrich themselves, to gain prestige, to use it as a stepping-stone to a finer post, and, in some cases, to wrestle with the problems of implementing Lisbon's colonial rule on the coast and in the *serto* ('hinterland').[22] The island remained the capital of the entire province well after its economic and political eclipse by mainland towns. In 1897, Lourenço Marques became the provincial capital. Before this, however, the island had protected Portuguese claims in Mozambique and had wrecked much Muslim coastal trade.

PORTUGUESE AND MUSLIM CLASHES

It was the Sofala settlement that first involved Portugal in Mozambique's hinterland, away from the strategic plan of island and coastal factories and forts. The desire for gold prompted the Portuguese to move inland. Without gold and to a lesser degree other Mozambican trade goods, Portugal's commercial position in the East stood in jeopardy. Caravels, brigantines, and naus might sweep Muslim vessels from the sea, but spices could not be acquired from powerful land-based kingdoms by these means; for this, pleasing trade goods were needed. The amount of gold at Sofala proved disappointing, and tales of unlimited gold in the interior inspired plans for inland expeditions.

Upon da Gama's return from India, King Manuel gleefully communicated to Ferdinand and Isabella of Aragon-Castile that Portugal's discoveries brought fantastic wealth to the country. He claimed that the Sofala mines were filled with 'infinite gold'. Over a period of 25 years, during which Portuguese factors confined themselves to the proximity of Sofala, the realities of wealth never matched anticipations. Nor have they ever in Mozambique. The Sofala gold trickled for a while, long enough to whet the Portuguese appetite but not long enough to outweigh the operating costs, let alone to pay for the spice trade.

The Portuguese commercial policies added to their difficulties. Their inability to undersell Muslim merchants with European cloth at a cheap cost was an insurmountable problem. Africans much preferred the Cambay material from India. Private traders subverted the crown's share in the turnover and contributed to the failure of the royal factory at Sofala.[23] Ironically, Lisbon's policy of paying its officials and missionaries with cloth for trade well into the nineteenth century promoted competition from the private sector.[24] Private trading in addition often led to fraternization with Muslim merchants—something to which the crown was decidedly opposed. Corruption, which ran rampant in the Estado da India, also took its toll of the crown's profits. Officials at every level had the incentive of minuscule wages and the opportunity of limited supervision to dip into the royal till or the returns of a distant merchant. Many succumbed to the temptation.

One of the first Portuguese profiteers in Mozambique was Manuel Fernandes, who strengthened the defences of the fort at Sofala by superintending the erection of a stone tower within its walls in 1506, for which he was later raised to the nobility. Less noble was his embezzlement of the factory's treasury by paying funds for a non-existent debt to himself and by manning the fort with slaves, thus filling his own pockets from the garrison's pay-roll. Fernandes escaped prosecution and returned to Portugal to praise and ennoblement.[25] As was to happen so often, a scoundrel in Mozambique was a hero in Lisbon.

Behind Sofala lay the kingdom of Quiteve, which had begun to move independently of the Mwene Mutapa's suzerainty about the time of the Portuguese landing. The Portuguese cultivated the friendship of Inhamunda, King of Quiteve, to win him away from Muslim influence. As with other chiefs, the Portuguese gave him presents and fire-arms to secure his position. Once he dominated the surrounding territory, Inhamunda closed the trade routes to and from the Sofala settlement in 1519 for six years. This land blockade was complete except for brief and infrequent liftings or smuggling by a handful of traders. He stopped commerce between Sofala and the lands of Mwene Mutapa and Manica as a means of economic warfare.[26] Such wars in the hinterland emphasized the precarious existence of trade confined to the coast. But Sofala's position was undermined more seriously by the competition of Angoche traders than by Inhamunda's warfare.

Even before d'Anhaia's ships anchored at Sofala, its trade had begun to fall in the commercial shadow of Angoche, at the mouth of the Mluli River, and to a lesser extent Quelimane, also on the northern coast. Angoche Island benefited from the Zambezi route to the interior fairs, which came into prominence when the Mwene Mutapa's court was moved in the mid-fifteenth century. Settled apparently by dissidents from Kilwa, who grasped the economic significance of the Mutapa's new *dzimbabwe* in the Mount Darwin area of what is today Rhodesia, Angoche was placed at the spout end of a new trade funnel. To avoid the Portuguese, gold and other goods were clandestinely shipped up the coast via the Querimba Islands to Kilwa and Mombasa or directly across the ocean to India. Portuguese captains greatly overestimated the Angoche's population, putting it at 12,000 inhabitants, mostly African or mixed, at the beginning of the sixteenth century, but in so doing called attention to the most prosperous trading settlement in Mozambique, as was their intention.[27]

By the 1520s, Portuguese officials realized that Sofala's reputed fame in gold traffic was hollow, and they complained to the crown that the 'Moors' of Angoche ruined the whole trade of Sofala.[28] Angoche's merchants understood the open-sesame nature of the Zambezi, and they exploited it to the full with their considerable business expertise. Some commodities, after being off-loaded from dhows on the river, were taken by porterage to Otonga fair on a mountain of the same name, and some hauled upstream to Sena and Tete, called respectively Sinna and Onhaquoro by medieval Arab geographers. These two riverine ports supplied many of the fairs with trade items. At the fair, Africans and Muslim traders met to exchange gold, ivory, and slaves for cotton textiles from Cambay, jewelry, and ornaments. African traders participated in the organization of the fairs, and chiefs exacted taxes from the Muslim merchants. The Arab trade network extended beyond central Mozambique to Kariba Gorge on the Zambezi, and African and Islamized black go-betweens carried on extensive trade prior to Portuguese penetration.[29]

Eager to cut-off the Muslims from the lucrative trade in the interior, the Portuguese resolved to exclude them from the shore by sweeping their vessels from the sea. The Portuguese attacked what was perceived as illicit coastal traffic, butchered crews, and confiscated goods as contraband when possible. With countless sandbars, coral reefs, and mangrove swamps interlaced by hidden inlets, the Mozambique coastline is a smuggler's paradise, and the trade persisted. The smash-and-dash raids had little lasting effect on the resilient and elusive merchants. Only an assault on Angoche, which served as a headquarters for commerce up the Zambezi and a haven for smugglers, was viewed with any success.

Captain Saldanha's three-ship squadron raided Angoche in 1511. The Portuguese believed that the settlement would yield to force, if not to competition. The destructive effects of the amphibious raid were slight and temporary; however they set fire to the town and sank a few leaky dhows. But when they retired, the damage was repaired and trade resumed. Permanent occupation in the face of the Makua allies on the mainland was beyond the thinly stretched human resources of Portugal, with its far-flung empire.[30] Towards the end of the sixteenth century internal disputes enabled the Portuguese to occupy Angoche for a century, by which time trade fell off, making the possession of the island worthless. It was then abandoned until the nineteenth century.

A dozen years after the assault on Angoche, another pillaging expedition sailed to disrupt the main Muslim trade settlement on the Querimba Islands. Located south of Cape Delgado, the Querimbas served as a terminus to overland routes and riverine commerce down the Rovuma as well as a link in Kilwa's southern trade. The islands also had a plentiful supply of coconut fibre used for rope-making — a strategic commodity for sailing craft. Their allegiance to Mombasa, the chief garrison-port and rival to the Portuguese on the east African coast, prompted the punitive raid. The crews of two ships wintering at Mozambique Island furnished the manpower. 80 men-at-arms crashed the sheikh's defences, ransacked the town, and departed laden with loot before reinforcements could be mustered. As in the Angoche raid, the townspeople rallied African support from the mainland, and they discouraged the Portuguese from tarrying after the sailors had gutted the settlement and burned the palm groves.[31]

These forays and the depredations on coastal shipping formed only a small part of Portugal's commitments and suffered ,like so many Portuguese enterprises, from shortages of men and ships. More strategic places such as Ormuz, Diu, Goa, and Malacca increasingly preoccupied the planners in Lisbon. By the third decade of the sixteenth century, rumours of gold in Brazil and the Moluccas (Spice Islands) diminished the crown's focus on Sofala, but not on the territory as a whole, from which Portugal derived enough wealth for some officials to consider the toehold in Mozambique to be their most prosperous possession during the seventeenth century. The steep decline in Portuguese fortunes in the Indian Ocean at the hands of Dutch, French, and English intruders, along with growing Omani Arab power, made Mozambique's prosperity relative to the crown's failures elsewhere. Mozambique Island cost the crown next to nothing to defend and administer, for corruption usually compensated officials for their administrative services, and the general lack of interest in the territory on the part of other Europeans saved a heavy defence budget.

Realizing they could not undersell their competitors or get rid of them, the Portuguese tried in 1600 to keep all trade in their own hands by forcing Muslim traders and shippers to purchase licences from their officials. These monopolistic regulations were tossed to the wind, for the Muslim policy was widespread 'free' trade.

By that time, much of the profitable Muslim commerce had come to an end after the Portuguese had established bases on the Zambezi before the middle of the sixteenth century. At the end of the next century, the trade of Angoche and other Muslim exchange centres in Mozambique had fallen to a fraction of its former size. It was to stay like that until the slave trade to Brazil and the Indian Ocean sugar islands revived Muslim fortunes on the northern coast.

Apart from their commercial competition, Muslim and Portuguese settled down to fairly amiable social relationships in remote offshore and inland regions untouched by the crown's dispatch of fervent priests to prevent the synthesis of African, Muslim and Portuguese religious practices. Once established below Cape Delgado, the Portuguese coexisted with Muslims much as they had for centuries in the Iberian peninsula — with a complex mixture of peaceful interchange and violent outburst. Barred from acquiring conspicuous wealth, Muslim merchants and sheikhs worked as go-betweens in trade with Africans in the *sertão*. Humbler followers of Islam worked as labourers, seamen, and servants.[32]

The expulsion of the Muslims from mastery over the lower Zambezi-Indian Ocean commercial network was to change the direction of Lisbon's practice and policy in Mozambique. Muslim destruction in south-eastern Africa forced the Portuguese to discard their coastal scheme of empire for penetration into the countryside; the cost to Africans was far higher, for it brought about the eventual subjugation of Mozambique.

3

PORTUGUESE PENETRATION AND DEFEAT

Mozambique from the start of the sixteenth century stood at the beginning of a complex and three-century struggle in which five main contenders at various times took part — Mwene Mutapa, Changamire, Portugal, Muslim merchants and Malawi kingdoms. No people had sufficient power or sustaining interest to control all of south-east Africa. Each suffered from a lack of unity within its own ranks and, except for Changamire, had undergone a diminution of territory and power by the mid-eighteenth century. When Portuguese crews waded ashore at Sofala in 1505 the Mwene Mutapa, Changamire and Malawi states dominated, or soon would dominate, large tracts of Mozambique and the Muslim trading system was uneasy at the prospect of a Portuguese challenge to its prosperity and expansion. 300 years of warfare, revolts, ambushes, massacres, sieges and isolated killings produced no clear victor. All contenders, save Changamire, experienced a decline that, coupled with the Ngoni invasions, brought not tranquility but anarchy to much of the country and left the lower Zambezi region in the thrall of the *prazo* residents and virtually all Africans to the tender mercies of the slavers whose calling underwent a devastating intensification toward the close of the eighteenth century.

THE MWENE MUTAPA AND THE PORTUGUESE

Encounters between different states have sometimes resulted in the destruction of one of them. This destruction is more often than not preceded by the internal breakdown of the victim state. What happened to the Mwene Mutapa kingdom, which reached out for shoring up to prolong its power only to become a dependent satellite, has been repeated in our own time in Asia. A declining state or leadership reliant on alien arms for rule may delay a fall but in time its identification with a foreign civilization makes the deterioration all the more unavoidable. For its part, the patron state often mistakes the durability of its puppet.

The Portuguese, as in the case of the Manikongos on the west coast, initially overestimated the strength and importance of the Mutapas, falsely identifying them as the supreme power over the entire hinterland. For their part, the Mutapas fostered this misconception and feared that the Portuguese would learn the truth of their growing weakness. During the sixteenth century the once-mighty Karanga empire drifted toward fragmentation; the eastern provinces of Barue, Manica, Quiteve and Madanda wielded greater autonomy, and Changamire to the south threatened the very safety of the parent state. So when local Portuguese meddled and intrigued in Karanga affairs, they speeded the withering away of the Mwene Mutapa's 'indirect rule' over its provinces. The Karanga empire, beset by internal power struggles, ungovernable provinces and the dangerous rivalry of Changamire, sought Portuguese assistance and in so doing opened a Pandora's box of ills.

The Mwene Mutapa court encountered its first European early in the second decade of the sixteenth century when António Fernandes set off from Sofala.[1] A *degregado*, or criminal, who hoped to atone for his wrongdoings to the crown by hazardous undertakings, Fernandes was instructed to gather information about interior peoples, their goods, fairs and above all gold. Tales of Mwene Mutapa's wealth circulated in Lisbon and convinced some that it was the biblical land of Ophir where the Queen of Sheba got her gifts of gold for Solomon. From 1512 to 1516 Fernandes made two, possibly three, trips into central Mozambique and eastern Rhodesia. His presence was welcomed by Mutapa Kakuyo Komun-yaka as an opportunity for trade and perhaps even for an alliance to underpin his fragmenting empire. Kakuyo showed the traveller gold, perhaps to entice his countrymen to ally themselves against Changamire, but he did not reveal the sources of the precious metal. Many of the mines were in his rival's lands. Ascertaining the whereabouts of the mines was the goal of much Portuguese activity during the sixteenth and seventeenth centuries.

Soon other Portuguese — criminals, deserters and fortune-hunters — followed in Fernandes' footsteps to escape the unhealthy low veld, stultifying regulations and unprofitable confines of the crown's forts. More Portuguese moved into the interior by the 1530s than the official population on the coast at Sofala and Mozambique Island. Brisk trading was transacted at many Muslim-established fairs. The immigrants acquired land, collected concubines and

Christianized a few Africans and Indians. The Portuguese captains on Mozambique Island were determined to restrict their nationals in the hinterland whose fraternizing with Muslims benefited neither the crown's treasury nor the Church's mission. In 1531, the crown set up a fair and lesser captaincy at Sena, 160 miles up the Zambezi:

At first the relationship between the 30 or 40 Portuguese *sertanejos* ('backwoodsmen') and the Mutapa or lesser chiefs of his provinces was one of subject to sovereign. The chiefs insisted on presents, usually rolls of cloth, before granting audiences, trade or favours. They also required these fugitives from the crown's monopolistic controls on the coast to conduct business within the limits of the fairs so as to collect a tax for the privilege. As a means to maintain order among the unruly *sertanejos*, the Mutapas obliged the Portuguese, like the Muslim traders, to select a headsman to represent his and their interests. They demanded that the traders at Massapa submit the elected captain for their approval. If the candidate was acceptable, then the Mutapas allowed the appointment to be confirmed by the captain on Mozambique Island. Because the Massapa fair served as a gateway to and from the Mutapa's *dzimbabwe*, the official carried the title Captain of the Gates (*Capitão das Portas*), and performed a host of duties: he collected trade revenue, arbitrated in disputes, sentenced offenders and regulated commerce under the direction and authority of the Mutapas.[2]

The first contacts between Muslim merchants and a few score of *sertanejos* had gone off amiably, but larger numbers of backwoodsmen and before long crusading missionaries were certain catalysts for economic and religious strife. Tension also mounted in the Mutapa's court with the steady influx of frontiersmen and missionaries during the 1540s and 1550s. The proverbial last straw on the camel's back came in 1561 with the Jesuit priest Gonçalo da Silveira's arrival at Mutapa Nogomo's *dzimbabwe*. Impelled by absolute faith in God and a steely determination to convert the 'heathen', Gonçalo da Silveira through his preaching had radiated a powerful influence on Africans near Quelimane before he journeyed to the Mwene Mutapa court. With characteristic missionary fervour he set about proselytizing Nogomo, and he baptized the young man as Sebastian. Hundreds of relatives and officials followed suit. Over the long term such conversions to Christianity made as little impact on the Shona as had Islam; the cult of Mwari met the spiritual and psychological needs of the people. But the political repercussions were felt almost immediately, for the Muslims believed their position jeopardized and Nogomo took alarm at the mounting Portuguese presence.

Fearful of losing their leverage in the empire with the conversions, the Muslims, according to the Portuguese version, sowed doubts in the mind of Nogomo Sebastian about the intentions of the Europeans, and he reportedly ordered the missionary killed. More recent analysts, however, have concluded that Nogomo was more responsible for the priest's death than the Portuguese cared to concede.[3] Although he was warned about the dangers surrounding him, Gonçalo da Silveira persevered in his religious labours until he was strangled and tossed into the Zambezi. His corpse eventually contributed to one of the last crusades against Islam. But not until after nearly a decade did an expeditionary force embark for Mozambique and even then its departure owed more to the grandiose vision of the young, enigmatic King Sebastian than a corpse in a faraway African river. At 14 years, Sebastian reached his majority in 1568. Once on the Portuguese throne, he undertook a series of campaigns to destroy Islam and to enrich the crown. Turning to southeast Africa this self-proclaimed Captain of Christ, despite some court opposition to the switch from peace to war, commissioned Francisco Barreto to drive out Islam from Mozambique and gain access to the goldmines of Mwene Mutapa.

Upstream from Sena on the right bank of the Zambezi Barreto's expeditionary army, arquebusiers against spearmen, fought a pitched battle for three days in 1572, and reportedly killed 4,000 Tongas, enemies of Portugal and Nogomo. This thumping victory became a foundation of sand upon which was built the stubborn myth of the invincibility of European troops and of fire-arms against less well-armed opponents in the tropics. Barreto's column of 800 soldiers, many of them noblemen, encumbered with armour, horses and unwieldly cannons, dissolved in the rain and pestilence of the Zambezi environment by the next year. But the myth endured.[4]

Despite its overall lacklustre performance, Barreto's army struck out at Islam. Encamped at Sena, his men dealt a severe blow to an upcountry Muslim community. Suspecting the Muslims of poisoning their fever-ridden comrades and horses, the men vented their anger and hatred on the small community according to the custom of the day. Men, women and children were exploded from cannons or ripped apart by various weapons. 400 years later and a little further up the river at the village of Wiriyamu a Portuguese-trained force went berserk massacring the villagers for their alleged support to the cause of independence and testifying to a continuity of Portuguese conduct in Mozambique.

Seeing the usefulness of Portuguese arms (and because of a series of natural disasters interpreted by the Mutapa as retribution for the Jesuit's murder), Nogomo had a change of heart. He ordered the execution of some Muslims at court. More importantly, Nogomo concluded in 1575 the first formal agreement that began the reduction of Mwene Mutapa's independence by signing over to Portugal the right to trade freely, mine gold, establish churches and expel Muslims from lands under his direct jurisdiction. Subsequent treaties and greater intervention into the affairs of Mwene Mutapa were needed to effect its subservience to Portugal, but the Mutapas found themselves in the increasingly unhappy position of paying the piper without calling the tune.

Nogomo's vacillation toward the Portuguese and then the Muslims was both a symptom and a cause of the Karanga empire's downfall. In time, other Mutapas did likewise. As the Mutapas struggled to preserve the empire, they practised a policy of greater dependence on the Portuguese punctuated by outbreaks of independence and continual backslides from Christianity. By vacillating they displayed an awareness of the Karanga's waning paramountcy. But having dealings with Europeans hobbled chances of building an African front against Portuguese encroachments, and in turn resulted in a greater dependence on the foreigners. A similar pattern of intervention and African independence had enabled the Portuguese to dominate Manica and Quiteve.

The reign of Gasti Rusere, Nogomo's successor, deepened Mwene Mutapa's dependence on the Portuguese. In return for military assistance to lash back at his enemies, the Mutapa signed a treaty in 1607 to turn over to the crown his gold, copper and iron mines and entrust two daughters and three sons to Portuguese education and the Catholic faith. Despite other military misadventures necessitating Portuguese arms, Gasti Rusere delayed revealing the sites of the mines.[5] The arrogance of local authorities in refusing to extend the customary *curva*, the payment—usually cloth—by a newly appointed officer to the Matapa or lesser chief, and the greed of the

Zambezi settlers for land and gold go a long way in explaining Gasti Rusere's obstructions.[6] Adept at the game of cat-and-mouse, he also wanted to keep the Europeans obedient to his wishes by withholding information on the valuable minerals.

Until his death in 1627, Gasti Rusere relied on foreign arms but contrived to thwart Portuguese designs. He frustrated Portuguese efforts to find his metal wealth by placing difficulties in their path and engineering treachery in their midst. As befitted the head of a shrinking empire, he fought rearguard wars and shifted allegiances. Contemporary European monarchs behaved no differently, and like them Gasti Rusere made and broke alliances as circumstances demanded. To consider the Karangas's dependence on Portuguese arms as a sellout of Africans to Europeans is to view their policy in light of a later day's racial and colonial problem as well as from the secure knowledge of hindsight. But Gasti Rusere's policy was only a temporary stay against inevitable disintegration, and it carried in its core the erosion of the Mutapa's legitimacy as an African chief.

The next Mutapa, Nyambo Kapararidze, squarely pitted the Karanga empire against Portuguese domination. He forcibly reminded them of the overdue curva, perhaps to reassert the empire's independence. Declaring an empata, he besieged the fairs. Help to the beleaguered traders arrived from the residents of Sena who counterattacked at Massapa, the principal fair. Afterwards the residents announced the dethronement of Kapararidze.

Alive to the dangers that a hostile Mutapa posed to gold trading and prospecting, the Portuguese decided on a departure from their customary policy in their dealings with the Karanga empire.[7] At the dzimbabwe, they enthroned Mavura, an uncle of the deposed Mutapa, who was more to their persuasion. Because of the foreign underpinning of his position, Mavura proved to be a Mutapa to the Portuguese liking, although he had streaks of independence. In 1629, he scrawled his mark on a significant treaty that made him a vassal of the Portuguese king, and this 'Lord of the mines of gold and silver' in addition opened his lands to Portuguese prospectors and traders. The treaty also provided for a wide allowance of evangelical pursuits, and stripped away many of the ceremonial obligations paid to the Mutapa, such as the required presents and deferential hand-clapping by persons of lesser station.[8]

Despite this capitulation, all was not well in the Zambezi region. Little gold fell into Portuguese coffers as a result of the unstable political situation. Kapararidze still lived biding his time in resentful exile. His hand can be discerned behind the uprising that shortly engulfed the 'Rivers' — a wedge of Portuguese influence extending from Chicoa to Sofala and Quelimane on the coast. The tinderbox ignited in 1631 with a xenophobic explosion. From Mavura's *dzimbabwe* to the coast, Portuguese settlers, missionaries and traders were killed. The resourcefulness of Kapararidze and his recognized legitimacy as the Mutapa provide a partial explanation for the dimensions of the rising, but the Portuguese themselves engendered fiery bitterness by their refusal to obey traditional customs, and by their king-making and king-breaking and their general arrogance. African chieftaincies on the land and river approaches to the Karanga lands harboured smouldering resentment of Portuguese trespassing and meddling. So much so that Manica, which paid only lip service to the Karanga chief, joined in the revolt.

Chaos fed on chaos until the rising ran its course reducing the Portuguese population of over 300 to some 40 panic-stricken survivors huddled in Sena, Quelimane, Tete and a couple of f...[9] With the less fortunate Europeans perished thousands of African adherents and their adversaries. Anarchy in the interior and Dutch and English threats to Mozambique Island brought double trouble to Portugal's hard-pressed hold on Mozambique.* Such twilights in Africa reinforced Portugal's tenacity and belief right up to contemporary times that it could outlast the dark hours until the dawn of changing fortunes.

The Portuguese retrieved the disaster with the inevitable winding down of the rising and the perennial African cleavages. Once again, Kapararidze's forces were put to flight and Mavura was reinstated. Foiled in two attempts to rule the Karanga kingdom, Kapararidze persisted in his efforts to recover the throne, albeit with caution and without success until his death. A restless peace gradually descended, and with it a measure of trade took place. The residents, the cause of much of the trouble, kept up their waywardness.

A brief account of the *prazo* ('estate') owners will be given in the next chapter, but for now these Afro-Portuguese residents of the

---

*   The Spanish throne's takeover of Portugal (1580-1640) made Holland and England enemies who threatened the Portuguese coastal defenses in Mozambique. The Spanish crown did not change administration in the colony.

Zambezi Valley, like settlers elsewhere, professed loyalty in sentiment but in practice clashed with the mother country's interference. Made up originally of *degregados*, deserters and ex-soldiers, these *prazo* holders, who became Africanized, broke the crown's laws, killed its ministers and fought wars against its African subjects. By mid-seventeenth century, the power and unruliness of the residents introduced a third force in the Rivers — a force acting contrary to Lisbon's and Goa's efforts to prop up their Karanga puppets and to gain a regular flow of gold. At the end of the century, the crown's authority was flimsier than a hundred years before, and it was as unwilling to open new problems as it was unable to act against the troublesome Rivers.

When Mavura died in 1652, a long and generally beneficial relationship with a pro-Portuguese Mutapa was finished. Rebels killed the next Portuguese favourite, Siti Kazurukumusapa, 'so they might approve the one to be chosen king'. [10] They replaced him with Mukombwe, a younger brother and stronger ruler. His dealings with the Portuguese, although more discordant than some of his predecessors, served as no substantial check on the Zambezi residents.

Mukombwe's reign of nearly 30 years witnessed continued Portuguese land seizures and arrogant mistreatment of the population. The depredations of their private armies lowered the prestige of the Mutapa in African eyes. By strong-arm tactics, the Portuguese had also begun to acquire mastery in Quiteve and Manica provinces. Under the Macombe dynasty, Barue, another eastern province, achieved a measure of independence, although it acknowledged some Portuguese suzerainty. But the zone between the Limpopo and Save rivers, never an integral part of Mwene Mutapa jurisdiction, slid into isolation with Karanga impotence. [11]

This sword-point marauding brought a tapering off in gold and trade profits for the royal treasury, for Africans refused to discover new gold diggings only to have Europeans dispossess them of the fresh finds. Wars with the Tonga, who inhabit the lands near the town of Tete, and the Manica kingdom further disrupted commerce. Still, the dwindling export of brazil wood from Brazil and the loss of Portuguese strongpoints on the Indian Ocean littoral in the late seventeenth century relatively raised the value of Mozambique's trade, although it alone could not stop the decline of the colony after 1700.

Plans to settle immigrants so as to dilute the *prazo* owner's power were abandoned in 1637, when more pressing manpower needs for defence called in Brazil and India. Again four decades later, Lisbon planned on halting resident abuses by the settlement of farmers and artisans in the Zambezi region. And again its dreams amounted to little real commitment. 78 men, women and children arrived in the Rivers in 1680, but, although their numbers more than doubled the Portuguese population, they failed to accomplish the crown's hopes, succumbing to fever or to the same wickedness of the residents.[12]

By the close of the seventeenth century—a century of active imperial interest and haphazard expansion in Mozambique—Afro-Portuguese affairs had fallen to an unsalvageable level. Portuguese actions had become bywords for land robbery and tyranny. Their puppet regimes in Mwene Mutapa, however, had not gone unnoticed, and it bred a hostility in the kingdom of Changamire whose counter-conquest nearly broke Portugal's fragile hold in east Africa. At the least, it weakened Portugal in Mozambique for over 150 years.

CHANGAMIRE'S ADVANCE AND MWENE MUTAPA'S DISMEMBERMENT

The Kingdom of Changamire—called Abutua by Portuguese chroniclers—split from the Mwene Mutapa empire near the end of the fifteenth century under Changa, onetime vassal of the Mutapa. Assuming the praise name of Changamire, this king founded a dynamic dynasty that at first collaborated with the adjoining province of Mbire against Nyahuma in about 1490 and then conquered that province, supplanting its Togwa dynasty during the seventeenth century. Throughout the sixteenth and seventeenth centuries, Changamire's sway spread as the Mwene Mutapa's jurisdiction contracted. Changamire's ascendancy in the face of its rival's collapse can be explained partly by its isolation from Europeans's corrosive infiltration.

Hewing to traditional commercial patterns, Changamire blocked Portuguese traders from entry. Its military prowess, which was in an ascendant phase, enabled it to shun the easy expediency of Portuguese firepower. It, therefore, maintained a sort of iron-curtain exclusion from the *sertanejos*.

Owing to the absence of Portuguese infiltration there is a corresponding dearth of information about Changamire. The Mutapas, who sought to use the Portuguese in their duel with the Changamires, also discouraged interest in Abutua lest the Portuguese learn the extent of Mwene Mutapa's decline and of its rival's gold. Something of Changamire, however, was recorded when it challenged Portuguese domination of the Mutapas.

The inevitable clash between African conqueror and European invader took place in 1683 in Maungwe, a minor vassal state of the Karanga, where a small number of residents and their armed retainers tried to repel Changamire Dombo's advance. Dombo hoped to take advantage of the Portuguese weakness. The day-long battle proved a draw despite possession of firearms by the Portuguese. Playing on his enemy's fears of reinforcements to decide the morrow's battle, Dombo ordered the kindling of many false camp fires that night. The ruse worked and the Portuguese force fled into the darkness thinking they were hopelessly outnumbered. A decade later Dombo followed up the victory. This delay can be explained by his takeover of the Togwa's kingdom of Mbire rather than any dread of his enemies. During the same period Dombo's foes also suffered domestic problems with a breach of unity.

Interregnums in southern African politics have often produced disorder and instability as claimants vied for the throne. Such crises in the Karanga empire had fitted into the designs of the Portuguese as they allied themselves with one faction or another in a policy of *divide et impera*. When Mukombwe died in 1669, however, the tables were turned, and they found themselves odd man out. True to form, they had baptized and groomed Mukombwe's son, Mhande, to follow him. But the dead Mutapa's brother, Nyakambiro, usurped the throne with popular support before the Portuguese puppet could be invested.[13] Either from hatred of the Portuguese or from the fear they would depose him, Nyakambiro welcomed the Karanga empire's chief rival and enemy to enter his lands and to expel them. His invitation to Dombo brought down not only the foreign domination but also reduced the Karanga empire to a remnant of its former size.

Dombo's armies descended on the unsuspecting settlements in 1693 and swept them away with the suddeness and destructiveness of a tropical storm. Fairs and estates in Manica, Karangaland and the country right to the outskirts of Tete were submerged before the Portuguese and their African allies could counter-attack. Then Mhande, the Portuguese-backed nominee, took to the field to repulse the attackers. His counter-assault recaptured the empire's *dzimbabwe* and compelled Nyakambiro to seek the protection of Dombo; but it recovered little else. The bulk of the empire was lost forever and the dynasty retreated eastward to the province of Chidima where the Portuguese propped up subsequent Mutapa puppets. Reinforcements and supplies from the coast reached Sena but these certainly would have proved inadequate if Dombo had wheeled his army from Manica toward the river town in 1695 as expected.[14] But one of the chance-factors of history intervened. Dombo unexpectedly died in the full tide of victory, and to the great rejoicing of his enemies the war ceased. The Portuguese never gained the initiative against Dombo or future Changamires.

Changamire's attack on Portuguese encroachments stemmed from economic as well as political considerations. Being a land-locked state, it wanted unrestricted trade access to the sea — also a *desideratum* of the present-day Rhodesian government. Dombo's triumph excluded the Portuguese from the Mashona plateau and confined their trading and settlements to a triangular zone in which one side ran from Cabora Bassa rapids down the right bank of the Zambezi. The coast from the river's delta to Sofala and then inland to the rapids formed the base and other leg of this triangle. Beyond the triangle of Portugal's indirect empire, European traders and fairs existed at the sufferance of Changamire or his vassals. Rather than permit Portuguese traders to cross into its territory in what is today's southern and eastern region of Rhodesia, Changamire, famous for its pure gold, relied on African porters and *mussambazes*, black professional traders, to service its fairs by routes established before Europeans entered Mozambique. Travelling inland from Zumbo on the upper Zambezi or up the Save, African caravans carried on a commerce in gold and ivory for Portuguese and Indian merchants. Some artifacts and documents also suggest a little trade to the Delagoa Bay region with the Dutch.[15]

In the kingdom of Quiteve, which was squarely in their wedge-shaped zone, the *sertanejos* reverted in 1699 to their standard practice of deposing a recalcitrant paramount chief for a pro-Portuguese puppet named Inhaunda, who was to open the gold mines to European production. This produced not gold for Sofala but a Portuguese retreat before hostile chiefs, the death of Inhaunda and a war among claimants that temporarily dislocated trade.[16] These reverses coincided with Portugal's loss of Mombasa on the east African coast to the Omani Arabs in 1698. Power politics were not discredited, just Portuguese power.

A word about warfare: Musket-fire often, although not always, proved decisive; but it was certainly overrated by the Portuguese. Much depended on the numbers and deployment of musketmen. Kapararidze's rebellion in 1631 and Dombo's campaign in 1693 overcame Portuguese resistance and expelled residents from fairs and settlements despite their weapons. Diogo Simões Madeira, an eminent *prazo* owner, skillfully employed small groups of armed men with Gasti Rusere's forces to turn the tide against the larger armies of his challengers. To protect themselves from African bowmen, the Portuguese plaited wicker screens, some of which shielded two scores of men and had apertures for return fire. Chiefs acquired firearms through trade, and their followers learned to shoot with skill. The Tonga chief, Chombe, on Bandari Rock at the mouth of the Zambezi's Lupta Gorge armed his forces with 'a hundred and fifty firelocks and muskets and two cannons' to exact payment for travel up the Zambezi.[17] It took no less a soldier than Medeira several months to break the blockade. One side or the other at times fought from behind palisaded stockades built from green tree trunks that took root and strengthened the wall as they grew. The strongholds of living trees about 100 yards in length that protected a village in the seventeenth century developed into *aringas*, giant fortified compounds capable of housing thousands of inhabitants, by mid-nineteenth century. The Portuguese built some stone and mud-brick forts but these were usually in a sad state of disrepair.[18] Once breached, usually by fire or axe, the occupants—men, women and children—were enslaved and the fort or stockade sacked. African and Portuguese alike were capable of cruelty as well as valour and tenacity.

The collapse of Portuguese power stripped the Karanga emperors of their secure undergirding, but the Mwene Mutapa empire ended not with a bang but a whimper. Dating from the Mhande-Nyakambiro feud, the position of Mutapa was never long free from aspirants who eliminated each other with almost wearisome regularity. The political interference of Changamires and Portuguese only escalated the rivalries by sometimes supplanting each other's candidates. These succession disputes kept the coals of civil strife burning, and the turmoil convinced the Portuguese residents to desert their *prazos* above Tete on the right side of the river.

Dombo's victory delimited the former empire to a chieftaincy in the unhealthy lowlands immediately south of the Cabora Bassa rapids, an area which straddled the undemarcated and turbulent frontier separating Portuguese and Changamire spheres of influence. This geo-political spot contributed to its further deterioration. Yet the Portuguese kept up the ceremonial appearances in their relations with the Mutapas whose coronation ceremony called for baptism to validate the chief's investiture.[19] Still referring to the Mutapas as emperors, they indulged the pretensions of succeeding rulers and strengthened their justification to territorial claims in Mozambique during the 'Scramble for Africa' on lands ceded by paramount chiefs in the sixteenth and seventeenth centuries. 1917 saw the destruction of the last significant dynastic citadel of the Karanga when the Portuguese crushed the Barue rebellion and ended the 400 year dual between Portuguese invaders and Karanga chiefs. The eclipse of the old Karanga empire in the 1690s drove home, however, the reality of Changamire's hegemony over much of the country south of the Zambezi.

From the Rhodesian plateau, Changamire exercised suzerainty over much of central Mozambique for almost a century and a half after the ejection of the Portuguese from all but the lower Zambezi region. In the 1830s, the invading Ngoni and Ndebele overran the Changamire empire, dispersing and destroying the Rozwi dynasty and its subjects. With them went a valuable source of oral history. Till then archaeological evidence points to the flourishing of an artistic and prosperous civilization. The fertile, salubrious highlands furnished the inhabitants with sufficient food to free the society for architectural pursuits. Zimbabwe was elaborated and enlarged, and many smaller stone structures were erected throughout the empire. Tools and ornaments of gold, copper and iron as well as soapstone carvings bare silent testimony to the achievements of the Changamires.

DELAGOA BAY AND THE SOUTH

Clustered around Delagoa Bay in southernmost Mozambique stood several small Rhonga chieftaincies which survived to the nineteenth century. The Rhongas are a group of the Thonga-speaking peoples who inhabit the region from the Save River to the bay. The Rhonga's occupation of malarial coastal lowlands and distance from Zimbabwe helps explain their freedom from Changamire and Mwene empires. To the west, less than 50 miles from Delagoa Bay are the Limbombo Mountains which hampered communication and no doubt interior control of the coastal peoples. The bay region is drained by a series of confluent tributaries and rivers that flow into the Indian Ocean. Slightly up the coast is the Limpopo, the largest river south of the Save. Although it coursed through the southern edge of Changamire, the Limpopo apparently carried little trade between it and the Rhonga peoples. None of the seven chiefdoms or small states encircling the bay probably ever had more than 15,000 subjects. Under capable leadership, one of the chiefdoms sometimes established sway over its weaker neighbour until displaced by a more skillful or powerful rival.

It is learned from sixteenth and seventeenth century documents, some from shipwrecked sailors, that relations among the Rhonga chieftaincies were at times stormy, and conflict was not unknown. The chief of Inhaca eagerly sought Portuguese trade and aid against a rival in 1552.[20] As a sustained Portuguese presence was absent in the early period of European contact in Mozambique, the catastrophic consequences of foreign penetration for this chieftaincy were postponed. Opportunities for Portuguese interference existed, however, for the Rhonga chiefdoms displayed signs of political instability so well-documented in the states to the north.

Until the 1540s, the Portuguese visits to the Delagoa coast were brief and made usually by shipwrecked survivors. But the disappointing Sofalan gold trade and the Muslim control of inland trade compelled the Portuguese to undertake a systematic investigation of the southern coast. In 1544, the same year the Quelimane factory was established, the crown dispatched Lourenço Marques at the head of an expedition. Because of his observations of plentiful ivory, which by this time the Portuguese had come to value, Mozambique Island sent an annual trading vessel with fair regularity. The ships carted away primarily ivory but also amber,

slaves, honey, rhinoceros horns and hippopotamus teeth — a sub-
stitute for ivory. A moderate long-distance trade for ivory as far
south as Natal developed with the Rhonga functioning as middlemen exchanging European goods. During the late eighteenth
century, the Thonga, who previously acted as immobile middlemen, began to seek out trade goods from the interior people.[21] No
attempt was made at first to set up a permanent settlement or
factory. Looked at from the Portuguese point of view such
permanency probably would not have improved trade and would
have subjected the settlers to the ravages of fever.

Sooner rather than later, difficulties arose from this sporadic
trading. Disputes broke out between certain Rhonga chieftaincies
and the Portuguese in which the latter were worsted in more than
one instance. War and sacked ships were considered by Africans as
proper retribution for Portuguese misconduct. Fear of reprisals
forced the ship captains to change locations and even to suspend
briefly transactions. But Portuguese difficulties arose not from
Africans alone, for by the last decades of the seventeenth century
English merchants were out-bartering their European predecessors
with fine brassware. The trade in highly-prized brass basins and
bowls depleted the ivory stocks compelling Portuguese ships to
return to Mozambique Island with near empty holds. At the
beginning of the eighteenth century as Mozambique's trade fell off,
the Portuguese stopped the Delagoa Bay vessels, and abandoned
posts at Quelimane and Angoche Island to spare the expense and to
shorten lines of defence. Inhambane, more than 100 miles up the
coast, however, enjoyed so much trade in ivory and most of all
slaves that it surpassed all the Portuguese centres in Mozambique
except Sena after mid-eighteenth century.

Toward the end of the century, the Portuguese reestablished
themselves at Delagoa partly as a result of the stimulus provided by
the departure of a Dutch East India Company post and the profitable trading of English and Austrian ships. Early in the next
century, they realized their goal of a monopoly by shutting off
foreign traders.[22] Fortunately for the Portuguese, the meagre trade
below Inhambane did not bring competition from Indian
merchants who began to arrive on the south coast about the 1840s.

Here in the south as in central Mozambique, African chiefs
looked to Portugal to survive their neighbour's expansion. The
Mfumo chiefdom, at the mouth of Espirito Santo River, depended

on Portuguese trade and power from the 1780s. When the Portuguese temporarily withdrew until the next century, Mfumo fell prey to the domination of Matoll. On their return, the Portuguese gained a toehold on the bay and the commercial contacts of Mfumo as compensation for their support.[23] In time, they extended a type of suzerainty over it. During much of the nineteenth century, Matoll thwarted Portuguese expansion. Portugal finally conquered the last Rhonga chiefdoms in the 1890s but not before they involved it in an ambitious campaign against the formidable Gungunyane.

NORTH OF THE ZAMBEZI

The historical evolution of the Malawi states lagged behind that of the Mwene Mutapa. Malawi expansion was still in progress when the Portuguese first proceeded up the Zambezi Valley in the 1530s. Sometime during the same century, the Kalonga's kinsmen split off after disputes, and took military-settlement expeditions from his headquarters on the south shore of Lake Malawi. As described in chapter 1, Lundu and Kaphwiti settled along the Shire River, and Undi occupied the region north-west of Tete. These Nyanja-speaking invaders apparently had gained superior state organizing abilities and perhaps developed military prowess from their expertise as elephant hunters. Their settlements hatched states that progressed to independent kingdoms as they enveloped smaller and weaker political units until most of Mozambique north of the Zambezi felt their influence, if not their subjugation.

The greater strength of the Undi's kingdom provides half the explanation why it avoided a sixteenth or seventeenth century confrontation with the advancing Portuguese, who spun fictitious tales of cannibals inhabiting the north bank in order perhaps to justify their timidity in crossing the Zambezi. The other half is that the gold fever of the Portuguese initially blinded them to anything but the known goldfields on the south side of the river. Yet violent repercussions above the river from Portuguese expansion to the south there certainly were.

Portuguese posts on the Zambezi had as one goal the elimination of Muslim traders from the route to the Mashonaland gold-fields. While the Portuguese were ultimately successful, they also disrupted the trade in ivory—a commodity of great importance to

Malawi commerce. Ivory from the country north of the Zambezi had become the staple article of trade to the coast and a source of wealth to Malawi chiefs. Knocking out the Muslim merchants on the river and coast generated tensions within Malawi societies deprived of their markets for ivory exchange. This dislocation in ivory commerce may have set off a chain of events culminating in the devastating Zimba upheaval. Professor Alpers offers a plausible explanation for the 'infamous Zimba migration' which spread death and destruction to the coast in the 1580s. The Portuguese used the name *Zimba* to denote truculence, although today a small ethnic group near Tete is called Zimba. But the Zimbas of the raiding migrations were for the most part followers of Lundu.[24] Lundu's forces surged eastward to the coast opposite Mozambique Island, subdued the Makua people and founded the Manganja kingdom. This eastern state, called the Bororo kingdom by the Portuguese, owed its origins to economic motives as well as the personal ambition of Lundu. The conquest opened a land route to the coast which lessened the reliance on the ruptured river commerce. Malawi traders also forged an overland route to Kilwa which received the new trade contacts with enthusiasm, for its pre-eminent commercial position had been overthrown by the Portuguese interlopers on the coast. Thus Malawi's expansionist drives may have been in part a response to Portugal's sixteenth-century policy to dislodge Muslim traders from southeast Africa.

The Undi's huge kingdom north of the upper Zambezi had more than just the autonomy of a distant province from the central authority of Kalonga. Indeed, it must have posed an economic and political threat to the mother kingdom, for the reigning Kalonga, Muzura, was not precipitous in checking his wayward vassal state. Setting right internal matters. Muzura next secured his flank by good relations with the residents in the vicinity of Tete. Then he scored a diplomatic *coup* of sorts in 1608 by forecasting and supporting with several thousand armed men the winning side in a challenge to Gasti Rusere's reign. Thanks to his reinforcements the Portuguese put to flight the Mutapa's enemies. Not long afterwards Muzura took advantage of the residents' appreciation and more importantly their alarm at Undi whose forces menaced their *prazos*. Together they defeated Undi's army, but Muzura allowed the Undi kingdom continued autonomy. The Malawi empire now extended from Mozambique's coast to the Luangwa River west of Lake

Malawi.[25] It stood at the peak of power and unity by mid-seventeenth century; but its descent was in the offing.

Gratitude and alliances were short lived in the rough-and-tumble politics of northern Mozambique. When Gasti Rusere died, Muzura attempted to wrest control of part of the Karanga empire. He failed but the attempt began a period of bloody feuds on the north bank of the Zambezi as the Undi and the Portuguese wrestled for its possession.[26] Already the residents had begun to cast covetous eyes across the river on seeing gold from recent strikes.

The possibility of silver and gold in the Undi's domains and the widening warfare south of the Zambezi switched Portuguese attention to the north toward the end of the seventeenth century. While silver exercised a magnetic pull on the first few prospectors and the crown's dreams, the actual get-rich rush to the north bank took place for gold. Scholars of this period are still puzzled by the source of the silver brought to the coast since silver deposits have not yet been found anywhere in Africa. Chiefs on both sides of the Zambezi became vague when pressed for details of the silver mines. Perhaps it was traded inland in bygone centuries. Gold veins were, however, discoverable, although quickly exhausted. The belief that gold lay in the next hill or stream drove men and even a couple of women estate owners mad with the desire for wealth: it drove them into a genuine gold rush.

Settlers from Tete and Sena, fugitives and even priests swarmed over the north bank from Lupta Gorge to Cabora Bassa. They set up mining camps and marked out land claims, obliging Africans to abdicate authority and withdraw from their territory. Hundreds of slaves working one site demonstrated not only the labour requirements to make the strikes profitable but also the vast power of Portuguese fortune seekers. Gifts were at first given for privileges and ceded land but then outright conquest, at times contrary to official policy, alienated land from Malawi chiefs. Their land grabbing undermined the Bive, a Undi tributary chief across from Tete, and weakened the Undi state system itself. By mid-eighteenth century, the Portuguese influx recreated the turmoil of the previous assault on the Mwene Mutapa empire. 'Feudal-type strongmen appeared on the north side of the river and again hacked out large estates with hundreds or thousands of armed African retainers.[27]

A united reaction to the Portuguese invasion was made impossible by the Malawi empire's disintegration. As early as the

beginning of the eighteenth century the empire, in reality a confederation of kingdoms and peoples, began to fall apart: the
Manganja kingdom divided into many chieftaincies; the Malawi
kingdom of Undi displayed growing autonomy; and everywhere
Kalonga incurred some form of disobedience. Challenged on their
southern and eastern frontier by the *prazo* owners the Malawi states
also faced commercial competition in their lands by Yao and Bisa
traders who trespassed to the coast in the commerce of slaves and
ivory. Yao and Bisa commercial ventures were probably both a
factor and sign of imperial Malawi's decay. With the growing drift
of the Makua-Lomwe peoples from its orbit, the Malawi empire lost
not only an outlet to the Indian Ocean but also witnessed its
acquisition by the Yao and Bisa. The Malawi state soon degen-
erated into petty struggles and frequent strife.[28]

The Yao people inhabited the region to the east of Lake Malawi
and acted as middlemen for goods to and from the interior. By the
last years of the eighteenth century, Yao traders also travelled north
of Cape Delgado to Arab markets to obtain greater returns than
from the Portuguese on Mozambique Island.[29] Bisa traders
travelled a much greater distance from the Lunda kingdom of
Mwata Kazembe, the capital of which lay near Lake Mweru in the
Luapula Valley of present-day Zaire; they also exchanged items
with the Yao. It was the accounts of Bisa traders that sparked the
famous Lacerda expedition to the Mwata Kazembe's territory in
1798. Originally sent to the Zambezi to blaze a transcontinental
crossing to Angola in order to substantiate Portugal's claims to
central Africa in the light of Britain's first occupation of Capetown
in 1795, Lacerda e Almeida decided instead on an embassy to
the Mwata Kazembe court to open trade relations.[30] Although he
died before reaching his destination, Lacerda's journey was
offered — along with similar undertakings made afterwards — nearly
a century later by Portugal as justification for international recognition to a land corridor connecting Mozambique and Angola. By
that juncture, Lisbon's claims to the hinterland were more dubious
than ever.

Leaving aside the notable exception of Changamire with its
Rhodesian base, the major states and empires of Mozambique by
the eighteenth century were in decline, disunity or exhaustion. The
Muslims trading network had been destroyed south of Cape
Delgado; Mwene Mutapa had been reduced to a contested pro-

vince; and the Portuguese had been expelled from earlier advances inland and on the coast, ending their supposed golden age of occupation in Mozambique. While village life wound its traditional passage through time, the resiliency of African society renewed itself the way luxuriant African foliage covers over the untrodden path. It is within this setting that Portuguese estates underwent an Africanization in what is one of the most fascinating episodes of African history.

4

THE PRAZOS: AFRICAN AND PORTUGUESE SOCIETY

Much of the history of Mozambique (what comparatively little there is written) is portrayed as the history of the *prazos da corôa*, or crown estates, in the Zambezi region. The explanations for this historiographical focus are plentiful: the Zambezi itself courses through a central part of the country and any settlement on its banks and tributaries assumes an inherent geopolitical significance; the *prazos*, some with immense lands and hundreds of armed retainers, were significant settlements in themselves; the very uniqueness of the hybrid institutions, part African and part Portuguese, was sure to capture scholarly attention; their institutional longevity warranted historical investigation; and their destruction involved Portugal in Mozambique's *sertão* for the first time in centuries as only military intervention could.

The *prazo* system emerged from the chaotic environment during the breakup of the Mwene Mutapa empire. Because of the disordered conditions, the Shona and Tonga peoples for security and sustenance reassembled around Portuguese strongmen who seized the advantage to establish their own chiefly rule over former chieftainships. The presence of the Portuguese altered African state formation around strong chiefs or dynamic societies that usually succeeded the collapse of an overlord state. Into the place of African *mambos* stepped Portuguese felons, ex-soldiers, female orphans and penniless officials to take up chiefly roles without upsetting the peoples' religious beliefs, social customs or economic patterns: they forcefully disrupted existing systems, however. Unlike the Boer communities to the south or most European societies in Africa, the Portuguese and Indian residents did not live in a closed world, self-sufficient to its own needs and cares. The *prazo* masters relied on Africans for defence, trade, food and women. Using African techniques as well as labour in mining gold, hunting elephants, raising food and building houses and forts, they gradually became Africanized. It was this adaptation that enabled them to survive. Alternately, they played up their Portuguese-ness when it suited their social aspirations or dealings with the crown's representatives. It was a dual personality and in some respects a dual system that over the generations became more African than European. The fusion of blood and culture produced the *muzungos* — to Africans, persons of black parentage who lived as Europeans, and to the nineteenth-century Portuguese, those of non-African extraction who adopted African modes of life.[1] The estate owner began as a sort of surrogate chief and by the mid-nineteenth century he had become virtually an African leader defending his way of life and territory against renewed Portuguese invasions.

THE ESTATES AND THE CROWN

The *prazo*'s historical basis lay in the Roman contractual arrangement of emphyteusis which provided the lessee with rights and a long-term hold over land, usually for three generations. The reasons for its usage in Portugal and under Portuguese application in Mozambique were similar — to allow the lessee freedom of action and length of tenure to encourage the development of land and yet not surrender the crown's ownership. Starting in the early seventeenth century, the crown issued land titles to the *sertanejos* (some captains of the forts and fairs began issuing them in the 1580s)[2] in a policy of expediency, for it had not the power to do otherwise. Thin resources and scarce manpower determined that the crown from the outset of expansion should delegate judicial, administrative and fiscal duties to individuals, the first of whom carried feudal values to the tropics. What it perceived in the *sertanejos*'s freebooting activities on the Zambezi was a means to insure a flow of gold and a rough administration at little expense to itself. By issuing land titles — in reality acknowledging already possessed land — the crown maintained the fiction of its ownership and prerogatives. A few respected members of Portuguese society, such as Madeira, received titles to land for their services.[3] For their part, *prazo* holders craved royal recognition of their claims against cutthroat rivals or revanchist African chiefs seeking to regain land purchased, conquered or ceded. Upon this slender reed hung Portugal's nominal control and international claims to east Africa for over 300 years until nearly broken by the Zambezi wars.

On both banks of the Zambezi from Tete to the Indian Ocean and 100 miles up and down the coast from the delta, the estates occupied wide swaths of territory.* Most titles were awarded for three lives but regrants to the same family were legal and common, because physical possession made it difficult to transfer property to other owners, and the paucity of residents dictated this continuation. Not all grants were subject to termination or renewal after three generations; the *terra em fatiota* was a perpetual lease requiring loyalty to the crown and a small rent. One novel aspect of the granting regulations developed with the transference of *prazos* from mother to daughter rather than through males. Grants of position and land had been first given in Goa to the orphaned daughters of noblemen and loyal servants. Unoccupied *prazos* by the early eighteenth century had become the dowries of worthy women so as to repay the services of their fathers, provide for the daughters and enable the girls to attract husbands to Mozambique. The arrangement was intended to enlarge the European population and to halt the *prazos* from falling under control of a few powerful families. It did neither.

The *prazo*'s dowries lured scarcely any metropolitan Portuguese husbands to the feverish Zambezi, and the *donas* married into established families whose strength afforded a means of safeguarding the grant, if not a European husband.[4] Not very surprisingly, a few of the *donas* were as deft and ruthless in wielding power as the *senhors*. Men also sought entrance to the *prazo* society and the protection of prominent families by marriage. Governors of the River (*Tenente-Geral*), who were not already *prazo* lords, as many were, married for allies to carry out their duties and to enrich themselves. Neither was possible without the support of some powerful resident.

The obligations of estate holders were as numerous as the times they were broken; indeed, the laws depict more what was common practice than what was enforced by the distant crown. Its dependence on the *prazo* colony for defence and administration made the crown rely on even its infrequent and cursory discharge of royal functions. Lisbon enacted regulations that prohibited officials from granting themselves or religious orders estates, required land to be given to settlers for cultivation, outlawed absenteeism of

* There were also some *prazos* on the Querimba Islands and around Sofala.

owners, demanded *prazo* owners to maintain roads and forts and later limited the size of the *prazos* to about nine square miles (some reached 1,000 square miles).[5] The Zambezi Portuguese paid little heed to the government's regulations. Lisbon's answer to the abuses of estate owners was to issue and reissue decrees in a mystifying belief that paper laws promulgated in Portugal would right the situation in Mozambique: it was a Portuguese failing that lasted as long as the east African colony.

THE *PRAZO* CHIEFS

The Portuguese acquired chieftaincies and smaller traditional lands for their estates. The whirling-swirling world of *prazo* politics, however, made for rapid acquisition and loss of lands. Instability among individual estates, especially small ones, was commonplace and yet the system as a whole endured for centuries. Such long-lived *prazos* as Gorongosa, Cheringoma and Luabo encompassing hundreds of square miles and governing thousands of inhabitants give rise, however, to the false impression of the imposition of alien rule over the indigenous people. Nothing could be further from the truth. In fact, the transference of lands and people to Portuguese control approximated the incorporation of one African entity by another or by an African chief.

Along with the take-over of African territorial limits went the assumption of a chiefly role and dependence on the African hierarchy. Manuel Barreto, a Jesuit priest, wrote in 1667:

> The holders of these lands have the same power and jurisdiction as the Kaffir fumos [chiefs] from whom they were conquered, for the deeds of lease were passed in that form . . . Sometimes they may commit great barbarities, but they would not be duly respected by their vassals if they did not hold the same powers as the fumos whom they succeeded.[6]

Except for changes at the peak of the bureaucratic pyramid, the traditional society remained largely undisturbed. Village headmen and *fumos*, or minor chiefs, functioned as before the *senhor*'s appearance, and on large territories the *mambos*, or great chiefs, retained their positions. The African hierarchy and common people related to the *prazo* chief much as they had to conventional rulers. But few European owners achieved acceptance as a legitimate African chief and most had to rely on the traditional structure.[7]

Apart from an owner's prolonged absences, the principal failure to legitimate his rule resulted from a poor personal relationship with the *mambo*, for often it was the political behaviour of the estate holder that determined his power. The scarcity of European women dictated the founding of African families and diplomacy necessitated marriages with the *mambo*'s families. The *prazo* chief also inserted himself into a traditional position by adapting to African customs, which narrowed the cultural gap between African client and European patron. Some *prazo* rulers 'went native' by adopting African life-styles, praise names, and trappings approximating those of African chiefs: they dressed in traditional costumes (even wearing loincloths), carried symbols of chiefly station such as drums or staffs and practiced African medicine and supernatural beliefs.[8] This acculturation was not merely African veneer over cynical Portuguese hearts. On the upper west African coast Portuguese traders, or *lançados* (from the word 'to throw' meaning to throw themselves into the African population), had previously undergone such an Africanization. The darkening of blood by miscegenation, the distance from Iberian cultural influences and the vitality of African civilization worked far-reaching changes on the Portuguese settlers. The prevalence of Muslim and African religious rites and beliefs among the Portuguese in Mozambique was denounced by an edict of the Goa Inquisition in 1771.[9] By mid-nineteenth century in fact most Zambezi settlers had only a poor knowledge of the Portuguese language.

Lest it be supposed that the Portuguese character alone possessed unique traits that enabled it to adapt to a new *milieu*, it should be borne in mind that what happened to the Portuguese in Mozambique has happened the world over to small immigrant groups and conquerors—they were submerged and assimilated into an alien culture. Nor did the Portuguese transform African society through miscegenation and Christian conversion into a new type of civilization which Gilberto Freyre, the Brazilian sociologist, termed Lusotropicalism. Their numbers were too small and their political power too weak to integrate and unify different ethnic groups into a Luso-tropical civilization without colour consciousness which Freyre believed evolved in Brazil and the Cape Verde Islands.[10] Except for vestiges of Portuguese dress, behaviour and language, the *prazo* residents became absorbed into African life.

INHABITANTS OF THE *PRAZO*

Occupying a chiefly place entailed much more than simply chiefly carriage: a *prazo* holder had to rule a traditional society in a traditional way. Most inhabitants of the estate remained unaffected by the imposition of a non-African *mambo*. The *colonos*, or free peasants, adhered to their customary life on a *prazo* much as they on an African chieftaincy. They lived in villages as they always had, and their pattern of life — birth and death, planting and harvesting, marriage and ceremonies — paced through time unaltered by a remote, although sometimes harsh and exploitive, foreign over-lordship. Like feudal serfs, they were according to *prazo* regulations to stay with estates during transfers of land. Many *prazos* were with-out *colonos*, and for those with peasants their sporadic contacts with Portuguese influence were slight. Only trade items, such as guns, liquors, Portuguese cloth and beads, broke with traditional goods. Serious disputes between *colonos* might reach the *prazo* holder, but in settling them he acted as a chief. Yet the life of a *colono* on a *prazo* was a hard one. Subject to the heavy taxes of the titleholder, the tyrannies of his armed slaves and the vagaries of African climate, they eked out an existence of barely subsistence level.

What shocks vibrated from the *prazo* chief were largely absorbed by the *fumos* or *mambos*, who upheld law and order, directed tax collection at harvest and recruited men for porters, maintenance projects and soldiers in times of crisis. The *fumos* tightrope walked between the two worlds of alien rule and traditional society. But his balancing came to naught, if the holder exacted too much from the peasants. Hostility to a *prazo* owner could cause the *colonos* to flee to a neighbouring estate, revolt or aid an attacking chief or another *prazo* holder. Much of the decision rested with the chosen *fumo* or *mambo*, who was accountable to the *senhor* for taxes and workers and to his own people for their well-being.[11] With generous presents, the *prazo* lord sweetened relations with traditional leaders, but with his force of armed slaves he bolstered his power.

Slavery was an ancient institution in Mozambique. Men of sub-stance owned slaves in proportion to their wealth or position. They acquired them through trade, war, raids or recompensation for wrongs and used them principally to enlarge and strengthen their lineages by absorbing the new members, often as though they were blood members. Marriage to free persons manumitted them or at least their children and slaves could rise in status by getting their own bondsmen.[12] During times of war or famine, Africans, like Anglo-Saxon peasants, voluntarily and temporarily enslaved themselves to royal or wealthy persons in return for security and food. The ritual for voluntary enslavement usually involved the candidate breaking a *mitete* — a utensil or cup — belonging to the strongman from whom he wanted protection.

The *prazo* chief took advantage of slavery to muster private armies and labourers, and with them superimposed his administrative apparatus over the traditional hierarchy. Domestic and menial chores were performed by personal servants who worked in the household, transported their master by dugout canoe or *machilla* ('palanquin') and carried messages. Women slaves mind gold as well as pleasured his life in concubinage.[13] Other slaves traded for the *prazo* chief on months-long commercial expeditions without European supervision. Still others were carpenters, blacksmiths and bakers.

The action arm of the *prazo* holder was the *chicunda* (or *achikunda*). They guarded long-distance trade caravans, policed the estate and marched in defensive and offensive wars in the service of the *senhor* or with his permission in the campaigns of the Portuguese officials. For their servitude, the *prazo* chief rewarded them in land, elephant hunting privileges and sometimes guns and cloth. Bondage to the *prazo* chief differed from traditional slavery in that it was a permanent status and passed on to the warrior's children. In times of wars and raids, they press-ganged captives into their ranks. Although equipped with some firearms and organized into *ensacas*, or regiments, for campaigns, the *chicunda* were normally scattered throughout the *prazo* to insure peace, to restrict flight from the estate and to spy out internal trouble. Some encircled the estate holder's dwelling and others were attached to the *fumo*'s village to reinforce the *senhor*'s authority. Their dispersal did not weaken their pride in arms or their professional soldier's disdain for the civilian *colonos*. Sent to enforce the *senhor*'s will, they preyed upon the *colono* for food and women. The *senhor*'s cruelty and arbitrary enslavement of the free peasants did little to discourage the *chicunda* tyranny.[14] It was one of the paradoxes of the *prazo* system that the free could be worse off than the enslaved.

The *senhors* and *donas*, who lacked wide sanction from the

mambo, often were forced to depend on the *chicunda* — a sometimes precarious buttress. A weak or absent *prazo* master could sow
disorder or revolt among the *chicunda* which could spread to the
colonos or the inhabitants of nearby crown estates. The *prazo* chief,
who failed to provide opportunities for his followers to loot, stood in
danger of their desertion to a more warlike master. Manuel Barreto
gave an example of how one *prazo* owner kept his adherents fearful
and respectful: 'by being very munificent in his gifts and very warlike, even cruel, in chastizing two qualities which will make any
man adored by the Kaffirs.'[15] In Mozambique, as in any slave
society, the ever-present fear of a rising pervaded throughout the
colony. Some *chicunda* set up slave communities, *musitu*, that can
be compared to the *quilombos*, or runaway slave groups, of north-
eastern Brazil and like them they possessed the capacity to
challenge Portuguese authority.

Much of the *prazo* chief's command over his private force hung
on his appointment of the *mukazambo*, or regimental commander.
He picked his *mukazambos* from the army, but the choice of
candidates was somewhat predetermined by their martial ability,
trustworthiness, peer's esteem and obedience to him. A few vast
estates could field armies of about a thousand warriors but the
many small *prazos* only a score.

Despite their ethnic diversity, the *chicunda* formed their own
group loyalties, developed their own language from Portuguese and
local tongues and they eventually merged into a distinct ethnic
group. Over the generations they assimilated people from far and
near (but mostly comprised of Chewa, Lomwe and Nsenga),
founded kinship ties and evolved from heterogeneous slave bands to
emerge as the Chicunda people who live in present-day Malawi,
Zambia and Mozambique. They became noted long-distance
traders and the finest elephant hunters in south central Africa.[16]
The Chikunda formation preceded the similar fusion of the
Macanga to the north of Tete and the Massingire on the Shire
during the Zambezi wars.

ADMINISTRATION OF THE *PRAZO*

Prazo administration was carried on by the *senhor*'s functionaries.
An important position within the slave hierarchy was that of the

chunga, a busy factotum, who collected taxes, transmitted orders and messages between owner and *fumo* and acted as the *senhor*'s eyes and ears on the village level. A *chunga* supervised each *fumo*'s collection of produce and game for the master; his labour was rewarded by a share of the revenue — an inducement to exact the utmost. Equally unpopular among the *colonos* was the *chunga*'s task of purchasing with poor quality cloth their agricultural products at below market prices. Such forced sales could enrage the *mambo* who owned large fields, and peasants alike, in spite of gifts to the traditional leader to oil the wheels of exploitation. Carried out regularly or harshly these purchases provoked migration or rebellion among the *colono*.

The *fumos* managed to maintain some independence on the *prazos*. So as to limit the autonomy of the *fumos*, who were chosen by the *colonos* from royal lineages, the estate holder paid them a small sum, but they remained outside the slave apparatus.

At the apex of the slave hierarchy stood the *mwanamambo*, who acted as an adviser to the *senhor*, took over in his absence and carried out trade and military assignments. Below the *mwanamambo* was the *mocasambos* whose key function was the command of the fortified villages on the perimeters of the crown estate. The larger the *prazo* the more *mocasambos* were needed.[17]

AGRICULTURE ON THE *PRAZO*

Armed warriors and obedient slaves might be the symbol of an estate's power, but the substance was the plentiful production of food and the prosperity of commerce. Without economic well-being, the *prazo* chief could neither attract slave volunteers nor halt desertion or rebellions. Predatory raids were not lucrative enough before the stepped-up demand for slaves toward the onset of the nineteenth century to sustain a *prazo*'s population, let alone increase the holder's wealth. Like mini-states the *prazos* engaged in home food production and 'foreign' trade.

Agriculture on the *prazo*, as so many other undertakings, conformed to pre-European methods; the Portuguese introduced no innovations and only some new crops. The *colonos* prepared the land in the customary fashion in which they fired trees and bushes and used the ashes for fertilizers. Since soil was exhausted after four or five years, farmers moved to new lands, leaving the spent earth to lie fallow. After the initial clearing, women planted in the southern hemisphere spring months of October and November and threshed crops during the second and third months of the new year. In the rich, moist soil of the Zambezi delta two crops could be harvested in one year. Cereal dishes from maize, millet and sorghum formed — and still form — the basis of the African diet out of which bread, porridge and beer were made. In bountiful years beans, melons, peppers and squash were picked to vary the fare. Wild sugar, coffee and rice were also gathered. Men tended herds, snared game and caught fish. The estate holder extracted tribute in all of these commodities, plus honey, wood, ivory, wax and *manchilla* — an African cotton cloth highly valued for trading.[18]

Slavery, land and European-valued crops would seem to have disposed the lower Zambezi to a plantation economy. Growing wild in the forest were such plantation crops as indigo, coffee and even sugar; yet no genuine plantation system developed before the last of the nineteenth century and some *prazos* had even to import sugar and coffee. Many *prazos* had no *colono* population and the *chicunda* by nature of their profession of arms farmed little. It was another paradox of the *prazo* slave system that it lacked an economic orientation such as the plantations of the New World, and most slaves whiled away years as guards, escorts, carriers or in similar nonproductive pursuits designed to protect the *senhor* and gratify his ego. It would not be until Portugal reinvaded Mozambique in the second half of the nineteenth century that the *prazo*'s feudalistic economies were destroyed and replaced by more modern capitalistic exploitation. But even then Portugal with its backward economy had to turn to foreign concession companies to usher capitalism into Mozambique.

Why did the *prazos* not evolve a plantation economy? Briefly put, the harnessing of labour for cash crops was as foreign to African subsistence farming as it was to the feudal-inspired *prazos da corôa*. Since the *prazo* holder imitated African organization and customs, it was small wonder that the Afro-Portuguese clung to African agriculture practices as so much else. This said, it should be acknowledged that no overriding economic incentive existed to spur the *prazo* lord into plantation farming or to introduce new agricultural organization.[19] The absence of an inexpensive, swift and sure transport to the sea worked against agricultural development then as it does today. Besides, the *prazo* chief had more promising endeavours.

THE SLAVE TRADE

Pre-colonial Mozambique was afflicted by a host of ills, not the least of which was the slave trade. Mozambique had yielded a trickle of workers, servants and concubines to the Indian Ocean world since ancient times but in the 1770s there arose an almost insatiable export demand for slaves. Almost simultaneously the interior trade picked up. Beginning in the 1830s and lasting through the 1880s different groups of invading Ngoni provided an alternate market for slave dealers. The Ngoni, like other Bantu conquerors, augmented their ranks by absorbing captives. They bought slaves, especially women, from the Zambezi traders who embraced the internal demand as the export commerce lagged. North of the Zambezi *prazo senhors* supplied slaves to Yao traders bound for the Swahili ports above Cape Delgado. The *senhors* sold their *colonos* and even *chicunda* warriors to reap a quick profit. Their greed helped to undermine the traditional *prazo* system (a topic discussed in the next chapter) but not before selling thousands of hapless victims down the Zambezi.

Toward the late eighteenth century in northern Mozambique, Makua chiefs also stepped up supplies of slaves to Portuguese dealers in a mutually profitable trade that temporarily lessened Makua opposition to Lisbon's coastal presence.

By the end of the eighteenth century, the expanding sugar plantations on the French Indian Ocean Islands of Réunion and Mauritius drew as many as four thousand Africans a year from Mozambique. Soon after, European states began outlawing the trade in slaves to the New World. When British naval patrols appeared on the west African coast, Brazilian suppliers exported from the safer east side of the continent. This, too, quickened the demand for Mozambican slaves and vaulted Quelimane and Ibo Island into the front ranks of African slave ports. Counting legal shipments and smuggling to avoid the tax, one modern authority estimated that about '15,000 slaves were being carried away from Mozambique each year during the 1820s and 1830s.'[20] The story of Mozambique's oceanic slave trade had its denouement after the start of the nineteenth-century pacification wars but can best be completed here at the cost of strict chronology.

So important had the trade become by 1825 that Mozambican slave interests echoed their Angolan counterparts' hopes of joining Brazil in its independence in order to perpetuate the degrading business and plotted a separatist scheme in 1839 to do so; it was not to be the last time that local interests planned independence from Portugal's crimping rule.[21] Under British urging, Lisbon had already issued in 1815 a law prohibiting Portuguese slave commerce north of the equator and banned the trade itself in 1836. Six years later, Portugal concluded a treaty authorizing the Royal Navy to board Portuguese vessels in search of slaves. But the trade flourished in spite of British gunboats and Lisbon's laws, for smuggling replaced the normal traffic of the ports.

The prosperity and power of the Muslim community on Mozambique's northern coast, down for so long, suddenly revived with the contraband trade, and eroded Portugal's influence still more. Portugal's presence, never secure in the mainland from European interlopers or African attack after a renewed eastward movement of the Makua in the late eighteenth century, hinged on the fictitious incorporation of the sheikhs of Quitangonha, Sancul and the Moçimboa area into the colonial administration. But army commissions and small wages achieved nothing, for the Muslim rulers only subordinated themselves when it suited their interests. A genuine puppet had a short life.

Portugal suffered a further weakening from the complicity of its own officials in the commerce of 'black ivory', for as one sheikh remarked: '[the slave trade] is a tree with sweet fruit that everyone wants to eat.'[22] Made up of Muslims, Portuguese, Africans and Indians, the slavers bought off the government officials, sometimes even the Governor-General. Most authorities accommodated themselves to the smuggling. Honest and energetic officials lacked sufficient forces to deal with the sultanates and sheikhdoms, and Lisbon itself wanted for the power to impose its will on the offenders. When in 1857, a Mozambique Governor-General, unlike his corrupt predecessors, seized the *Charles et Georges*, a French barque from Réunion with 110 *émigrés* (supposedly voluntary labourers) on board, Lisbon was forced under the shadow of French warships in the Tagus to return the ship and pay an indemnity. Britain, which had pressured Portugal for half a century to stop the slave traffice, stood by lending neither moral nor material support as the Portuguese were humiliated into surrender.[23] Such an incident was unlikely to promote zealous enforcement of the abolition laws. But British interference, which was motivated by humanitarian disapproval and imperial ambition, and the fears that it would lead to territorial losses in Mozambique did propel Lisbon into action. What proved most worrying to Portugal was the Royal Navy's attacks on slave ship operations along the shore, lest they lead to permanent interventions. Joint Portuguese-British amphibious assaults were launched against Muslim strong points for a time after Lisbon prohibited British cruisers from entering Mozambique's ports in 1847. But when 'effective occupation' became the criterion for territorial claims at the Conference of Berlin in 1884-5, it behooved the Portuguese to establish control on at least the 1,750 miles of Mozambique's coastline.

MINING AND GOLD TRADE

Until the expansion of the overseas slave trade, mining and long-distance trade furnished attractive alternatives to agriculture. Mining and much of the trading activity had as their goal the acquisition of gold. In Changamire and its vassal states where Portuguese control of mining was disallowed, the *prazo* trader sent trading caravans to procure the yellow metal. It was the less powerful Malawi states north of the Zambezi that bore the brunt of rapacious gold seekers in the eighteenth century. From their estates, *senhors* and *donas* dispatched mining caravans north across the river. Here women slaves dug pits and panned alluvial deposits in streams.[24] Guarded by the *chicunda*, the mining settlements also doubled as trading fairs with the local peoples, and led to trade with the distant north. Gold was not the only item of exchange; ivory, copper, wax and slaves figured as important commercial goods. This interior trade and that to the coast had been begun in pre-European times and it proceeded in the *prazo* era. So once again, the Portuguese had left undisturbed the existing system, except, of course, they had uprooted many Muslim merchants with hopes of insinuating themselves into the role of middlemen.

Some 'domestic' trade took place within the large *prazos* in addition to the forced sales. This freed the *prazo* trader from reliance on imported food and furnished the *manchilla* cloth necessary for inland exchange. Trade beyond the region of the states was directed by *mussambazes*. Following the procedure of chiefs and African merchants, the estate owner employed professional traders to head his caravans, although he selected the agent from his most trusted slave officers. Accompanied by guards and porters, the *mussambaze* was accountable for the success of the commercial journey; he chose the routes and fairs to be visited; conducted the negotiations; and oversaw the caravan's safety.[25] With responsibility came reward, for he probably turned a handsome profit by his own trade and that of the *prazo* owner. His skills made the undertakings 'pay' and without him the Portuguese could not have traded with the wary Changamire—the principle source of gold by mid-eighteenth century. He was a worthy successor to the Muslim trader.

From the Zumbo and Manica fairs, all-African caravans travelled southward into the rich goldfields under Changamire's domination. Tete's trading routes looked north to the nearby Malawi peoples and, with less profit, to the more distant southern Lunda of Kazembe where the Portuguese encountered stiff competition from Yao traders who offered lower prices by evading the crown's custom fees and trading to the north of Cape Delgado. The Zambezi towns of Sena, Tete and Zumbo acted as collection and distribution sites for the goods of the *prazo* trade. Here the traded items were sold to Indian merchants, and here Indian cloth and beads and Portuguese brassware arrived from the coast.

The sale and purchase of trade commodities until 1755 lay in the hands of the captain on Mozambique Island. Generally, he bought the position which had been awarded by the crown to a loyal servant, who auctioned the office to the highest bidder. By manipulation, the captains used the royal monopoly to line their pockets at the expense of the *prazo* trader and ultimately the crown.[26] Inflated prices on items bought by the *prazo* trader resulted in smuggling and shifting the source of goods to Arab merchants to the north beyond Portugal's control. Considered as the reason for lost revenue and corruption, the crown abolished the mercantile system and introduced only an export tax. But the *prazo* trader never fully reaped the sweet desserts coming with the termination of the factorial system, for another group of merchants replaced the royal officials as the profiteers of Mozambique's trade.

Transporting goods up and down the river demanded capital and business expertise, and Indian merchants, the financial masters of Indian Ocean commerce, had both. Two classes of Indians migrated to Mozambique. From British India arrived Hindu bankers who loaned money to Zambezi residents and traded merchandise on the river. Called *Banyans* along the east African coast, these clannish folk intermarried and refrained from social mixing with the residents of the Rivers. This and their propensity to return money to India, which the Portuguese blamed for the economic stagnation of the Rivers, raised up many enemies against them as in the African territories to the north. Thinly disguised hatred of them existed in Mozambique for centuries, and occasionally has burst into the open with beatings and killings. Another ambitious Indian group also came to seek wealth and position among the *prazo* settlements. The Canarins — Catholic Goans — differed from their Hindu countrymen in that they moved outside a strict commercial career and into administrative and military posts in the colony. They viewed themselves as Portuguese and despite regulations to the contrary married *prazo* heiresses and acquired estates.[27]

The Indian merchants', particularly the *Banyans*, monopolistic controls, high prices to competitors and racial exclusiveness in choosing company agents all worked to bring the Zambezi route within their trading sphere. Caravan trade from the river-staging ports continued to be a *prazo* operation, but indebtedness to Indian firms became a fact of *prazo* life. Through peaceful competition, the Indian trading houses eliminated the Portuguese from control of river trade as effectively as European guns had expelled Muslim merchants almost two centuries before.

One can only speculate on what might have been the outcome of *prazo* trading had not first the more lucrative commerce in slaves sidetracked the hunt for gold and elephants, and then had not the Ngoni invasions disrupted the *prazo* trade system. No speculation, however, is necessary on the changed composition of *prazo* society. Not very surprisingly, the Goans intruded into *prazo* life by marriage and control of several estates. As wealthy merchants or occupants of government and military posts they made good catches for the *donas* saddled with debts and deficient in suitable European suitors. So prominent were Goans on the Zambezi that by the middle of the nineteenth century their economic and political standing was linked to the preservation of Portugal's claim to

Mozambique. In high posts or as the owners of several *prazos*, their loyalty to Portugal during the nineteenth century was virtually the only support Lisbon had in the rebellious Rivers.

THE *PRAZO* COMMUNITY

The influx of Goans to the ranks of estate holders further diluted European blood and Portuguese influence on the hybrid *prazo* community which was already heavily Africanized. By 1800, the count of *prazo* holders in actual residence was indeed small — probably less than 20 — despite the crown's best efforts to enlarge the number of Portuguese owners along with the European population, as well as to limit the size of each holding. There were, of course, more estates than titleholders and as many as six were held by one person. Some domains, such as the Pereira's nineteenth-century lands on the north bank of the Zambezi from Zumbo to the Shire River, never had a *prazo* title. Nor did most titleholders stay on their land; instead they could collect their rents in Portugal or India. The consequence was not only abandoned estates but also the concentration of power in fewer families which discouraged small proprietorships. Examples abound of the crown's settlement schemes designed to break up the *prazo* families. Little came of them as they foundered on Mozambique's climatic reputation and Portugal's meagre resources. Settlement of Mozambique by European immigrants proved as elusive in the seventeenth and eighteenth centuries as it was in a more modern period.

Untrustworthy figures and imprecise racial categories make a census nearly guesswork, but one scholar estimated that the entire *prazo* community of Portuguese, Indians and mulattos never numbered 500 and it probably decreased by mid-nineteenth century. Yet this small population owned over 100 estates.[28] When that century opened, slightly more than 10 per cent of the registered Christian population were Portuguese and nearly two-thirds mulatto with the final quarter Indian.[29] Malaria decimated the newly arrived officials and criminals sent to boost the Portuguese population and to rid Portugal of undesirables. Lacking white women, the *senhors* married or disported themselves with African or mulatto women. Private harems were widespread and denounced by the Church although its own servants set far from exemplary standards. The world was too much with the priests and friars increasingly careless about the things of the spirit. The un-restrained indulgence of Portuguese sexual appetites in the tropics far from the constraints of Iberia sprang from the absence of European women and not a special tolerance of non-European people. African polygamous marriages provided an example to the Portuguese as did the extended family which some *prazo* residents adopted. The Zambezi *donas*, who for unknown reasons outlived their male counterparts, were likewise obliged to wed non-European husbands for security, except when officials married them as a passport into *prazo* politics. While some *prazo* ladies followed the male titleholders in loose relationships, the majority remarried at the death or desertion of each husband. One re-doubtable *dona*, Caterina de Faria Leitão, as an octogenarian married for the fourth time.

Marriages among the top *prazo* families were not affairs of the heart but shrewdly planned alliances with each other or African chiefs to expand territory or tighten security. In striving for wealth and power, *prazo* chiefs married polygamously and established wide family connections: kinship networks could achieve and retain power. On occasion, the community banded together to save one of its members from government prosecution. But since the *prazo senhors* bribed or overawed most officials, the government's writ usually failed to run on the Zambezi.[30]

Rather than a tight community always braced against a hostile world, the estate holders frequently crossed swords in bitter feuds. Private armies, land grabbing and the desperate thirst for riches bred a no-holds-barred competition. The allies of one war became the foes of the next. Clashes between retainers, a reflection of the rivalry between owners, moved officials in Tete and Sena to pro-hibit armed slaves from entering town. A neighbour could be as much an enemy as an independent and bellicose chief. Lourenço de Mattos, the father-in-law of the famous Sisnando Baião, for example, swept back an invading African chief from lands occupied by Portuguese settlers only to keep them for his own.[31] Such was the morality of the Zambezi Portuguese.

The Portuguese towns of Quelimane, Sena, Sofala and Tete were little more than squalid settlements with less than 100 non-Africans each. As an extension of the 1752 administrative separation of Mozambique from Goa, these four settlements were granted in 1763 municipal status (the town on Mozambique Island became a city) with the right of electing their own councils (*Senado da Câmara*) as in Portugal. Life changed hardly at all, however, for the same powerful residents who dominated the Rivers before the introduction of local government continued to do so from their council seats. Political power and social prestige were based on the possession of land, not in the urban centres.

The forts, whose decaying walls, rusty cannons and grossly understrength garrisons testified to Portugal's crumbling military power, offered no protection against serious attacks. At Quelimane the cannons lay in the sand and in one 'an ear of green millet was growing from the touch-hole.'[32] The dilapidated storage houses and churches also reflected a waning in commodity trade and evangelizing pursuits in Mozambique before the close of the eighteenth century. It was recorded that in 1835 'only ten priests lived in the remote parts of Eastern Africa.'[33] Only the island town of Mozambique escaped most censorious comments of travellers and officials who remarked admiringly on São Sebastião, the extraordinary four-bastioned fortress built from granite carted from Portugal in the sixteenth century, and the charming white stone buildings that gleamed around it. Lying on the coast, Sofala and Quelimane were more unhealthy than the upland sites, but all exacted a high toll in lives. Made of stone and mud, the walls of buildings and forts looked as if they would dissolve in the next rain unless repaired; but no labourers would make repairs. The settlers' houses in the towns and on the estates, which were ringed by the servants' huts, decayed in the tropical ravages, in the indolence of the *prazo* system.

The *prazo* residents, even the most Africanized ones, clung to the traces of Portuguese origins or values. Apart from security against Dutch, French and English predators on the coast, there existed reasons of sentiment and profit why *prazo* owners wanted the continuation of Portugal's rule in Mozambique in spite of their defiance of its laws and officials. It is almost a historical platitude that colonial societies long for sentimental attachment to the mother country and attempt to emulate what they believe is life there. Despite their darkening skins, the *prazo* holders retained Portuguese surnames along with African praise names and practised nominal Catholicism while at the same time consulting witch doctors. Powerful *prazo* chiefs with huge estates and large slave armies measured part of their success by obtaining titles of nobility. The Order of Christ and a patent of nobility were the most coveted, and helped to retain some estate owners' loyalty and their assistance for campaigns on behalf of the government. Ranks and titles carried prestige, and for the less status conscious they brought a small pension and exemption from punishment of minor offences. Government grants of arms to loyal settlers also furnished an incentive for duty to the crown by sitting on town councils or crushing rebels.[34]

Still, the Zambezi residents resisted government efforts in any project that might interfere with their livelihood or way of life. The bitter complaint of António Pedroso Gamitto, who served as second in command of an 1831-2 expedition to establish trade with the inland kingdom of Kazembe, about the *prazo* residents setting up obstacles out of fear of losing their rich position in the slave trade might well apply to any government scheme:

> These people, living in sloth and indolence, which their wealth effortlessly acquired enables them to do, have been indefatigable in rendering useless any government measure or any individual enterprises, which they imagine could influence directly or indirectly their speculative arrangements.[35]

At no time was resistance more determined than during the Zambezi wars in the second half of the nineteenth century, but settler opposition to the far-off Lisbon government reoccurred again and again.

To assert their Portuguese ties and to compensate for the harshness of African life, the *prazo* holders lived in baronial fashion. Home in Portugal or India these men and women would have been impoverished nobles, day labourers or peasants; here they lived as petty monarchs, lording it over their flunkies, armed slaves and domestic servants on African fiefs. Just as they warred against each other, so too they competed in displays of 'wealth, power and largesse' to retain their lackeys and slave retinues. The great lords usually lived in European-type stone houses of thick walls and the smaller *prazo* owners dwelled in huts. The best-off *prazo* barons set richly dressed tables with Portuguese wines, imported cigars and silver tableware.[36] They prided themselves on their hospitality to visitors, some of whom later turned out to be sharp critics of the estate system and its residents while remembering a generous reception. Less well-off Zambezi Portuguese pretentiously indulged themselves and their guests. No matter what their standing on the river, high or low, they commanded a few armed retainers or at least household servants. Some may have truly believed themselves Portuguese; others, especially darkly-hued titleholders, wanted Portuguese identification as a means of acceptance in the *prazo* community.

Professor M. D. D. Newitt, a knowledgeable scholar of *prazo* history, noted that this hybrid culture reached its climax in the life of Manuel António de Sousa, a late-nineteenth century *prazo* lord of great renown. Almost simultaneously, he commanded Portuguese forces with an army colonelcy and announced himself the Macombe, or paramount chief, of the Barue Tonga.[37] That Sousa met a combat death while in the cause of Portugal's re-invasion of Mozambique and that the Africanized estate system it-self was destroyed by Lisbon points up the hybrid-ness of the *prazo* institution — neither wholly Portuguese nor African. It was unsuited to the modern colonial age.

5

INVASIONS: NGONI AND PORTUGUESE

The nineteenth century in Mozambique opened with an African invasion and closed with a Portuguese reinvasion. From Natal province in South Africa, the Ngoni swept northward in the first decades leaving rack and ruin in their wake before establishing a new political state in southern Mozambique. The French attacked Lourenço Marques, Inhambane and Mozambique Island during the Napoleonic Wars, and in the same period Sakalava bandits from Madagascar raided the Querimba Islands. Commencing in the second half of the century Portugal launched occupation and pacification campaigns that, although initially less havoc raising than the Ngoni storm, fixed a colonial rule over the country which was not seriously challenged until 1964. Mozambique in the last century then witnessed a continuation of its past history of invasion by yet other alien peoples. The historical cycle of this strange land where the conqueror so often became the conquered persisted.

The government on the Zambezi, weakened by laxity, slave trading and Ngoni incursions, allowed power to slip from its fingers. In the disordered conditions, the great *prazo* lords subdued their lesser neighbours and created local sovereignties independent from Portugal's rule. Uncontrollable slaving and intractable *prazo* barons called into question Lisbon's feeble authority in southeastern Africa. Faced with the prospect of territorial loss to other European powers, Portugal responded to the challenge by conquest.

THE NGONI INVASIONS

Two years before they made their first forays into southern Mozambique in 1821 the Ngoni fled from the *mfecane*, or times of troubles, in the Natal region of South Africa. Having part of its origin in the intense population pressures and struggles for grazing lands, the *mfecane* upheavals plunged southern Africa into conflict and forced migrations for nearly half a century. In 1818, the brilliant and tyrannical Zulu chief Shaka embarked on campaigns of conquest that ravaged the countryside and created a powerful kingdom of the Zulu, who had been one of several chieftaincies of the Ngoni. His military innovations in tactics and weaponry—short jabbing spears, large shields and relentless attacks—revolutionized warfare and enabled his *impis*, regiments, to shatter their enemies. Other chieftains, unwilling to accept Shaka's rule but able to imitate his methods, split off to lead their own armies and set into motion far-reaching conquests as group ricocheted against group.

In about 1830, Zwangendaba pierced the declining Changamire empire, sacked Zimbabwe and scattered the Rozwi rulers. Five years later his *impis* devastated the remnant of the Mwene Mutapa empire and crossed the Zambezi into the Luangwa River region of what is now present-day Malawi. Mzilikazi, another Zulu commander, whose followers acquired the name Ndebele, undertook a permanent occupation of much of the old Changamire domains, although his forces were engaged in ongoing battles with the Shona for decades. Just north of Natal, Sobhuza established the modern kingdom of Swaziland.

Other spin offs of the *mfecane* convulsions spilled into Mozambique. One Ngoni group raided the Portuguese fair in Manica in 1832, and others attacked the *prazos* and independent chieftaincies in the Zambezi Valley occupying about half of the legal estates until 1840 when they were pushed northward by the Ngoni of Soshangane. Across the Zambezi, the fleeing Ngoni disrupted many Malawi societies and hence fed the Arab slave caravans en route to Kilwa and Zanzibar. Acting under orders of Dingane, Shaka's brother and successor, a Zulu force with auxiliaries from some Rhonga chiefdoms nearby Lourenço Marques attacked the town in 1833 and put to death the Portuguese governor, possibly for his policy of local expansion. The south shore of Delagoa Bay stayed under Zulu influence until the defeat and exile of Cetewayo, the last great chief, in 1879.[1]

Soshangane founded the Gaza kingdom in southern Mozambique and a dynasty that harassed the Portuguese to the twilight of the nineteenth century. At the zenith of the Gaza Ngoni sway, about 1850, they dominated the country between the Zambezi and the Incomati rivers. Nomadic by nature of their cattle-based economy, they ranged over large areas. Yearly, the *impis* struck as far as the Zambezi delta to collect tribute and instill fear in the Portuguese who paid the *danegeld* rather than risk annihilation. For military hegemony, the Gaza Ngoni chiefs relied on regiments (called *mangas* or *impis*) which were commanded by *indunas*, or lieutenants. Modelled on Shaka's regiments these organizations of professional soldiers, grouped by age and toughened by rigorous training, dominated the local peasantry. Later their fighting skills and detachment from *prazo* politics made them excellent mercenaries, and thus the Portuguese hired Ngoni soldiers in the conquest of some Zambezi estates.

Intermarriage with conquered Rhonga, Tonga and Chopi to expand their numbers diluted the Ngoni ethnic distinctiveness. The Portuguese came to refer to them as 'shangana' from the name of their first king in Mozambique, Soshangane. The Ngoni overlords tried to offset the loss of homogeneity by requiring their subjects to adopt their customs, such as pierced earlobes. Not since the times of Mwene Mutapa dominance had a foreign invader overrun and subdued so much of the country below the Zambezi.

The Ngoni whirlwind ripped over Mozambique aggravating wretched conditions. Plagues of locusts, lack of rain and widespread hunger beginning in 1823 brought added misery to the life of the peasants already hounded by slavers. When the warlike newcomers appeared from the south and west, life on the *prazos* had changed for most of the *colonos* and many of the *chicunda* warriors, for they had become fair game for the slave trade. So eager were the *prazo* holders or renters to gain from the new 'gold' that they rushed to sell the inhabitants of their lands, when the supply of captives failed to keep pace with demand. First, they enslaved the free peasants of their estates and then discarded the ancient bond between slave and master in order to fill the coffles bound for the coast.

Sometimes the *chicunda* revolted and occasionally made common cause with the *colono* against the involuntary sales of the *prazo* master. Other *colonos* fled to the delta estates where they fell into the rapacious hands of slaving bands. Deserted by the *colonos* and abandoned by their owners, the *prazos* disintegrated. They were dealt further hammer blows by chieftaincies above and below the Zambezi which took advantage of the chaos to reconquer lands or expand their rule. *Prazo* resistance, already enfeebled, crumbled before the armies of Barue, Manganja, Quiteve and Malawi states. At least 12 estates in the vicinity of Sena, including the large estates of Gorongoza and Cheringoma, were overrun until the 1830s. At mid-century, an official report listed only 20 *prazos* out of 83 in the Sena and Tete regions that escaped invasion or abandonment.[2] Small wonder that the beleaguered *prazos* put forth only anaemic opposition to the Ngoni onslaught.

Chopped by the triple axes of invasion, drought and slave trade the conventional *prazo* sank only to resurface as part of the larger domains of grand *prazo* lords into whose grasp power grew and concentrated out of the previous ruin. Portugal's influence and prestige in Mozambique ebbed with the development of giant *prazo* states. In the last third of the century, it strove to salvage its standing as mightily as the *prazo senhors* fought to maintain their life and society against an alien invasion and westernization.

THE ZAMBEZI WARS

The diminishing of the Ngoni raids and the subsiding of Barue succession strife brought neither peace nor stability to Mozambique. Indeed, the territory stretching inland on both sides of the Zambezi from the coast to beyond Zumbo was cast into a *Götter-dammerung* conflict from the 1840s to 1902 that destroyed the *prazo* system. The struggles of the Zambezi warlords also merged into the wider circle of Portuguese imperial ambitions and beyond to the European 'Scramble for Africa'. These wars, in which African fought African, further paved the way for Portugal's control of vast regions of the country. In all of this, the *prazos* stood at the centre of the storm.

Except in the old Quelimane district Lisbon's writ ran not at all, and there it ran poorly. The realities on the Zambezi would have made a dead letter of the formality of emphyteutic contracts had it not been for their termination. Several estates became the possessions of a few *senhors*; others rendered tribute to the Ngoni. The destitute *colonos* and *chicunda* warriors were compelled to put themselves under the protection and at the disposal of *prazo* lords, who could give them food and security. The *prazo* barons grew powerful and established local political hegemonies. During the eighteenth century, debate of the estate system centred on its unproductivity, unruliness and unceasing hostilities. To encourage settlement and expansion, Sá da Bandeira, a liberal politician, wrote a law in 1858 abolishing the emphyteutic title grants, none of which had been issued since 1838. But it was not until the 1870s that the government gingerly began to experiment with direct administration on the secured estates in Quelimane. Up river, the Portuguese reversed their past policy and pushed the *muzungos* to acquire land from independent chiefs by any and all means. Portugal then proclaimed the territory crown land hoping to convince other European states of the legitimacy of its claims to the African hinterland. Usually, it rented the captured lands to the *muzungo conquistador*. Lands formerly outside of Lisbon's domination in this way came under the control of increasingly powerful *muzungos*, and through them they fell into Portuguese hands.

By the dint of war and its ruthless application, the *muzungos* extended their control; retained their followers with bounty captured in fighting; virtually ruled their preserves as independent states; and some blocked Portugal's occupation of the *sertão* with arms from Muslim traders. Lisbon tried to win over the *muzungos* so as to further its territorial ambitions by commissioning them as a *capitão-mor* ('captain-major') or *sargento-mor* ('sergeant-major'). Some *muzungos* assisted Portuguese pacification, and others resisted. The government's advances threatened their independence and the abolition of slavery altered their consent of a rule that formerly had fostered a slave society. Portuguese governance now promised change.

Many great *senhors* of the war era claimed foreign origin. The Pereiras of Macanga, the Vas dos Anjos family of Massingire and Manuel António de Sousa traced their descent to Portuguese India and Catholic Goanese families. The first da Cruz came from present-day Thailand as a soldier in the mid-eighteenth century. Only the Silvas contended that their founder arrived from Portugal in the early nineteenth century to take up trading. They all adopted African wives and customs. Contemporaries described them as dark complexioned and obviously the products of mixed parentage. The grand *muzungo* chiefs were a power in both African and Portuguese worlds.

The Zambezi wars began with the expansionist drives of the Pereira chiefs in 1840.[3] The first Pereira acquired an extensive trading and prospecting network among the Chewa on the upper north bank of the Zambezi in the eighteenth century. Gradually their power increased with their wealth until the north riverine region from Zumbo to the Shire, known as Macanga, was under their thumb, although they never held a *prazo* title to it.

The principal challenger to the mounting Pereira hegemony was the da Cruz, who had come lately to power. With wide family connections, they rose quickly to dominance, and in 1849 rented the Massangano estate from the Portuguese who were glad of the defence that the da Cruz could offer against Ngoni raids from the south. Situated among the Tongas on the right side of the Zambezi above the Lupata Gorge, it commanded the river. From their formidable *aringa*, the da Cruz mastery of the water route distressed the Pereiras and in time the Portuguese. Their spreading sway also worried the Barue kingdom which shared borders with the south bank *prazos* between Sena and Tete. Fear of the da Cruz united the Macombe, paramount chief of the Barue, and the Pereiras for a disastrous siege of Massangano in 1853.

Nothing succeeds like success in rising up rivals and enemies, and the da Cruz triumph over the Pereiras and Barue was no exception. No sooner had word spread of the latest da Cruz success than a fresh coalition assembled for another assault on Massangano. In late 1853, the first governor of the newly created government in Tete arrived with 200 European soldiers in hopes of establishing Lisbon's authority in the war-torn region. River traders and downstream slavers furnished the bulk of the troops and Portuguese arsenals supplied weapons and ammunition.

Half a thousand African auxiliaries supplied by anti-da Cruz *senhors* and augmented by the fever-wracked Portuguese troops set out in a frightfully mismanaged campaign to besiege Massangano. The presence of metropolitan soldiers did not forestall the expedition's rout nor the mutiny against the Portuguese commander. An uneasy peace descended on the lower Zambezi at the start of 1855 with the deaths of first Joaquim da Cruz and then Chissaka Pereira. The family feud between the da Cruz and Pereiras quieted for a while. It was over a decade before the government undertook another expedition to lay siege to Massangano. This was due more to Portuguese distraction than the amiability of the new da Cruz family head, António Vicente, or Bonga (the 'wild cat'), who raided riverboats or charged them a safe passage fee.

The victories of the da Cruz over Lisbon and its *muzungo* allies in 1853 and 1854 ironically worked in favour of the Portuguese, for they loosened the Pereira's grip on the region from Cabora Bassa to the long-since abandoned fair at Zumbo and beyond. The re-establishment of the Zumbo fair in 1862 began an active Portuguese influence on the upper river. Lisbon supplied weapons and military titles, and *muzungo* chiefs conquered vast stretches of territory from Tete to the Luangwa Valley, territory that now lies within Zambia and Malawi. When the 1891 Anglo-Portuguese treaty delimited Mozambique's borders, Portugal lost some of the *muzungo* gains.

While the conquest of the Tete highlands pursued its bloody course, events downstream moved toward inevitable and direct participation of Portugal in the Zambezi wars. Up to now its involvement had been fitful and indirect. By the early 1860s, Lisbon resolved to crush the da Cruz of Massangano or be forced to admit internationally the invalidity of its interior claims. Resolution was one thing, execution quite another. What should have been a minor military affair against the piratical da Cruz, one of the less powerful families, developed into a touchstone of martial ability on which the Portuguese measured poorly. Each of the four expeditions, in the late 1860s sometimes numbering 400 to 600 regular troops along with auxiliaries, encountered ambushes, malaria, desertions and mutinies in varying degrees and all ended in bloody and shameful defeat. After mauling the Portuguese, Bonga da Cruz's men adorned the stockade walls with the skulls of their enemies as a warning. Not since the sixteenth-century Barreto column had such large numbers of metropolitan troops been sent so recklessly to their death in Mozambique. Skirmishing continued until Bonga and the Portuguese signed a peace treaty in 1875, in which he was pardoned in return for recognition of Portugal's paper sovereignty.

While the Pereiras' and to a degree the da Cruz's wheel of fortune slowed, that of Manuel António de Sousa accelerated. By the third-quarter of the century, Sousa, widely known as Gouveia, was on his way to becoming the most powerful *muzungo* in Mozambique and the longest and strongest ally of Portuguese expansion in the colony. Arriving from Goa at about 20 years of age to manage a dead uncle's trading business, young Gouveia enjoyed a meteoric rise in the topsy-turvy Zambezi politics. He built a stronghold in the rocky highlands of Gorongosa and repelled Ngoni raids from the Gaza kingdom. This and other services to the government got him the title of *capitão-mor* of Manica. His titular control over the

Manica chieftaincy after 1874 was used by Lisbon to buttress its territorial claims against encroachments from Cecil Rhodes's British South Africa Company, although in the end it lost out but to no fault of Gouveia.

Already the largest land-holder in the colony, Gouveia laid plans to acquire the ancient Barue kingdom. Acting as regent after the Macombe's death in 1880, he forcibly occupied the Barue lands and brutally squashed potential opposition. It was at this point that Gouveia's full utility to the Portuguese cause was realized by Joaquim Carlos Paiva de Andrada, a major in the artillery. Of the same stripe as Cecil Rhodes, but much less wealthy, Andrada hoped to spread Portugal's rule and enrich its treasury by use of the Mozambique Company, a commercial enterprise financed mostly by non-Portuguese capital and chartered by Lisbon in 1891. Lacking funds and military forces, the energetic imperialist teamed up with Gouveia to further his goals.

The seizure of Barue and Gouveia's wholehearted support of Portuguese penetration, by now a full-blown reality, pitched the Zambezi region into an upheaval of new alignments. The Pereiras, old-time enemies of the da Cruz, and the deposed royalty of Barue all rallied to the defence of Massangano in hopes of staying the Portuguese advance.

Preceding the Portuguese destruction of Massangano was another nearly as momentous event on the Shire River — the Massingire rising of 1884. Before this the Shire had been a sideshow to the main theatre along the length of the Zambezi. The roots of the Massingire rising go back to the 1860s. When the Vas dos Anjos family disrupted the Manganja villages during their retreat up the Shire from Portuguese-directed assaults, many of the people drifted into their ranks at the Massingire *aringa*. The Vas dos Anjos afforded the refugees a measure of safety. Over time, the refugees evolved into a distinct group, the Massingire, just as the Chicunda had developed a separate identity under foreign stimulation.

Almost from the establishment of the Vas dos Anjos on the Shire, they combatted devastating raids from the upriver Makololo. Originally from what later became Zambia, the Makololo first arrived in Mozambique in 1856 as carriers for David Livingstone's transcontinental journey from Angola. Awaiting Livingstone's return, they settled on the middle reaches of the Shire where they came under the sympathy and protection of the Scottish missionaries in

Blantyre, Malawi. Like the *prazo* chiefs they probably imitated, the Makololo amassed a military machine. With their armed bands, they raided the Massingire lands. The Massingire people in desperation ousted the *aringa senhors* and ceded the country to the Portuguese who promised protection — a promise not kept.

In 1884, two years after the cession, Massingire blazed in revolt against Portuguese taxation, interference in the appointment of headmen and want of protection from the Makololo. From Sena to the coastal port of Quelimane, the Massingire people and collaborating groups, including some *libertos*, killed European traders and residents, besieged the towns and shook Portuguese authority to its foundations. The Portuguese turned to Gouveia, who with a 4,000 man army, quashed the rebellion six months after it began. This would not be the last time that Manuel Antónia de Sousa pulled Portuguese chestnuts from an African fire.

The pan-ethnic rising represented not only the strength of traditional chiefs in unity but more importantly a mounting discontent and resistance to wider European encroachments. Census taking (a prelude to taxing), taxes, replacement of the *liberto* status in 1876 for a system of contract labour, direct administration of estates in the Quelimane area, European commerce in the Zambezi region — all began to tear the traditional fabric of society woven for centuries.[4] After quelling the Massingire rising, Gouveia wheeled his army southwestward for a drive against several small chieftaincies west of the Luenha River and then toward Mashonaland in Rhodesia. Gouveia and Andrada's goal was to head off the British South Africa Company's designs on what is today eastern Rhodesia.

The first phase of Gouveia's campaign established control over nearly a score of chiefs in 1886, but the second against the Mtoko chieftaincy, south of Mazoe headwaters, met defeat. Troubles come doubly in Mozambique, and the Mtoko and Massangano spirit-mediums negotiated an alliance that hurried a da Cruz relief column to the chieftaincy. Ringed by what seemed a wheel of enemies Gouveia and Andrada made a fateful decision to suspend the war on Mtoko and strike at the hub — Massangano. This decision was a strategic mistake, for Gouveia and Andrada allowed the British South African Company to steal a march on them.[5] Hence a wide slice of Mashonaland slipped into British hands.

The campaign launched in 1888 to smash once and for all the da Cruz at Massangano was one of the most elaborately organized campaigns of Portugal's colonial wars. The colony's Governor-General, Augusto da Castilho, personally took charge of the attacking force that first knocked out outlying *aringas* before it laid a siege with heavy cannons to the Massangano stockade that killed an estimated 6,000 inhabitants in a bloody testament to modern weapons. The attackers pulled down the *aringa* and built a fort on the hill overlooking the site. Today the African bush covers all but a few traces of the former citadel.

The last decade of the century saw the Barue revolt which was occasioned by a fluke of history. In the fall of 1890, the British South Africa Company captured Gouveia in the Manica mountains and held him captive until the following spring. His immense personal empire between the Save and the Zambezi erupted in his absence. As with other *muzungos*, Gouveia's supremacy rested on his presence and without it his lieutenants pursued their own ends. The Barue princely houses also asserted their claim to the throne, although they achieved no unity. Portugal's shadowy claim to Gouveia's domains darkened with the collapse of his power. Not since the contraction of the Mwene Mutapa suzerainty in the 1690s had Portugal lost such a substantial prop to its informal empire in Mozambique. Had Gouveia's *aringa* commanders, the da Cruz remmants and the Barue princely houses buried their rivalries, the outcome may have been different. But the Portuguese were spared, and the recently chartered Mozambique Company carried on a chaotic administration amid the disorder of the region until the turn of the century. At that time Portugal resolved in the face of British and German territorial avarice to wipe out the last stubborn spots of African independence. Up to then, Hanga, a Macombe of Barue, had managed to put up some resistance with refugees from various down-river ethnic groups.[6]

The Portuguese hired Ngoni mercenaries to help extinguish the independence of the Pereira enclave of Macanga in 1902. A similar fate befell the Barue rebels in the same year when a large mercenary force snuffed out the ancient kingdom's independence in 'the campagne war'.[7] Its victory closed the era of the Zambezi wars.

The Zambezi wars began in the 1840s with the attempts to establish or resist what Professor T. O. Ranger has called 'dominance or sub-imperialism'[8] of one African group over another, and continued after the 1880s with appeals to wider unity against the extension of Portuguese sovereignty; but as elsewhere in Africa, there never evolved a long-lived unified African resistance to European colonial expansion. The Zambezi potentates and mercenaries both aided and defied Portuguese advances. Yet the story of the Zambezi wars is more than a chronicle of brigandage, battles with un-pronounceable names or the 'gyrations of barbarious tribes in picturesque but irrelevant corners of the globe.'[9]

Toward the wars' conclusion some participants manifested an evolution, a dawning, of conscious African-ness that reached beyond narrow ethno-nationalism. The alliances between the da Cruz, Barue, Pereiras and others, the rolé of the spirit-mediums in the resistance and support of the freed slaves and disaffected *colonos* are manifestations of an incipient African unity. On the other hand, collaboration of some *muzungos* with the invader continued to the end of the fighting. Indeed, Portugal capitalized — then as it did in the independence war — on the splits within African ranks. Still the inchoate African opposition to European conquest took on greater significance in the last quarter of the twentieth century. During the early 1970s, the name Massangano reappeared in the guerrilla's military communiqués, and the Shona people of the region, remembering their traditions of resistance, staunchly backed the nationalist forces. Looked at from the vantage-point of Dien Bien Phu, for example, the Massan-gano defence and the Massingire rising jut out from the 'irrelevant corners of the globe' to take on new and unaccustomed prominence among reactions to western domination.

OCCUPATION OF THE NORTH

The curve of Muslim power on the northern coast rose with the growth of the slave commerce. Angoche Island, the centre of Muslim coastwise trade in the sixteenth century, again came into its own. Its independence and the existence of the slave trade made a lie of Lisbon's claims of sovereignty over Mozambique's northern tier. Forgetting much of Muslim resourcefulness and foreseeing little of African determination, Portugal's northern campaigns dragged on until the early twentieth century.

In the 1850s Angoche's defence passed into the able hands of Mussa Momadi Sabo, nicknamed Mussa Quanto, whose family contacts and personal connections from former Islamic preaching tours on the coast later served him well in uniting opposition to Portuguese military ventures.[10] Mussa Quanto's devastating forays on the mainland near Quelimane moved Portuguese officials and *prazo* owners to repay tit for tat. A complicated series of campaigns followed after the capture of Angoche in 1861 by a *prazo senhor*, who was supplied with Portuguese firearms.

The fall of Angoche was only a temporary Muslim setback and the slave trade thrived. Before his death in 1877, Mussa Quanto controlled most of the coast from Mozambique Island south to the Licungo River above Quelimane and inland about 100 miles.[11] His death triggered a succession crisis. Seven claimants struggled for the Angoche sultanate setting off internal conflicts until a distant relative of Mussa Quanto, Mahamuieva, known to history as Farelay, emerged on top. By 1890, Farelay, as much a diplomat as a soldier, forged enough of a common front with Makua chiefs, disgruntled sheikhs and Muslim factions to repel Portuguese attacks until 1910 when Lisbon at last sent the 'first well-equipped and well-led expedition' to the north coast.[12] The export of slaves was ended and a way of life as well as independence was lost.

Islam's religious impact proved more durable and survived into the present in some parts of northern Mozambique. The Muslim community exerted a powerful influence inland during the late nineteenth century. Both Mussa Quanto and Farelay had religious backgrounds. Makua and Yao middlemen brought slaves to the Indian Ocean, and with these traders Islam spread inland reaching back to the Lake Malawi region. Here Islam as an appealing fashion and as an effective challenge to the growing Portuguese presence took hold more rapidly than at any time in the three previous centuries of contact with the Islamized coastal chiefs and traders.[13]

The northern hinterland was the last to be subdued in Mozambique and the first to bristle in the nationalist revolt of the 1960s. Geographic remoteness from Portugal's already over-extended authority and borders with rival European-controlled territories, which afforded sanctuary to rebels, partially accounts for the regions defiant resistance and volatile rebelliousness. In the northwest, now part of the Niassa district, a Yao chief, or Mataka, resolutely hurled back the expeditions of the government and the Niassa Company—one of the three principal foreign-financed concession companies formed in the 1890s to exploit Mozambique's resources.

Not unlike the nationalist war of fifty years later, the Portuguese faced the difficulty of sealing off the Rovuma River border — in the early part of this century a source of arms from German East Africa (Tanganyika). A string of small forts along the river and a final campaign in 1912 against the Mataka's kraal near today's city of Vila Cabral overwhelmed the Yao's last-ditch military resistance.[14] The last pacification expeditions in the north were mounted against the Makonde by the Niassa Company as late as 1920.

GUNGUNYANE AND SOUTHERN MOZAMBIQUE

Portugal's interest in the Delagoa Bay region rekindled early in the nineteenth century and blazed with the European 'scramble'. The discovery of gold in the Transvaal in 1886 and the commencement of a railway between the Boer republic and Lourenço Marques in the same year pointed up the importance of the extreme southern section in the development of the country. This was recognized by naming Lourenço Marques the capital in 1897. Yet much of this vital gateway to the interior was still under African jurisdiction as late as 1895.

The southern third of Mozambique from about 100 miles north of the Save to below Lourenço Marques comprised the Gaza kingdom a legacy of the Ngoni invasions. While its founder Soshangane reigned, the kingdom maintained ascendancy; but by the death of his successor Muzila in 1884, the realm witnessed not only the usurpation of the throne by Gungunyane over the legitimate claim of his brother but also disconcerting problems. Epidemics and alcoholism struck at the Shangana (also known as Gazas, Vatuas and Landeens), as the Portuguese called them. Cattle died from rinderpest. Land was neglected, and the military ranks went unfilled. Young men emigrated from the 1860s onwards to work on the farms and mines of South Africa where their labour was rewarded in cash. Internal weakness accounts for one reason why Gungunyane strove to avoid war with the Portuguese despite the urgings of a powerful war party in his capital. The decrease of manpower could be worrisome in itself to a conquest state and doubly so to one confronted with Portuguese, British and Boer ambitions for control of Delagoa Bay, a fine natural harbour and access to the sea for the landlocked country below the Zambezi.

Gungunyane, Mozambique's most famous monarch, and the Portuguese first crossed swords over the kingdom of Manica.[15] Gouveia had established a fragile and unexercised sovereignty over Manica by the mid-1870s by driving out Barue and Maungwe invaders. At first, this did little to persuade Gungunyane to renounce his control. Finally in 1889, Portuguese influence replaced Gungunyane's sway over Manica in return for Gaza paramountcy in the Limpopo Valley where the Shangana hoped for improved farming and a place from which to attack the restive Chopi. Since before 1870, the Portuguese had infiltrated the Inhambane district and won the allegiance of a nest of Chopi chiefs who increasingly looked to them for protection from the Shangana raids. The Chopi-Shangana wars divided and eroded resistance to Portuguese penetration.

Gungunyane moved his royal kraal and some forty to sixty thousand people from Mossurise on the Rhodesian plateau, near mount Selinda, to Manjacaze about 30 miles north of João Belo (now Xai Xai). The move, however, jeopardized the Portuguese position at Inhambane and Lourenço Marques. There they were already under pressure from the British South Africa Company which desired access to the sea.

The canny Gungunyane sought to take advantage of the contending interests for his new lands in order to preserve his independence. António Enes, Royal Commissioner who marched on the Shangana king, described the goal of Gungunyane's policy as 'real and practical independence'.[16] To this end he manoeuvred between British and Portuguese. Professor D. L. Wheeler called him 'a master of playing both ends against the middle to maintain his freedom of movement'.[17]

Lisbon regarded Gungunyane as a hoary and skilled intriguer whose treating with the British could imperil its position in southern Mozambique despite the guarantees of the Anglo-Portuguese treaty of 1891. It justified war. Another Portuguese reason for war against Gungunyane stemmed from their discredited view of themselves after the British ultimatum and the ungenerous terms of the 1891 treaty that set Mozambique's borders. A military triumph over the Gaza kingdom would do much, in the eyes of Portuguese super patriots, to restore the lustre to Portugal's tarnished prestige for yielding to Britain. But local officers, even the conquest-minded Enes, cautioned as late as 1893 against a precipitous attack, lest a reverse lead to British intervention. It seemed better to await the right moment and allow the ills besetting the Gaza state to sap its resistance. But as so often happens in inevitable conflicts, the outbreak was occasioned by a third party.

In summer 1894, two minor Rhonga chiefs, Mahazul and Matibejana, laid siege to Lourenço Marques in retaliation for Portuguese interference in a succession dispute and demands for higher hut taxes. The town's inhabitants with the assistance of a few companies of *Angolas* (black mercenaries from Angola) beat off the attack until reinforcements arrived. The residents beseeched Lisbon for aid. The appeals bore fruit in the famous campaign of 1895 — one of the most celebrated of Portugal's colonial wars.

Enes was appointed Royal Commissioner with extensive powers and placed in charge of the campaign. Authoritarian, toughminded, bold and an imperialist, Enes determined to offer no compromise nor quarter to Gungunyane. He assembled a mixed force and went on the offensive. A brief but bloody encounter at Marracuene on the Incomati River in February 1895, introduced Gaza's forces to the lethal machine gun.[18] Encouraged by the victory, Lisbon hastened an expeditionary force of 2,000 troops to Enes's command. Heartened and strengthened, he issued several demands to Gungunyane that, if accepted, would have cost Gaza's independence.

Still preferring peace to war, Gungunyane offered to meet some of Enes's demands for a tribute to Portugal, but not the surrender of the two rebel chiefs who had been granted asylum. Internally, he faced rising pressure to break off negotiations by a war lobby headed by Maguiguana, his chief advisor and war minister. Enes held firm. Attempts to gain assistance from the British and Boers proved unfruitful. Gungunyane stood alone.

War continued in September, and the Portuguese won a lopsided victory to the west of Manjacaze. Outgunned by modern weapons and debilitated by smallpox and famine, Gaza power wilted. A series of skirmishes preceded the bloody battle at Lake Coolela where Portuguese firepower left a hecatomb of African dead. Portuguese casualties were less than 50.[19] His army shattered, Gungunyane fled to the village of Chaimite. There he communed at the remains of Soshangane, his grandfather, for inspiration and recovery until overtaken by Joaquim Mousinho de Albuquerque. Dashing, charismatic and a suicide Mousinho de Alburquerque rode into Chaimite, humiliated Gungunyane in front of his followers, and then transported him a prisoner to Lisbon where he was paraded through the streets in Roman fashion. Mousinho de

Albuquerque's swashbuckling raid through hostile country with a small troop of soldiers captured the Portuguese fancy for decades, and his belief in a mystical Portuguese nationalism made him a fitting hero for the ultra-nationalism of the future Salazar regime. Soon after Gungunyane's arrival in Lisbon, he was shipped to the Azores Islands to live out his life in comfortable exile. Mousinho de Albuquerque's life ended differently. Unfit for the thrusting and parrying of political life as Enes's successor, he shot himself to death in 1902. Pushed by his generals for a war impossible to win and by the Portuguese for a surrender of independence, Gungunyane parleyed, played for time and lost. Professor P. R. Warhurst wrote: 'If tragedy is the approach to inevitable catastrophe, in which the central figure is pushed to the edge by factors over which he has no control, the story of Gungunhana is tragic indeed.'[20]

The removal of Gungunyane from Mozambique brought only a hiatus in the fighting, for Maguiguana led a rising two years later. The reopening of the fighting was occasioned by the hut tax, the government's confiscation of the former monarch's cattle and the misconduct of the African auxiliaries who used the opportunity to settle scores with their onetime masters. A non-Shangana, Maguiguana had risen through the ranks to become Gungunyane's best general. But good generalship could not compensate for modern weapons. He lost the decisive battle of Macontene in today's Gaza district and fled toward the Transvaal. Considered more arduous than the first Gaza campaign, it finished with the old general's death in 1897. Cornered by his enemies, he went down heroically firing his revolver rather than ignominiously surrendering.[21]

So ended the last full-scale war in southern Mozambique. The Portuguese conquered those that had conquered. Their success did more than eliminate a threat to Portugal's occupation. Gugunyane's defeat and capture were touted as evidence of superior Portuguese 'moral forces' and as a redemption of Portugal's national prestige and martial vigor bespattered by diplomatic failures. In reality, the machine gun and rapid fire rifle made the outcome anticlimatic when compared to earlier wars on the Zambezi. But soon the tales of Portuguese arms at Manjacaze and Coolela, magnified and distorted by a golden mist, became triumphs over the foes of the fatherland, hallowed in memory and proclaimed in ideal.

Out of the military occupation in Mozambique and Angola came what Professor James Duffy called 'the generation of 1895, those soldiers and administrators who faced the task of reconstruction in the African colonies,'[22] where underdevelopment and poverty pervaded and local interests thwarted government control. In Mozambique, the authoritarian stamp of Enes and Albuquerque's imperishable words on administration, development and policies toward Africans left their mark on Portuguese colonial government until the nationalist insurgency. The occupation wars produced 'heroics' for Portugal; for Mozambique they laid the groundwork for colonial rule.

EXERTIONS OF THE SCRAMBLE

The 'scramble for Africa' wrenched Portugal from its centuries-long slumber in Africa. Livingstone's journeys catapulted central Africa into European headlines and roused Lisbon to the dangerous ambitions of rival European powers. Belgium's Leopold II's empire building in the Congo (now Zaire), German treaty making to the north of the Rovuma and the British South Africa Company's extension northward challenged Portugal's exclusiveness in Africa and placed in peril the long-cherished dream of a transcontinental corridor between Mozambique and Angola.

Portugal's decline and impotence since *O Século Maravilhoso* cast into doubt its pretentious claims and whetted the appetite of other European scramblers. Much of Portugal's decline was relative to the industrial and military rise of other European states. Historical circumstances in the nineteenth century further crippled its power. The Napoleonic Wars ravaged the Iberian peninsula, Miguelist civil war and political tumult unsettled the country for decades leaving the monarch perched uneasily amidst republicanism. It was innocent of modern technology and balanced budgets. As a consequence Portugal, unfavoured with industrial raw materials or financial expertise, lacked sufficient wherewithal to play power politics in European chancelleries where African boundary questions were ultimately decided. Its withered laurels counted for nothing in the age of Salisbury, Bismarck and Leopold II.

As late as 1890, Portugal's hold on Mozambique was pitifully infirm and confined to a half-dozen deteriorated forts or emaciated garrisons at Lourenço Marques, Sofala, Tete, Sena, Quelimane and on Mozambique and Ibo islands. Despondently, Albuquerque complained: 'in the rest of our possessions in this part of Africa we had no authority of any kind.'[23] A young Portuguese officer lamented: 'The province of Mozambique belongs without question to the blacks who live in it.'[24] Twenty years later Portugal, although never realizing its extravagant territorial aspirations, had occupied nearly all of the country.

Portugal's first significant round in the 'scramble' went favourably. It centered on Delagoa Bay. The sorry state of Portuguese defences at Lourenço Marques and obvious strength and independence of surrounding African chiefs belied protestations of control and occupation to such early nineteenth-century visitors as Captain William F. Owen. At the head of a British coastal survey of east Africa from 1822 to 1825, Owen appraised Delagoa Bay to be of high value to Britain's recently acquired Cape colony, and urged, as did subsequent Britons, the establishment of a British settlement. Disdainful of Portuguese claims, he signed protection and friendship treaties with chiefs to the south of Lourenço Marques; ran up the Union Jack at Catembe on the opposite shore from the town; arrested slavers in the bay; and initiated a simmering diplomatic controversy on who held jurisdiction to the region. The Transvaal's recognition of Mozambique's border below Delagoa Bay in 1869 brought the issue to a boil. Arbitration by French President MacMahon in 1875 awarded Portugal with the bay and the country to the south already set by the Portuguese-Transvaal treaty. MacMahon's award proved crucial to the economy and future development of Mozambique, for it placed within its borders not only an excellent harbour, but also the profitable traffic to and from the interior via Delagoa Bay.

On the west coast, the giant chess game turned badly for Portugal. Convened by Chancellor Otto von Bismarck, the Berlin Conference of colonial powers in 1884-1885 denied Lisbon's claims to territory north of the Congo River (except for the now oil-rich Cabinda enclave) in favour of Leopold II's Congo Free State. It also established the principle of 'effective occupation' for international recognition of claims—in the Portuguese view a doctrine always more rigidly applied to their possessions.[25]

In Africa itself, Portugal also faced clear and present dangers to its goals. The aggressive British South Africa Company, often a forerunner to Britain's imperial actions, moved toward what is today the central zone and the northern section of Mozambique. In the central zone, Rhodes wanted a right-of-way to the sea from his company's base on the Mashonaland plateau to the port city of Beira. His designs on what became Northern and Southern Rhodesia (Zambia and Rhodesia), and his grandiose vision of a British 'Manifest Destiny' from Cape to Cairo soon unhinged Lisbon's hopes for o mapa côr de rosa ('the rose-coloured map') of Portuguese territory stretching from the east to the west coast colony.* In the north on the upper Shire in what is now Malawi, Portuguese and British interests again collided. The Scottish missionaries pressured the Foreign Office to assume control of the region. In the tradition of Livingstone, they mounted a virulent campaign on what they perceived as the inveterate slaving of the Portuguese and their moral and racial degeneracy in Mozambique. Thereupon, Rhodes pushed for consent to allow his company to administer the disputed region.

Encroachments on its African territories were viewed with alarm in Lisbon where interest and concern had grown since mid-century. Amplifying the imperial sentiments was the Lisbon Geographical Society.[26] Founded in 1875, it promoted exploration and the idea of empire in its influential bulletin. The goal of Portuguese explorers, colonizers and campaigners was to assert what the British disparagingly called Portugal's 'archaeological'[27] claims. One of these explorer-colonizers precipitated a head-on collison between Portugal and Britain in south east Africa.

Major Alexandre Alberto da Rocha Serpa Pinto, renowned veteran explorer, embarked up the Shire at the head of an ostensibly scientific expedition (but in reality an occupying force) that comprised 700 armed African auxiliaries. The Scottish missionaries were distressed by the advance of the column and its battles with the Makololo. Reports of Serpa Pinto's actions coincided with cables from Rhodes that the Portuguese were constructing stockades in Mashonaland. Prime Minister Salisbury in 1890 issued the famous ultimatum to Lisbon to cease all its operations on the Shire and in Mashonaland, and he backed up the demand with a dispatch of British warships to Mozambique Island. The Portuguese government bowed to *force majeure* and withdrew

---

* Minister of Foreign Affairs, Henrique de Barros used a rose-tinted map in 1886 to explain Portugal's historic claims across southern Africa to the Cortes, or paliament.

its forces from Mashonaland and below the confluence of the Ruo and the Shire.

The British ultimatum and Portugal's subsequent loss of territory in the 1891 Anglo-Portuguese treaty dealt a severe blow to Portuguese national self-esteem, and rocked the monarchy which toppled twenty years later. Portugal's politics were once more strongly influenced by events in Mozambique when in 1974 nationalist advances there were the single greatest African determinant of the military *coup* against the Caetano regime.

Electrified by the news of the government's capitulation to first the ultimatum and then the treaty, popular sentiment over-whelmingly espoused a hardline toward Britain in the short run and an entrenched commitment in the long run to the idea of a new African empire. Large demonstrations throughout Portugal voiced indignation and hurled charges of cowardice and betrayal at a government lucky enough to salvage what it could. Attachment to the belief in an African empire at that time ignored Portugal's economic difficulties or international powerlessness, it reached a kind of national madness. The loss in Mozambique tilted the Portuguese national character in the direction of what F. C. C. Egerton, an English observer of Portugal, classified as *loucura*, or heroic madness, away from its counterbalancing *siso*, or sound judgment and prudence.[28] Mobs stoned British consulates in Lisbon and Oporto; peasants, artisans, housewives and bankers subscribed to a national fund to send a cruiser and soldiers to Mozambique; and the nation's focus was riveted on occupation campaigns and colonial activities for the next twenty years. Students in Lisbon gathered about the statue of Camões whose sixteenth century epic poem *Os Lusíadas* extolled Portuguese exploration and valour, and pledged their lives to hold African lands — a pledge that was to be honoured, however reluctantly, by their grandsons.

From the crucible of defeat, anger and wounded vanity was forged a soaring nationalism and emotional link to Africa non-existent before. The glorified exploits of the 'generation of 1895' served to restore a badly shaken self-esteem and raised up heroes for the New State to call forth to examplify its virtues of Duty, Faith, and Service. It became fashionable to speak of the future lying in Africa. As second 'Brazils,' Mozambique and Angola could provide Portugal with wealth, settlement lands and a means to transend the tiny homeland.

But what mattered to the people of Mozambique was not the

difficulties Portugal encountered during the scramble nor the exploits of its explorers and soldiers. What mattered most were the policies, practices and prejudices that emerged from Portugal's renewed commitment to Mozambique. The twentieth century would judge how well Portugal put pilings under its castles in the sky.

PART TWO

Colonialism and Nationalism

Portugal's military conquest of Mozambique, sketched in the preceding pages, ended the competition of indigenous polities for local or wider hegemony. Something much more than military power determined the outcome. By African standards, Portuguese power was, of course, great; the Industrial Revolution insured that Enes's soldiers were more lethally armed that Barreto's arquebusiers. As so often happens in warfare, the armies and tactics employed by the combatants reflect their respective underlying social structures and register differences of more than military significance. A more modern state with superior technical skills in this case overcame foes with ancient disunity and archaic weaponry. This victory ushered in social and economic change, the seeds of which in time destroyed the victor.

Lisbon's colonial rule, weak and temporarily shared with chartered companies though it was to be, marked a division in Mozambique's history. For the first time, the various peoples from the Rovuma to the Maputo rivers were lumped together under one rule. By creating a Mozambican state with fixed boundaries, Portugal poured the foundation for a national unit. By proclaiming Africans to be black Portuguese, it lessened ethnic distinctiveness, but stimulated a national identity. Exploitation of the Africans gave birth to a common experience and raised up hatred for the hypocrisy of Portuguese citizenship. By introducing Mozambican Africans to the modern world of education, urbanization and Lusitanian fallibility, Portuguese colonialism begot a hope that lifted them toward independence.

The unfolding of these themes of Portuguese colonialism and African response are the subjects of the following chapters where in retrospect the story of Portugal's collapse proceeded toward a fate almost as certain as that of a Greek tragedy. Its exertions during the European 'scramble for Africa' brought down the monarchy; its exertions against Mozambique's independence contributed to the fall of the authoritarian regime. At its worst, Mozambique's colonial period was as if the violent past went forward into contemporary times; at best, the current of political, social and economic forces flowed in a new direction.

THE IMPOSITION OF ALIEN RULE: PORTUGUESE COLONIALISM TO WORLD WAR II

The Portuguese had come and they had at last conquered: now they must rule. Portuguese colonial rule from the end of pacification to World War II worked for a new order dominated by concerns for an effective administration, the profitable exploitation of Mozambique's resources and the formation of a comprehensive 'native policy.' These were old and troublesome problems to Lisbon now under fresh impetus to transform order and peace from anarchy and war, profit from loss, development from destruction. Portuguese plans involved an intensification and codification of former practices and programmes, not a revolutionary break with the past. Scarce material and human resources hampered implementation. Political tumult in Portugal that swept aside the monarchy for a Republic and then threw it out for a stern and uncompromising dictatorship added to the national debate on the right course of colonialism. The dictatorial regime reversed the previous policy of development for schemes designed to entrench Lisbon's rule still further, to place political stability ahead of economic growth, and to tie forever Mozambique to a tiny country on the western rim of Europe.

The 'generation of 1895' exercised a deep and lasting influence over the legislation, attitudes and projects of successive Portuguese planners and administrators. The Salazar regime enshrined their mystical nationalism, dedication to the colonial empire and belief in Portugal's imperial destiny in order to shape a colonial mentality. Taking advantage of the strong nationalistic and imperial currents in Portuguese thought, which had been imbued for centuries with legendary figures, heroic feats and the bombast of chroniclers, the New State ideologues amplified and moulded a colonial consciousness in a way that was in keeping with the authoritarian creeds and demagoguery of neo-Roman empires prevalent in Europe during the 1930s and 1940s. Chief among their much vaunted goals was a multi-continental Lusitanian community so cemented to Portugal that one New State philosopher exalted it as 'one State, one Race, one Faith, and one Civilization.'[1] Scarcely less important in the imperial rhetoric was a renewed commitment to the ancient *missão civilizadora* of Portugal. Shorn of its lofty phrases, this civilizing mission was a form of pacification by which the colonizer imposed on the colonial people a new order, law and nationality with the goal of defusing resistance.

Enes in his report on needed administrative reforms, published as *Moçambique (1893) Relatório*, advocated replacing civilian administration for military as soon after pacification as feasible, continuing temporarily the *prazos* where they still functioned and granting concessions to great land companies to exploit and develop Mozambique. He also justified foreign investment and pushed for the wide use of African labour to make the colony prosper. A devoted imperialist, his ideas on sources for government revenue, administrative procedures, character traits of officials and prejudices toward the African whom he considered a 'big child' were minutely detailed and exhaustively argued. They moulded beliefs and formed policies for decades.

THE ADMINISTRATIVE SYSTEM

The administrative reorganisation of Mozambique started in 1907. It was at first confined to thoroughly pacified regions and those not under the jurisdiction of the Mozambique and Niassa chartered companies. The government introduced the *circumscrição* ('circumscription'), the fundamental rural administrative unit of Portugal, and phased out the military rule of the *capitanias-mores*. Headed by a Portuguese *administrador*, the *circumscrição* was imposed in predominately African areas, and was split into two to six *postos* ('posts').[2] Placed under the control of a *chefe de posto*, the nearest Portuguese official to the African population, the posts grew to encompass usually some 40,000 inhabitants by the 1960s.

In some respects a white chief, the *chefo de posto* superintended the collection of taxes, presided over disputes, dispensed punishment, and he oversaw village agriculture and small government projects. Depending on his temperament, he could be sympathetic to his charges, or he could abuse his authority for purposes of spite, profit or lust. His tyranny, especially in the early years, forms a bitter and violent chapter in Mozambique's colonial history. Underpaid and poorly trained, he came as a bird of passage not to create but to squeeze what he could from his lowly position and return to Portugal. Corrupt, cruel and incompetent, he came to represent Portuguese rule to many villagers. Later colonial authorities strove to increase his skills and curb his use of the *chicote* (whip) and *palmatoria* (perforated paddle). The Overseas Organic Law of 1963 changed his title to *administrador de posto* in a belated attempt to refurbish his image.

The head of the *postos* worked through an African administrator-chief, known first as a *régulo,* and then *regedor.* This sometime uniformed official had the responsibility of a *regedoría* or a group of villages. Outside the *regedorías,* the migratory African was often subject to *regedores* in towns or on plantations. The *regedor* came to his position in the colonial administration by succession, election or appointment by the government for his loyal service in the army or lesser civilian bureaucracy. Not unlike the *fumo* on the *prazo,* he was charged with assisting in tax collection, persuading his people to contract their labour or work on their own fields, insuring order and gathering information. As late as 1965, about 90 per cent of the *regedores* were still traditional chiefs. Whether traditional chief or government appointee, they incurred the enmity and opposition of the nationalists in the 1960s and 1970s for their exploitation and collaboration.

Africans also came to serve the colonial government as policemen, clerks, messengers, interpreters for pay, prestige and self-advancement. They soon found, however, that an African or even *mestiço* could not advance far in the colonial bureaucracy. Since the 1895 war and the use of *Angolas* the government established separate black companies in the army with white officers.[3] A similar pattern was followed in the colonial police force.

The local administrative apparatus was different for Europeans in urban areas or settlements. The 1907 organization set up *concelhos,* or townships, for European and 'civilized' Africans. Modelled on metropolitan municipalities, the *concelhos* ('councils') enjoyed some limited self-government, but in keeping with the Portuguese political tradition, local government was never strong. The internal colonial regime remained highly centralized as 'the generation of 1895' wished. The few Europeans concentrated in Mozambican towns had since the mid-eighteenth century some form of municipal organization that was patterned on the *câmaras municipais* of Portugal's urban areas. After the outbreak of nationalist fighting in Angola, Mozambique's colonial administration accelerated the elevation of circumscriptions to townships. Under the 1963 Organic Law, all district capitals and *concelhos* with 500 or more registered voters were granted such municipal councils. By 1973, there were listed 60 townships and 43 circumscriptions.[4]

The administrative system provided loopholes for settlers to avoid subordination to African officials in black areas by permitting the establishment of the *freguesias* ('parishes' or wards) — a subdivision of the *concelho*. This allowed white rule in rural areas. The entire system froze the demarcation between black and white living areas. Whenever possible, the Portuguese recreated Iberian towns and architecture with outdoor cafes, inlaid sidewalks and red tiled roofs. The core of the cities and towns were made European; the shantytowns surrounding urban centres housed the African worker and servant.

The European townships and the African circumscriptions comprised the administrative districts of the province. In 1974, there were eleven districts in Mozambique;[5] five had been established in 1907. The district governors answered to the Governor-General of the colony. Governors-General, both military and civilian, had wide powers and responsibilities, although their fiscal reins had been tightened since the economic excesses under the Republic. As the highest official in the colony, he coordinated the civil service, oversaw African welfare and implemented Lisbon's policy. The colony's Legislative Council, largely a consultative body, never held any meaningful legislative power. Its delegates were selected or elected in a manner not likely to foster parliamentary growth.

With the coming to power of the New State, the Governor-General reported to the Overseas Minister, who as the chief administrator of the colonies, had the most extensive control over the administration, policies and finances of Mozambique. He had the prerogative of consulting with various groups, particularly the Overseas Council, in directing general colonial policy. Until the military coup in 1974, the Council of Ministers and the Prime Minister — the Portuguese government — exercised executive powers on colonial matters and acted on recommendations of the Overseas

Ministry. Portugal's National Assembly had slight impact on Mozambique and other colonies, except during a time of crisis such as the 1961 upheaval in Angola. Then the overseas deputies (23 in all and 7 representing Mozambique) modified the liberal proposals from the Overseas Minister Adriano Moreira. In quiescent periods, the 130-member assembly virtually legislated automatically what was presented to it from the Overseas Ministry via the Council of Ministers, although development plans were scrutinized closely.[6]

Over the years there were to be many modifications in labour codes, in Lisbon's centralizing-decentralizing orientation and in legislative definitions of citizens, *assimilados* and *indígenas;* but the basic administrative organization within Mozambique remained substantially unchanged by bureaucratic shuffling, upheavals in the colony or political turmoil in Portugal until the end of the independence war.

THE CHARTERED COMPANIES

Portugal needed help in expanding its authority, making the colony 'pay,' and having it administrated. To set up a network of administration and a system of transportation to facilitate communication and exploitation, to revitalise certain *prazos* and even to undertake military operations and police duties demanded investment capital. Portugal had little, and the government looked to foreign investors and the establishment of chartered companies.

The commissioning of concessionary companies was both a break with the past policy and a continuation of it. On the one hand Portugal, as well as other empire-building states since the heyday of mercantilism, had fought the introduction of alien commerical enterprises and denationalizing influences in its colonies. On the other hand, from the times of Prince Henry the monarchy had parcelled out bits and pieces of its authority along with trading privileges, revenue and mineral rights to Portuguese *donatários,* *prazo* holders, factors and custom agents. Just as the crown had delegated political and fiscal functions for lack of resources to *prazo* owners, so, too, the government handed over wide powers and vast lands to foreign-backed companies when conditions demanded it.

Beginning in the 1870s, Lisbon granted transporting and trading rights to a few British, Dutch and French firms on the Zambezi. The Lusitanian entrepreneurial spirit was not entirely lifeless and some small Portuguese companies undertook the production of sugarcane liquors. At Mopea on the left bank of the lower Zambezi, an opium company started growing poppies but failed when its crops were destroyed during the Massingire rising. The conquests of the next-to-last decade of the nineteenth century, however, stimulated the formation of great land companies for administration and exploitation.

Three principal companies came to dominate nearly two-thirds of the colony—the Mozambique Company, the Niassa Company and the Zambézia Company. Efforts to fulfill their goals carried the companies into the arena of politics, military actions and forced labour. The Mozambique and Zambézia companies acquired *prazos* which they subleased to smaller companies or collected the *mussoco* ('head tax') themselves. In any case, they prolonged the life of the *prazo* companies until the first years of the New State.

The Mozambique Company, creation of Joaquim Paiva de Andrada and oldest of the trio, evolved from a mining firm and other stillborn ventures into a *companhia majestática* whose lands coincided with present districts of Vila Pery and Beira (the former Manica e Sofala district) with its charter in 1891. By a fifty-year charter, Lisbon granted the company extensive governing powers and a tax holiday for 25 years in return for 10 per cent of the sold shares and 7.5 per cent of the profits. The company had exclusive control over mining, fishing, public works, African taxation and communication services. Tasks imposed on the company included the settlement of one thousand Portuguese families, the establishment and maintenance of schools, town administration and public order. The paper powers were only partially exercised, and the obligations went virtually unmet. Want of capital limited its activities, and the military missions thrust on it were beyond the company's capabilities. Continued resistance in the company's territory obliged the colonial government to mount a campaign against the Barue kingdom in 1902.

A similar charter for thirty-five years was given in 1891 to the largely British-financed Niassa Company for the region north of the Lúrio River comprising the present districts of Cabo Delgado and Niassa. Despite areas of fertile soil, the Niassa company failed in its agricultural pursuits, and its surveys uncovered no mineral deposits of commercial worth. At the time of the African guerrilla attacks in 1964, the northern region was the least developed and least influenced by Portuguese domination. Except for the construction of port facilities at Porto Amélia, the company's plans never materialized. The intended railway from the port to Lake Malawi went unconstructed, and its labour practices and high hut taxes caused Africans to flee to neighbouring territories.

The Zambézia Company differed from the other two companies in that it was more clearly a commerical enterprise, and it enjoyed the most diversified foreign investment. Founded in 1892 without a charter, the company avoided an administrative burden. As the largest of the three, the Zambézia Company occupied today's Tete and Zambézia districts where it fell heir to many *prazos*. Possession of much good land enabled the company to turn more of a profit than the Mozambique Company. The Zambézia Company's demand for taxes to be paid in labour caused large numbers of Africans to flee to the Mozambique Company's lands where the payment could be made in goods or money. Evolving from a mining concern into a company with a variety of holdings, the Zambézia Company subcontracted a number of its *prazos* to specific agricultural firms. One of the largest and most successful, the Sena Sugar Estates — a British outfit — had mills on both sides of the lower Zambezi which still crush sugarcane and distill alcohol. Another important sub-company, the Boror Company, which had German backing, cultivated coconuts, sugar and sisal, but failed in coffee growing.[7]

In accordance with their charters, the Niassa Company and the Mozambique Company transferred their lands back to Portuguese control in 1926 and 1942, respectively, although the latter had surrendered most of its administrative responsibilities in the 1930s. Outspoken critics had long since doomed any chance of renewal. Alfredo Augusto Freire de Andrade, Governor-General from 1906 to 1910, argued that the colony had not benefited from the 'privileged companies' and thanked Providence for disallowing the formation of a company in Inhambane district.[8] Advocates of the 1930 Colonial Act endorsed its tough controls on the grounds of foreign penetration in the colonies and the companies' semi-sovereign powers. Américo Chaves de Almeida, an editor in Lourenço Marques, stated that: 'Anyone who wants the Companhia de Moçambique to continue expanding within the province of

Mozambique. . . will have to undertake. . . . the responsibility of having denied his vote to a motion [1930 Colonial Act] which sets out to regenerate the colonial policy of Portugal.'[9] British capital was perceived as having an Anglicizing influence and Beira, the Mozambique Company's headquarters, was viewed as an English settlement. The prevalence of 'English' money (in reality Rhodesian and South African with pictures of British monarchs), the growing use of English in the south and even English titles on the cinema marquees evoked condemnation from Portuguese anxious about the colony's powerful neighbours. A handful of settlers formed the Liga de Propaganda e Defesa da Colónia de Moçambique which advocated 'economic independence of the colony' and strong cultural ties to Portugal. The termination of the company contracts put all of Mozambique under Portuguese rule and influence for the first time in history.

Portugal was well served by the *companhias majestáticas* and their subcontracting companies. The British shareholders' interests in the companies worked against the expansionist drives of London and the British South Africa Company. Their efforts strengthened Lisbon's hand during the 'scramble.' While in Portugal the monarchy collapsed and the Republic spiraled into near chaos, the companies began an economic infrastructure that, although woefully incomplete, at least initiated what the Portuguese were incapable of doing at the time. Until 1930, foreign investment subsidized all large-scale development; it was not until the end of the decade that the government undertook a few carefully studied projects from revenues in the colony or funds from Portugal. The companies launched and encouraged cotton, tea, sugar, rice and coconut cultivation on a commercial basis; conducted preliminary mineral surveys; established a skeletal communication and transportation network; and revived stagnant commerce and dying towns. Foreign investment financed the building of ports at Lourenço Marques, Beira and Porto Amélia. For good and ill, non-Portuguese elements stimulated systematic economic colonialism in Mozambique.

Africans benefited little from the start of European commercial enterprises. Indeed, their lives in the beginning were made harder. The government collaborated with commercial ventures to press-gang labourers and lay robber hands on land. A celebrated but by no means an isolated case involved Manuel de Brito Camacho,

High Commissioner (the Republic used the title instead of Governor-General) from 1921 to 1923, who gave the Sena Sugar Estates 'facilities—only facilities' to recruit annually 3,000 workers for twenty years.[10] His help was attacked by humanitarians who reflected some of the concern for Africans that prevaded the Republican years, but was endorsed by other local interest, some of whom thought he should have done more to assist companies in their labour shortages. The latter, however, compared him favourably to Angola's High Commissioner of the same period, José Mendes Ribeiro Norton de Matos, who decreed an end to forced labour for private employers. At the start of the modern colonial era, Africans were exploited with a certain ruthlessness absent from traditional life or *prazo* slavery. Gone were the checks on *prazo* tyranny that migration and rebellion offered the oppressed *colono*. Anger and hostility to the new regime and the commercial ventures were vented during World War I.

MOZAMBIQUE AND THE GREAT WAR

Portugal's entry into World War I in February 1916 involved Mozambique in disastrous hostilities with Germany that matched the metropole's poor showing on the Western Front. In Mozambique, the government rallied to the Allied cause by launching an offensive across the Rovuma into German East Africa (Tanganyika) in 1916. It was a short-lived advance. A German column of 2,000 Askari and European officers commanded by Paul von Lettow-Vorbeck, evading a British force pushing it southward, waded across the Rovuma in November 1917 and lunged almost to the Zambezi Valley. It lived off captured Portuguese stores and ammunition. For a year the invaders roamed virtually at will through the northern interior. The German-led column worsted its enemies in several engagements before inflicting on them a major defeat at the Namacurra River, near Quelimane. Here they put to flight a Portuguese, African auxiliary and English ('infected by the example of the Portuguese,' said the English) force. Half of the over 200 killed, drowned in the river while retreating. The Portuguese smarted under the British and Rhodesian jibes during and after the war, and the Allies overlooked that they also had been unable to halt General von Lettow-Vorbeck's tatterdemalion army. The

German force recrossed the Rovuma in September 1918. At the time of the armistice in Europe, von Lettow Vorbeck had struck in Zambia and was poised for an invasion of Malawi.

The Treaty of Versailles restored the Quionga triangle (a wedge of ground between the mouth of the Rovuma and Cape Delgado) from almost three decades of German control to Mozambique. It was Portugal's only territorial compensation for participation in the war. In its case for financial reparations, Portugal claimed the loss of 130,000 African lives. In 1930, it was awarded the scaled-down sum of $11 million.

A Portuguese historian blamed the lack of success against the German-officered invasion on 'native revolts against Portuguese authority' wherever the enemy appeared.[11] It would be closer to the mark to say that Latin martial spirit buckled under Teutonic assault. Yet the Portuguese had done little to win African loyalty in the recently pacified northern region where vivid memories of resistance lingered. Von Lettow-Vorbeck wrote that the Makonde around Negomano on the Rovuma 'fled before the advance of the Portuguese, fearing their ruthlessness and cruelty.'[12]

Actions taken by the colonial administration during the war in fact precipitated a widespread uprising. To defend the northern frontier, the government impressed an estimated 25,000 men into the supply columns as carriers — a common practice in colonial Africa. Disease and starvation marched in the carrier corps, and only one-fifth of the men returned. Coming on top of harsh colonial rule and famines that plagued Mozambique at the start of the century, the impressments set the flashpoint for rebellion.

THE BARUE REBELLION

The largest traditional rebellion against colonial rule in southern Africa, during the war erupted in the Barue kingdom in March 1917. Initially, the Barue Tonga spread the rebellion in all directions and gained adherents with every victory over Portuguese station or relief column. Soon the rebellion blazed with a momentum of its own. After pinning down a Portuguese force in Tete, the Chicunda peoples around Zumbo joined the revolt; the Tawara above Tete and the Zimba on the north bank of the middle Zambezi then cast their lot with the rebels in April; along the river to the south the remaining Tonga chiefs of the Sena estates came over to the revolt; and invidivudals left their jobs in the colonial economy as waiters and policemen to rebel. This was the high tide of the pan-ethnic revolt and it appeared that Portuguese rule would be washed away. Several agents of the Zambézia Company perished, and its posts went up in smoke. Except for the surrounded town of Tete and one small military site, the Portuguese military presence was no more on the middle reaches of the Zambezi.

Then on the eve of the intended strikes on the last government holdouts the rebellion lost steam, and no other groups sided with the rebels. The Ngoni instead soldiered for the Portuguese as they had in the last years of the Zambezi wars. Power from ancient times, the times of the Muslims and *sertanejos* down to the Portuguese colonial epoch, had shifted frequently enough for rank and file to be wary of joining a struggle before it had a better than even chance of success.

After the May high point, the Portuguese counteroffensive slowly and with effort rolled back the rebel gains. Not until November 1920, however, did the last remnants surrender to the Portuguese near the Rhodesian border, although heavy fighting had subsided when the Macombe slipped across the frontier in the same month the European war ended. For several years after 1917, the memory of the Barue rising was an important political fact. The revolt rattled Portuguese sovereignty which simultaneously faced a serious threat from the German invasion. The colonial administration tried to connect the two challenges by accusing local German missionaries of fomenting the rebellion, but its causes were of Portuguese making.

The ancestors of the Barue kingdom split from the rising Mwene Mutapa empire and migrated from Chidima province to the country between Tete and Sena on the south bank sometime in the late fifteenth or early sixteenth centuries. Except when it was briefly conquered in the late 1600s by a powerful estate owner the kingdom maintained its autonomy, despite the proximity of the Sena *prazos,* until colonial rule was imposed after its defeat in 1902. The Portuguese had intervened from time to time in Barue politics. An aspirant to the throne sought Portuguese recognition of his dominance. At the investiture ceremony, the Portuguese sent their endorsement of a successful claimant in the form of the *madzimanga* — a type of baptismal water that had pre-Portuguese origins.[13] Usually, the Portuguese authorities at Sena withheld the *madzi-manga* until the strongest claimant secured the throne, because he alone could guarantee security for European trade and the nearby *prazos*.

Centuries-long contact with the Portuguese had strengthened rather than weakened Barue customs and institutions. Thus vaccinated the Barue Tonga proved more resistant to the newly imposed virus of colonialism than other little-affected people. It was in fact the traditional religious and secular authorities who organized the revolt—the last of its kind in Mozambique and indeed south central Africa. Before the revolt, the Barue princely houses had been divided over the claims of two aspirants—Nongwe-Nongwe and Makosa—to the Macombeship. Nongwe-Nongwe's call for rebellion struck a responsive chord and gained him *de facto* recognition as the Macombe during the revolt. The deep grievances that united first the Barue kingdom and then other groups behind Nongwe-Nongwe stemmed from the recent imposition of Portuguese rule. The conquest of Barue had taken place only 15 years before the rebellion and was followed by forced labour without pay for many Barue Tonga and finally by conscription of them as carriers in the war. A particularly large draft two months before the rebellion coupled with injustices of the government and its *sepais* ('African police') turned sullen passivity into desperate revolt.

Aware of the Portuguese preoccupation with the Germans and the division among whites, the Barue kingdom co-ordinated the revolt with other groups through their spirit-mediums to give it a pan-ethnic expression. The method and purpose of the spirit-mediums to transcend ethnic separation was revolutionary in approach. The aims of the rising evolved from a dramatic way of manifesting grievances, through a hoped-for restoration of the traditional order, to finally a sought-after substitution of British rule for Portuguese by inviting Britain to occupy Mozambique territory. In light of British actions during the scramble, this last goal was not farfetched at that time, but the world war and Britain's need for European allies made it unlikely in 1917. British support for the hard-pressed Portuguese was, however, anything but wholehearted. The Portuguese, who had dispatched a small detachment of troops from Sena to Blantyre in 1915 during the John Chilembwe rising (in which the inflammatory preaching of the Mozambican Charles Domingo helped foment) in Nyasaland

(Malawi), fully expected reciprocal aid from another white government. But the British and Rhodesian officials showed a certain
sympathy for the Africans burdened by misrule and brutality, and
evinced a disdain for the Portuguese who they viewed with undisguised antipathy—a sentiment that long afterwards radiated
from Salisbury. Although the British supplied small arms to the
Portuguese, they were deaf to requests to close the frontier and
hence deny the insurgents a sanctuary. Toward the end of the
rebellion, about 100,000 people crossed the border to safety in
Rhodesia, Zambia and Malawi as the Portuguese and their Ngoni
irregulars crushed the last rebels with fire and terror.[14]

The Portuguese repression of the rebellion shattered more than a
revolt; it destroyed the Barue polity and with it the last refuge of
ruling Karanga aristocracy whose ancestors established the Mwene
Mutapa empire. As history was to show, the destruction of African
last-ditch revolts which were answered not by the colonial government's amelioration of grievances but by tighter oppression determined that Mozambican politics would be shaped in an environment of violence and bloodshed.

THE EMERGENCE OF THE ESTADO NOVO

Mozambique's fate became inextricably interwoven with Portugal's
history in this century. Political events in Portugal were to have
dark and bloody consequences for Mozambique. Already gone was
the informal empire of the past, the half-dozen crumbling forts and
impotent garrisons. With the new regimes came restrictions on
African freedoms, forced labour, settlers out for profit, and blue-
prints to transform Mozambique into a Portuguese province in
language, custom and identification. Out of the political tumult in
Portugal came also a new and intense colonial rule.

The Portuguese monarchy collapsed in 1910 and was supplanted
by a wobbly republic for the next 16 years. Both were the victims of
mass disillusionment, institutional instability, career ambitions and
chronic economic difficulties. The Portuguese in Europe and in
Mozambique ushered in the Republic amid jubilation and hope
that were soon dissipated. Presidents and ministries rotated in and
out of office with the rapidity and impact on the nation's problems
of a revolving door. The corrupt vied with the incompetent for

power while a few men of rectitude and ability sank in the task of building institutions to replace a discredited monarchy and sullied Church. By 1926, the country stood at the brink of anarchy and the economy was paralysed by fraud and debt. The army, the most unified and decisive of Portuguese institutions and arbitrator of political wrangles and questions for more than a century, intervened to end the strikes, disorders and violence. It had toppled the flagging Bragança monarchy and now allied itself with the Catholic Church hierarchy, large land owners, bankers and industrialists (the powerful 'hundred families') to bring down the Republic.

Two years of military government failed to solve the economic problems, and the newly elected President António Oscar de Fragoso Carmona, one of the generals of the *coup* and later figurehead of the New State, gave the financial portfolio to a youngish economics professor at the University of Coimbra, António de Oliveira Salazar. By applying new taxes and pruning expenditures, the Finance Minister began the reduction of the huge national debt. Over the years, Salazar's balanced budgets and careful spending built up reserves that transformed the *escudo* to one of the world's soundest currencies. But even the most enthusiastic Salazarist has admitted that the tight money principles, so applauded in the interwar years, arrested the industrial and commercial development of Portugal and the colonies after 1945.

Authoritarian, humourless, solitary and austere, Salazar took charge of Portuguese finances and then Portuguese life for 40 years. From his financial post, Salazar exerted an influence on every facet of government so much so that Carmona appointed him President of the Council of Ministers (i.e. Prime Minister) in 1932. He held this office until suffering a crippling stroke in September 1968. He inherited a poor and illiterate country, and he bequeathed one. Salazar resisted change as sternly as he strove to preserve the past in the present and into the future. To do otherwise, he believed, would invite social and political disorder, perhaps even Communism with its atheism and disruption of the natural ordering of elite and masses. He once remarked: 'The Portuguese must be treated as children: Too much too often would spoil them.'[15]

In 1933, the small Portuguese electorate accepted Salazar's Corporative Constitution and the *Estado Novo* ('New State'). With the blessing of the National Assembly of regime politicians and conservative establishment, he ruled in an authoritarian manner, and characterized his regime as 'anti-parliamentarians, anti-democrats, anti-liberals.' His watchwords for the metropole and the colonies were Order, Unity, Duty and Hard Work. To heal the wounds of the Republican period, Salazar sought to depoliticize the nation, and his regime employed all the devices of control and manipulation associated with a modern totalitarian state: censorship, supervised education, indoctrination, government-managed organizations and an efficient and ruthless secret police.[16] Like most imperial states, the obsessions and injustices at home were magnified in the colonies.

The Salazar regime was determined to manufacture a neo-imperialistic spirit as well as a belief in the political and economic solidarity of the empire. By education in the classroom, government publications, much-publicized state visits to Africa and colonial week celebrations, the New State nurtured a growth of interest and pride in the colonies. The goal was Portugal's rejuvenation. Without the wealth and prestige of a colonial empire, Portugal was only a tiny, impoverished nation in Europe. Historically, the reliance on colonial possessions as a means to a national regeneration was as old as the decline of the empire in the sixteenth century; but the systematic amplification of Portugal's heritage and mission belonged to the New State. It also furnished a mainstay to the ruling establishment, for a grand mission in Africa justified sacrifice, discipline, poverty and authoritarianism at home.[17] Such grandiose trumpetings called for abrupt reverses in the Republic's colonial policies.

The advent of the Republic added impetus to the trends of autonomy and decentralization which appeared in the last decade of the monarchy. Demands by Governors-General for increased freedom of action in the colonies, although not for officials below them, had been voiced by the 'generation of 1895', and the 1907 administrative reorganization of Mozambique had pointed in that direction. In 1914, the Organic Law on Civil Administration in the Overseas Provinces defined the colonies as 'autonomous administrative bodies', but the war interrupted the expanded powers of the High Commissioners until 1920, when the colonies also received financial autonomy. What followed, particularly in Angola, was thundering debt. Mozambique weathered the crisis better than Angola because it did not have as ambitious development projects as its sister colony, and its railways — Lourenço Marques to the

Transvaal, completed in 1894 and Beira to Rhodesia, finished in 1896 — accounted for a steady source of revenue in transit trade. Still, Mozambique's financial situation was so critical that by 1926 Lisbon had to guarantee a loan of 100 million *escudos* to the province. Mismanagement of finances arose in part from the indecisiveness or unsound judgment of Governors-General or High Commissioners and in part from their rapid turnover. Between 1910 and 1926, Mozambique had 13 different heads of colonial government. Decentralization and political instability opened the way for pervasive corruption and manipulation of the colonial bureaucracy by special interests, such as the Banco Nacional Ultramarino, the official bank of Mozambique.

The New State swept away the concept of provincial autonomy in the *Acto Colonial* of 1930 which switched the 1838 designation of 'overseas provinces' back to 'colonies' in a 'Portuguese Colonial Empire', reintegrated the African territories into an administrative system that placed ultimate authority in Lisbon, terminated administration by private companies and abolished the office of High Commissioner for the more subservient post of Governor-General.[18] Thenceforward for the next generation, the New State attempted directly to tackle the intertwined problems of development and native policy. The Colonial Act was in tune with the New State's centralizing of power within Portugal, and it coincided with heightened apprehensions of foreign economic infiltration which Salazar closed out of the colonies and Portugal. Two other acts laid the foundation of the New State citadel in Mozambique: the 1933 Organic Charter of the Portuguese Colonial Empire and the 1933 Overseas Administrative Act. 'The cornerstone principle, of course,' as Professor D. L. Wheeler wrote, 'was *political unity* (his italics), a euphemism for Portugal's colonial sovereignty in its African territories, which meant political centralisation as opposed to the greater autonomy allowed under the republic.'[19] Later modifications did little to alter the essential provisions of these acts until the gains of the nationalists compelled Lisbon to set up an assembly in the colony and to fabricate Mozambique's status as a state within the Portuguese nation.

NATIVE POLICY AND PRACTICE TO WORLD WAR II

The overseas export of slaves decreased as British gunboats patrolled the coast, the French scrapped the *émigré* system in 1864 and the Portuguese moved to cut off traffic from the main ports. Slavery within the country, however, was undisturbed by the shutdowns on the coast. Rooted in the traditions of the *colono* and voluntary enslavement, slavery evolved from a form of serfdom to forced labour on European plantations or government projects by the end of the nineteenth century. As Portuguese colonialism spread over the country, so also did the exploitation of African labour. The enforced planting of tea, cashews, sugar, sisal and cotton as cash crops warped the African concept of slavery, to which the *prazo* colony had accommodated itself, and established a system of harnessing workers, who now had an obligation to labour for the 'development of the colony', a euphemism for Portuguese interests.

Missionaries, consuls, naval officers and travellers, most of them British, condemned slavery in Mozambique and the participation of government authorities in it. The foremost critic was David Livingstone, the most famous European explorer and missionary in Africa. What he saw on his journey from Angola across the continent and later his expedition up the Zambezi enraged the Scottish missionary with the extent of human bondage and suffering: 'The Portuguese at Tette, from the governor downward, are extensively engaged in slaving.'[20] With the uncompromising rigor of the recently converted, the British humanitarians reproached the sinful Portuguese for the lack of progress in their colonies, for tolerating slavery and for not being Anglo-Saxons. Outraged, the Portuguese considered the criticism as hypocrisy, meddling and an attempt to rob them of African lands by denying their ability to halt slavery.

The anti-slavery regulations from Portugal were not merely a trimming of sails to the gusts from the British Isles. Within mid-nineteenth-century Portugal there developed, along with the establishment of a constitutional monarchy, liberal pressure for the abolition of slavery which has been obscured by the authoritarianism of the Salazar-Caetano period. As was typical of the age, liberal sentiments against slavery accompanied imperial expansion. Starting with Prime Minister Sá da Bandeira's decree outlawing the slave trade, Portuguese governments promulgated four major laws and many decrees to abolish slavery without suffering the loss of African labour considered so necessary to exploit Mozambique and Angola. The most frequently legislated method in theory gave the African his freedom but in practice obligated him to work for his former master for a specified number of years. This *liberto*, or so-called freedman, status contributed to the idea that an African might still be a slave without a declared system of slavery. It was this masquerade and this gap between law and practice that so roused the government's foreign and domestic critics.[21] Still worse, it helped to perpetuate the master-servant relationship between Portuguese and African long after the *liberto* classification was dropped in 1875, even up to independence in some white Mozambican circles.

The significant Regulation of 1899 dashed flickering hopes for a progressive code to crown the preceeding three-quarters of a century of laws moving Mozambicans and Angolans, at least on paper, from slavery. Instead, the new code reintroduced forced labour and justified the legal turnabout on the survival of Portugal in Africa, for without a steady labour supply no economic development was deemed possible. In high-blown phrases characteristic of turn-of-the-century colonialism, the 1899 law required Africans 'to civilize themselves through work'. Enes's hard-nosed philosophy of forcing Africans to work for the prosperity of the colony was embodied in the new Regulation. Section I stated:

> All natives of Portuguese overseas provinces are subject to the obligation, moral and legal, of attempting to obtain through work the means that they lack to subsist and to better their social condition. They have full liberty to chose the method of fulfilling this obligation, but if they do not fulfill it, public authority may force a fulfillment.[22]

Much to the rejoicing of settlers and imperialists the 1899 Labour Code reversed the legal restrictions against compulsory labour contained in the Regulation of 1878, which in their view resulted in economic stagnation, because few Africans voluntarily entered the colonial economy. In practice, the liberal code had been ignored, evaded and defied.

For the next half century, subsequent codes incorporated the premises of the 1899 Regulation: Africans would not seek wage employment without compulsion and Lusitanian values were to be transplanted through work. The new legislation signalled an end to liberal values and replaced them with authoritarian beliefs and laws. In this turn toward authoritarianism, Mozambique and Angola foreshadowed what was to happen in Portugal under the Salazar regime.

The Republic inherited African forced labour both in law and in practice from the monarchy. Limiting the contract term to two years and providing stiffer penalties for corporal punishment by employers, the Republic's 1911 Regulation adopted essentially unchanged the Enes-inspired code. Three years later, the Republic in a pretty example of its republican spirit for the fraternity of mankind issued a new code that retained the 'moral and legal obligation' to work but specified the months of obligation for each year.

So much for the Republic's policy. In Mozambique, Thomaz de Almeida Garrett, district governor of Inhambane, advocated in 1906 changes in the labour code—increased head taxes, higher fines for vagrancy, reduced work exemption for farmers and compulsory work for women—so as to oblige more Africans to labour for Europeans.[23] The colonial government also made a deal (to be discussed below) with first the Transvaal mines and then the South African government for labour recruitment privileges in Mozambique. The sometimes artificial procedures could not hide the fact that in southern districts a form of the slave trade existed during the first couple of decades of this century.

Despite the questionable recruiting devices, Mozambique escaped the international controversy that swirled over São Tomé's contract labour methods with the publication of Henry Nevinson's *A Modern Slavery* in 1906. At about the same time, however, British missionaries and consular staffs reported official dragnets for labourers on railway construction as well as gold mining in South Africa. There were local efforts to diminish the evils of the *shibalo*, or forced labour, system in Mozambique occasioned by the notoriety gained by the Portuguese on the west coast. In the next-to-last years of the monarchy, Governor-General Alfredo Augusto Freire de Andrada, one of the dashing officers in the Gungunyane campaign and Commissioner Enes's former chief of cabinet, sought to check the rampant acquisition of *shibalos* by private firms. In 1906, he issued a *portaria* that held 'a person free to choose the mode, time and place for fulfillment of the obligation' to work.[24] Like Enes, Freire de Andrada carried no brief for Africans in positions of authority over Europeans, but unlike his illustrious predecessor, he implemented reforms to curb the abuses of compulsory labour. But these had little lasting or practical effect, except to awaken local concern to the injustices of *shibalo* recruitment and government's collusion with business firms in its perpetuation.

Unlike Angola's Norton de Matos, Mozambique had no prominent government abolitionist against forced labour during the Republican years. To be sure, Brito Camacho's extension of government assistance in recruiting workers for the Sena Sugar Estates in 1921 did, however, rouse loud objections from a few Portuguese in Lourenço Marques. But their efforts were singular and ineffectual.

Toward the close of the Republican epoch, Professor Edward A. Ross (accompanied by R. Melville Cramer, a New York doctor) observed the labour situation in Mozambique and Angola. He submitted a report to the temporary Slavery Commission of the League of Nations in 1925. While Ross, a sociologist from the University of Wisconsin, focused his report on Angola, he spent 24 days in Mozambique and travelled about 800 miles by car and rail visiting the country between the cities of Lourenço Marques, Inhambane, Beira and Umtali, Rhodesia. Assisted by Protestant missionaries and English nationals who secured interpreters and interviewees, Ross in a series of case studies presented a chilling account of women road-building crews, embezzled wages, government enlistment of workers for private interests and extortion and mistreatment by *sepais* whose beatings were encouraged or condoned by the Colonial government. In conclusion, Ross deprecated the labour system as 'virtually state serfdom', and Portuguese efforts at development with forced labour as 'veneered barbarism'.[25]

Such a scathing blast brought forth an official defence of Portugal's 'compassionate and educational policies' for Africans and an assault on the American's findings, his methods and Protestant missionaries. A former Angolan district governor, Dr. F. M. de Oliveira Santos, retraced Ross's itinerary in Mozambique and Angola. In Mozambique, he reportedly coerced, with threats of restrictive regulations, American missionaries into retracting their previous statements to the Wisconsin professor.[26] Oliveira Santos in a public lecture on completion of his tour eulogized Portugal's contributions to Africa, and branded the Ross report as a 'bluff carried out with the cooperation of some American missionaries.'[27] Lisbon disputed the report before the Sixth Assembly of the League of

Nations, and no further international attention was given it at Geneva. In Mozambique, official reports written within the province and books such as Eduardo de Almeida Saldanha's *Colónias, Missões e Acto Colonial* confirmed Ross's findings of bribery, inefficiency, defrauding of African wages and overcharging of taxes. The Portuguese reaction was the characteristic promulgation of another labour code.

The 1928 Native Labour Code maintained the 'moral duty' to seek work but prohibited 'compulsory labour for private purposes'. It laid down three main limitations on the freedom of work choice; compulsory labour for public projects, such as road building; compulsory work for African benefit; and forced labour for judicial sentences. For the private sector, it contained detailed regulations on contracts, wages and working conditions. The code served the New State and, although modified in 1955, remained in force until the Rural Labour Code of 1962.

Abuse of the *mão de obra indígenas* ('native workers') continued apace under the New State's administration, and the practical effect of the new code was negligible in Mozambique. Irregularities in execution of codes or regulations made the African little more than a toiler for Portuguese interests. Forced labour for commercial undertakings persisted not only for the old reasons of government weakness in Mozambique (few honest, adequately paid authorities and collaboration between officials and companies) but also because under Salazar Portugal closed out foreign capital, relied on manual labour to raise productivity and elevated work to a national ideology. Life in Mozambique was to be no different.

Governor-General José Tristão de Bettencourt (1940-7) issued a circular in 1942 outlining the proofs required to satisfy the labour obligations of African males between the ages of 18 and 25. Five of the seven methods required the African to engage in European enterprises in Mozambique, whether state or private, or migrate to Rhodesia or South Africa for work. Only a small percentage of males could fulfill the requirements of the other two conditions as a herder of 50 or more cattle or a registered *agricultor africano* in production of rice and cotton.[28.] Proof of employment was difficult particularly for labourers who had returned from work outside the province, and vagrancy laws were sweeping. The temporary labour migrations caused shortages which had to be made up. Not until 1959 did Mozambique's Director of Public Works, anticipating instructions from the Overseas Minister, terminate the policy of government officials directly recruiting labourers for public schemes. Government mistreatment of labourers in road building and port construction set a poor example for private employers. Legal niceties were seldom observed under Republic or New State.

LABOUR EMIGRATION TO THE TRANSVAAL

No single aspect of Portuguese labour policy in Mozambique was as subject to foreign and domestic criticism as the migrant worker flow to South African mines and industries. The discovery of gold in 1886 some 200 miles from the Mozambique border escalated the Thonga, Chopi and Shangana immigration already underway to South African farms since the 1860s. 100 years later, the exodus reached 250,000 workers per year of which 100,000 were perhaps illegal. To regulate the flux of workers and to profit from it, the Portuguese entered into a series of international agreements starting in 1897 with the Transvaal Republic and capped by the Portuguese-South African Convention of 1928 that set provisions lasting until Mozambique's independence. Only slight modifications were made at renewal times. In return for labour recruiting privileges south of parallel 22°S, the Portuguese got a guarantee for 47·5 per cent of the seabound-rail traffic from Johannesburg, Pretoria and Kurgersdorp. Other monetary advantages came to the colonial government: payment for each worker recruited, custom duties on the goods of returning workers and deferred wages at the mines given to the Portuguese in gold — the labourer once in Mozambique got provincial escudos.

During the early part of this century, the Witwatersrand Native Labour Association (WNLA), which was consigned in 1901 exclusive recruiting rights, resorted to 'blackbirding' (beating the bushes for labourers) and more fraudulent acts to fulfill quotas. When supply could not keep pace with rising demand at the Rand mines, the WNLA turned to bribing chiefs to meet quotas, deceiving Africans by dressing recruiting agents in uniforms similar to provincial police and buying the complicity of lower-echelon authorities.[29] Soon higher wages, improved working conditions, Portuguese forced labour and the opportunity to earn enough money to purchase bicycles, record players and ploughs induced

African males to sign up voluntarily.

The sector south of the Save gained the most from the labour traffic to the Rand. A steady source of revenue flowed to the government and a lucrative transit trade enriched the port of Lourenco Marques. Higher wages also came to the migrant worker than could be earned at home. The inflow of South African money to the southern part of the colony brought the population into greater participation in a cash economy than the agriculturally orientated north. African taxes reflected the separation. Below the Zambezi the annual rate was 300 *escudos* in 1960, whereas above the river Africans were assessed 90 *escudos*. The amounts in each area were viewed as excessive.[30]

On the other side of the coin, the emigration was held responsible for depopulation and denationalizing influences in the colony. Government critics pointed to the unwelcome impact of non-Portuguese values, language and religion on returning Africans which compounded the difficulties of assimilating them into a Lusitanian community. Some returning 'East Coast Boys' brought back the Anglican faith or various Ethiopian sects (independent African churches ambivalent or hostile to Europeans) that caused concern among the authorities.

Depopulation, a more broadly felt consequence, was blamed for the low level of agricultural cultivation below the Save. Government spokesmen contended that the 'unfavorable ecological conditions' were responsible and not its labour policy. They took the position that the migrations absorbed the unemployed Africans and the low rainfall and sandy soils propelled the rural Thonga and Chopi males 'to throw themselves into the system of capitalistic economy.'[31] Settlers condemned the government for not only reducing their labour supply but also driving Africans from farming. The editor of *As Notícias de Lourenço Marques*, Manual Vaz, who was often at loggerheads with Lisbon's policies, wrote again and again favouring higher prices for African produce, technical schools for Africans and an end to African immigration to South Africa and Rhodesia.[32] One renowned farmer, Eduardo de Almeida Saldanha, became so embittered at the chronic manpower shortage that he accused Brito Camacho of being bribed by the Chamber of Mines to facilitate their recruitment. His books peppered the international convention with criticism, and he demanded forced labour for agricultural development *sul do Save*.

There was, of course, much self-interest in the settler's protestations which represented one example of their discontent with Lisbon's control.

Non-Portuguese criticism attacked the callous exchange of labour for money. One detractor charged that the government exploited the Bantu sexual division of labour among the Thonga to such a degree as to foster a female agricultural specialization greater than the original situation in which the male only fells and burns the heavy growth in preparation for planting and the female tends to lighter but lengthier chores. Marvin Harris, a professor at Columbia University, wrote in 1957: 'Free of the responsibility of buying food for their wives and children, the migratory mass has been able to accept wages below what would be required to maintain a work force patterned after a nineteenth-century European industrial proletariat.'[33] *Mutatis mutandis* the Portuguese-South African labour agreements were viewed as a variation of Mozambique's earlier slave traffic. Working prospects in Mozambique were worse, however. It was hardly surprising that the young African faced with a Hobson's choice of labour at home for a pittance or of going to work abroad chose the mines, exotic and profitable.

RACE, ASSIMILATION AND MISCEGENATION

Forced labour, government-arranged labour migrations and prejudicial contracts were justified in mind and policy by their ultimate worth in uplifting the African through cultural assimilation to a civilized level. Any discussion, however brief, of Lisbon's policy in Mozambique of assimilating the African into a Portuguese community must also survey Portuguese racial attitudes.

There are no sure generalizations about Portuguese racial views. What is more, they have varied from place to place. In contrast to Angola where a greater number of settlers arrived before World War II, Mozambique was spared some of the early, bitter conflict between black and white job seekers. Conversely, the Portuguese presence in Mozambique did not produce the racial homogeneity nor the lessened-colour consciousness of the Cape Verde Islands. Rather practice had often diverged from stated policy with instances of violence, cruelty and discrimination toward the Mozambican African alongside examples of genuine acceptance, tolerance and well-meant paternalism.

Over the centuries, Portuguese racial attitudes have been influenced by Mozambique's place in the *Estado da India*, relatively greater distance from the metropole, small white immigration, and later proximity to South Africa and Rhodesia. If Mozambique's cultural and racial synthesis ('mulattoization') was hindered by its isolation from the Portuguese Atlantic triangle — Angola, Brazil, Portugal — its racial awareness was sometimes more sharply defined.

Race relations between Portuguese and African began on an upbeat in Mozambique. Vasco da Gama's crew were greeted by friendly peoples on the beaches, and even that arrogant captain appears not to have embittered the first encounters. Soon afterwards his ships, however, bombarded the Muslim entrepôt on Mozambique Island. King Manuel instructed Francisco de Almeida not to 'hurt either their [Africans] persons or their property, for it is our wish they be protected'[34] in the viceroy's blasting of the Muslims from the Indian Ocean commerce. From the Muslims the Portuguese acquired the name *cafre* ('unbeliever'), applied it to the African and used it for centuries, sometimes pejoratively, other times affectionately, but always racially. A fact which belied future declarations of nonracism.

Mozambique's malarial climate encouraged race mixing. The absence of white women in Mozambique drove the *sertanejo*, trader, soldier and Goan immigrant to racial fusion not by fancy or government design (as in Asia) but from libidinal urge that went unrestrained away from Portugal. From the beginning of the Portuguese presence in Mozambique, partly westernized individuals had augmented white settlements and served as businessmen, merchants and *prazo* chiefs. For all that, the *prazo* community still made careful distinctions as to the racial composition of the *mestiço*. In the colonial period, these 'naturalized foreigners' were barred from top government posts on the basis of race alone. Miscegenation proceeded to such an extent on the lower Zambezi that the African very nearly biologically absorbed the few European and Indian interlopers. This and a high white death rate caused concern in Lisbon which planned settlement schemes and endowed women with estates to increase the Portuguese population and strengthen its hold on the Rivers.

An accurate recording of the *mestiço* population has never been completed. Statistics in 1960, the last year of a published racial census, put the figure at 31,465, but the number certainly exceeded that listing as mixed children (most were born out of wedlock) not accepted by their European or non-African fathers were counted as African. The influx of white women to Mozambique altered the acceptance of *mestiço* children by non-African fathers that had so favourably impressed Livingstone. Rejected also in traditional society, the *mestiço* was relegated to a limbo status in colonial life, frustrated and angry.

Miscegenation, which became under the New State much-trumpeted evidence of racial harmony, was scorned by some of Portugal's most celebrated heroes. Serpa Pinto conspicuously abstained during his exploratory journeys; Enes heaped invective on the 'negress' for causing the 'proud conquerors of the Black Continent to fall victim to the sensuality of the monkey . . .';[35] and Freire de Andrada opposed miscegenation as a planned policy advocating instead the settlement of Portuguese peasant families in Africa.

The New State officially ignored the racism of the imperial evangelists and proclaimed nonracism as an historic constant. But the same small ruling class who put to rest their conscience on the African labour question by viewing the Portuguese peasantry equally hardworking, likewise considered miscegenation as acceptable only for ordinary folk. In Mozambique's urban society, a white man cohabiting with a black woman was a sort of social outcast and regarded *cafrealized* ('gone native').[36] African males saw this as another form of exploitation.

That miscegenation explained the key to the Portuguese special aptitude for colonialization was an argument postulated by Gilberto Freyre and his many disciples in Lisbon. Freyre, a Brazilian sociologist whose theories are heavily imbued with intuition and literary imagination, asserted that the long Muslim domination of Portugal instilled in the Portuguese an inimitable racial toleration that prepared them to be inherent colonizers who mated uninhibitedly with dark-skinned women. The Luso-tropical civilizations they produced in southern latitudes, Freyre argued, were the result of peaceful social contact and sexual relations with the Moors during their 700 year occupation of the Iberian peninsula. According to Freyre the Muslim invaders, who possessed superior political organizations and cultural achievements, gained the admiration of the Portuguese and led them to idealize the Moorish enchantress (*moura encantada*) in life and folktales. Equally significant but unobserved by Freyre, the same folk stories and fairy tales that recount their physical attraction for the Muslim princess also grimly picture the Moor as the embodiment of evil; one reason there are more Moors than dragons or ogres in Portuguese folk literature.

It may be that the Muslim occupation was distinctively formative in another more important way. Professor Magnus Mörner in discussing the Muslim imprint on Portuguese conduct in the Americas stated what is also true of it in Mozambique: 'the same kind of strange mixture between savage warfare and pacific exchange, including miscegenation, between intolerance and tolerance in inter-ethnic relations . . .'[37] existed in Portugal during the Middle Ages. Whatever the vigour of the imprint, a small *mestiço* population fathered by lusty men in the absence of European women fails abysmally to substantiate a thesis of racial tolerance for the African.

Compared with Angola, the large-scale export of slaves from Mozambique came late, but the lateness did not exempt the east African province from its corrosive effects on racial attitudes that no amount of mating with the daughters and sisters of the enslaved could obliterate. One striking example of colour prejudice in Mozambique, as Charles Boxer reminds us, involved the unwillingness of the white clergy to train and ordain Africans and *mestiços* in the priesthood. Even the 1761 decree of the Marquis of Pombal, Portugal's famous and dreaded dictator, to establish a seminary on Mozambique Island was quietly pigeonholed, and no black clergymen were ordained in Portuguese East Africa for 200 years. This was markedly at variance with the situation on the west coast where the ordaining of Africans was not infrequent.[38] Hence, the Church as an assimilating force was restricted in Mozambique. Yet, it is dangerous to generalize from one episode. Just as white churchmen defied Lisbon's directives, so other white men could exemplify and instruct with a model of racial egalitarianism. At the height of the Mozambique slave traffic, Captain Owen observed in 1825 an interracial ball at Mozambique Island's government house during which he noted that 'the complexions varied from the most brilliant black to the pleasing red and white of our more favoured race.'[39]

Nineteenth-century Portugal legislatively abolished the slave

trade and slavery, and issued parchment decrees of liberal sentiments. Twenty years before the imperial revivalists uttered ideas of
white superiority, Sá da Bandeira penned in 1873 'that the
Portuguese inhabitants of the provinces of Africa, of Asia, and of
Oceania, without distinction of race, colour, or religion, have rights
equal to those enjoyed by the Portuguese of Europe.'[40] A modern
historian, Richard J. Hammond, pointed out this was something
that 'did not command universal approval among the Portuguese
governing class.'[41] It would be almost a hundred years before the
1961 decree-law again erased the legal distinction between citizen
and *indígena*. Too little too late, it could not then stay the dissolution of the African empire.

The intervening years saw Lisbon construct its first comprehensive racial assimilation policy. For all its paternalistic and
hallucinatory rhetoric, it worked for the tighter and more efficient
repression of the black Mozambican. In the matter of assimilation, the New State drew upon the legislation of the Republic to reverse the nineteenth-century liberal policy of *assimiliação
uniformizadora* that allowed all Africans to be governed by
Portuguese laws and institutions. The Salazar regime replaced it
with individual or selective assimilation. Taking a definition of
citizenship requirement from the 1914 Organic Law (command of
Portuguese, service to the government or in the army, good
behaviour and self-sustaining employment), the New State
rigorously applied it. Fulfillment of these standards, or proof of a
high school education, a job in the colonial administration, or
proprietorship in business or industry could secure the issuance of a
bilhete de identidade. Because of red tape, the perversity of officials
and the woeful want of educational and employment opportunities
other than manual labour, less than 1 per cent of the non-white
population underwent the change in status from *indígena* to
assimilado in a policy operating in Mozambique since 1917. The
law's racial content was evident by the fact that Africans had to
meet qualifications to obtain the status of *não-indígena*, whereas
the Europeans—no matter the degree of illiteracy or lowly
occupation—were never classified *indígena*. This insured a predominately white electorate in Mozambique. The 1950 census
reported 4,353 *assimilados* in a population of 5,733,000 people.
Some individuals who met the qualifications were naturally hesitant
to seek the *bilhete* which entailed higher taxes, dubious benefits and

an ambiguous status in colonial society. The meagre results speak for themselves in condemning Lisbon's avowed mission to elevate and assimilate the black Mozambican.

The non-assimilated Africans, by far the great bulk, were termed *indígenas* and officially defined in the 1954 Statute of the Portuguese Native as 'individuals of the black race, or their descendants, who having been born and usually living there [colonies], do not yet possess the education and the individual and social habits assumed for the integral application of the public and private law of Portuguese citizens.'[42] The male *indígena* carried a *caderneta* (identification card and working record) and fell victim to the labour codes, manpower needs and vagrancy laws of the government. For them, the transplanting of Lusitanian culture was to have been achieved through hard labour and to await the march of centuries.

In modern times, the harsh 'native policies' of South Africa and Rhodesia hardened Portuguese prejudice but not formed it. South Africa and Rhodesia, esteemed for their economic and technical development, encouraged the 'respectability' of racism in the south and in Beira where their tourists and businessmen congregated. Their influence, however, may have been over-stressed. Before a definitive answer on the transference of racial attitudes can be given, much more should be known. Equally important is the fact that the same areas had undergone considerable Portuguese immigration after World War II, creating economic competition and social friction between races. The government's stress on 'civilization', meaning Portuguese language, manners and customs, made the culture bar virtually synonymous with the colour bar. It has been noted that Mozambican African behaviour included 'defensive reactions of clowning and fawning subservience typical of a group made to feel inferior.'[43] Two years before independence this writer's observations confirmed the oral and written testimony of others on the racial surliness with which many Portuguese addressed black waiters, cooks, messengers and servants, who were little more than paid slaves. Just as unmistakeable was the bitterness toward whites expressed in the eyes of a few black workers and passers-by in the urban centres.

The conclusion is inescapable, although hardly surprising: Portuguese expansion and colonial rule were accompanied by a conscious feeling of white over black. Lest this seem too bald a verdict under a comparative lamp, it could be added that Boxer's judgment about the Portuguese being more liberal than the Dutch, English and French before 1825[44] would serve in some cases during the peacetime period after that date. The post-World War II era would deliver some rude shocks to Portugal's professed nonracism; the stresses and strains of the nationalist war would crumble the façade.

RIDING OUT THE WINDS OF CHANGE

World War II, a watershed in western history with the collapse of European power, the rise of the United States and the Soviet Union to super-power status, the division of the world into ideological blocs and the establishment of a nuclear age, was also a watershed in African history. The war quickened the rise of anti-colonialism Africa. Former imperial domains transformed themselves into a mosaic of politically independent states from the Mediterranean coast to the 'white redoubt' at the foot of the continent. Situated between the newly independent states to the north and the white settler regimes to the south, Mozambique soon felt the crosscurrents of anti-colonialism and nationalism, although during the 1950s it appeared a placid island in a stormy sea. Against criticism in the United Nations from emerging nations, Portugal battened its diplomatic hatches while it anchored itself more firmly in Mozambique, determined to ride out the winds of change. Black independence and white separatist expressions received the careful attention of the colonial authorities who moved swiftly to quash protest and disloyal groups. As part of its effort to weather the approaching storm, Portugal altered policies, implemented long-overdue reforms and speeded development in Mozambique.

PORTUGAL AND ITS CRITICS

Thanks to Portugal's neutrality and the absence of a hostile neighbour, Mozambique avoided fighting in the 1939–45 war. During this second global conflict, Lisbon's only commitment to Mozambique's armament involved the dispatching of about two troop battalions to reinforce the colony's defences in light of Japanese advances early in the war. World War I had plunged the territory into some of the heaviest combat on the continent but left the colonial structure unimpaired. Ironically, World War II, which brought no conflict to Mozambique's soil, resulted in far greater ramifications for Portugal's presence. The war stimulated the need for Mozambique's agricultural products and stepped up the demand for manpower to South African industries on which Britian relied for part of its material and products. Anxious to maintain an uninterrupted flow of labour to South Africa and the use of the Lourenço Marques port, the British consulate watched with apprehension the German sisal farmers who had come into the country after World War I rather than return to Tanzania. To counter a potential fifth column movement, British officials pressed successfully for wide circulation of Allied propaganda. Most editorials in Mozambique's newspapers were sympathetic to the Allied cause. Allied propaganda condemning the imperialism of the Axis powers by implication subverted Portugal's colonialism in Mozambique. It served to legitimate the aspirations of black Mozambicans for independence and statehood. Unwittingly, the Portuguese contributed in a small way to the weakening of their own position.

Portugal's neutrality in World War II called for deft management; the years afterwards proved no less demanding. If Portugal were to survive the chorus of disapproval, orchestrated by the recently independent states of Asia and Africa, then it must change its colonial policy and end its isolation begun with the formation of the New State. The post-war world with its division into Communist and non-Communist blocs suited Portugal's plans. Long a foe of Communism, Salazar strengthened Portugal's stand on the anti-Communist side and was encouraged to do so by the United States and Britain. Portugal joined the North Atlantic Treaty Organization at its formation in 1949. Its participation paid off, for it relied on NATO prestige and material aid, some of which found its way to the African wars.

Portugal traded on its membership in NATO, its strategic position overlooking the western Atlantic and Mediterranean straits and its mid-Atlantic islands. Strategically vital as a refuelling base during the Cold War tensions over Berlin and later the Arab-Israeli wars, the Azores Islands served Portugal well in its relations with the United States. Except during the months following the outbreak of the Angolan war, when the new administration of John F. Kennedy voted against Portugal in the United Nations, the value of the Azores and European solidarity secured American support for its African policy.

From another quarter dark clouds blew up for Portugal. The self-determination articles in the UN Charter and a swelling General Assembly membership hostile to European colonialism pointed to an end of the halcyon days of imperialism in Africa. Recognizing that the times were against colonial holdings, Portugal redesignated its possessions 'overseas provinces' in 1951 and announced their integration into a Portuguese nation. Apologists of the change contended that the term *province* had alternated with *colony* in Portuguese decrees and legislation down through the ages. Critics charged that the relabelling was a calculated sleight of hand to dodge UN scrutiny and interference in professed domestic areas. Arriving with the anti-colonial surge, the timing can hardly be construed as coincidental; it was simply a modernizing of the imperial lexicon.

Again and again, Portuguese spokesmen took the position in the UN and other forums that Mozambique and their other colonies were provinces of Portugal. From its entrance into the UN in 1955 until the granting of independence, Portugal fought a rearguard defence of its heavily assailed stance in Africa. To Lisbon, the vehement anti-colonialism of the UN forced the pace of de-colonization in Africa with the consequences of civil wars, military dictatorships and the spread of Communism. In its own possessions, Lisbon believed the international agitation fuelled the nationalist assault on legitimate rule.

When the nationalist blow fell in India, it had consequences for Mozambique. The Indian government seized Portugal's enclave of Goa in December, 1961. In retaliation, the Portuguese expelled an estimated 15,000 Indians from Mozambique. Many of those expelled had their Portuguese citizenships revoked, their property expropriated and their pensions cancelled.[1] The Goans and British Indians had always enjoyed a precarious existence in Mozambique as elsewhere in east Africa. Officially tolerated, they worked as clerks in business or government administration where some officials welcomed them for being loyal to Lisbon and closer to the African level of civilization, or they lived as petty traders in the cities and along trade routes. Their minor success called forth periodic outbursts of violence from lower-class Portuguese and Africans who saw themselves cheated by quick dealing Indian traders. Expulsion of the Indians was a break with the government's policy of racial equality but an expression of long nurtured prejudice. This revenge evoked protests from India but no support for subsequent African movements in Mozambique despite Afro-Asian solidarity before the seizure of Goa. India lost interest in the anti-colonial struggle after repossession of the enclave, and Africans learned a lesson of self-reliance.

Just as Portugal was buffeted in the UN, so, too, Portuguese and foreign detractors such as Marvin Harris and Basil Davidson attacked misrule and inhumane practices in Africa. During the 1930s and the war years, Mozambique escaped international examination, and the renewed attention signalled a return to an earlier period. Foremost among the domestic critics was Henrique Galvão a high inspector in the colonial administration from 1946 to 1949. Galvão captured world attention when in 1961 he and a small band of followers seized at gunpoint the Portuguese luxury liner *Santa Maria* in the Caribbean and sailed it to Brazil in a demonstration of opposition to the Salazar regime. Galvão was no advocate of African independence. He favoured democratic reform in Portugal and white autonomy in the colonies.

As an Angolan deputy to the National Assembly, he rebuked Lisbon for the abuses of African labour and the deficiencies of the colonial government. In 1948, the National Assembly heard Galvão's *Report on Native Problems in the Portuguese Colonies* in which he detailed inadequacies in health services and misdeeds in labour practices that led to 'demographic anaemia' as Mozambique's workers fled to other territories.[2] He attacked the forced cultivation of cotton — 'slave cotton' — north of the Zambezi whereby African farmers grew and harvested a predetermined quota of cotton for several large white concession companies. The low prices paid for the cotton and exclusion of other crops caused malnutrition, famine and exodus to Malawi and Rhodesia. The Lomwe-speaking people of Mozambique were so attracted to the better conditions on the tea plantations of Malawi that their numbers jumped from nil there at the turn of the century to an estimated 380,000 by 1945.[3]

Galvão was later imprisoned for treason but managed to escape and carry out his swashbuckling raid on the *Santa Maria*. Unlike improvements made in Angola, his report accomplished little in alleviating the plight of African cotton growers in northern Mozambique which persisted in some form until the outbreak of the insurgency in 1964.

Less well known than Galvão but equally troublesome gadflies existed among the members of Catholic and Protestant clergy. Fewer Protestant missionaries entered Mozambique than Angola because of the Muslim influence in the north, the predominance of Catholic missions in the Zambezi Valley and the authorities' fear of British expansion after the close brush with the 1890 ultimatum. Since Mousinho de Albuquerque suspected Protestant missionaries of at least indirect inspiration of the Rhonga revolts in 1894, colonial governments excluded them or kept a wary eye on the activities of their two dozen mission stations in the colony. The Portuguese managers of the Mozambique Company barred them from most of the company's lands.[4] Among the most intractable missionaries were those of the Swiss Mission, of whom the distinguished anthropologist Henri Junod was a member. Their criticism of the native policy and concern for specific cases of official misconduct raised the government's ire more than once until the New State in 1930 compelled the Swiss Mission to shut down its secondary school in Lourenço Marques, one of the two in the province at the time. They continued to operate mission hospitals in the country.

During the 1950s, the major critic was Sebastian Soares de Resende, Bishop of Beira. He wrote several critical pastoral letters and articles in the newspaper, *Diário de Beira*, (later called *Notícias da Beira*), over which he was said to have exercised some control. Later Resende's successor sold the paper to a group headed by Jorge Jardim, a prominent businessman and *éminence grise* of conservative white politics in Mozambique.[5] Before Jardim turned the *Notícias da Beira* into an instrument of colonial propaganda, Resende used its pages to question the wisdom of the government's sanctioning the cotton concessions. In the liberal reforming tradition of Sá da Bandeira, the Bishop pressed for a termination of African mistreatment but he did not go so far as advocate a discontinuance of Portuguese influence in Mozambique. A much quoted passage from his book *Ordem Anticomunista* condemning the cotton concessions states:

In practice, at least, what difference is there between the activities of these natives [cotton farmers] and those who work as contracted labourers on farms? None. Or better yet, a difference does exist: the contract labourers receive clothing, food and board; here, nothing of this is supplied; whether the farm produces or does not produce, the contract workers receive a salary; here they receive the price of the cotton if the seeding is successful, and in case it is not, as occurs in bad years for this kind of crop, they receive nothing.

. . . .

There belongs to my diocese a region in which for six months the black spectre of hunger reaped the lives of the inhabitants . . .[6]

Outspokenly critical of the forced cultivation of cotton, absence of health facilities and especially educational opportunities for Africans, he finally suffered mild government disapproval and removal from the directorship of the secondary school in Beira. His high ecclesiastical position protected him from worse.

By the early 1960s, he felt that the lot of Africans in Mozambique had become better than those in other countries as a result of government labour reforms and a favourable improvement in material conditions of all black Mozambicans. It was an opinion not shared by many Mozambican Africans. Bishop Resende's earlier criticism was an exception to the staunch and undeviating endorsement of the Church hierarchy which only wavered during the nationalist war. Then denunciations poured forth from foreign Catholic missionaries and Portuguese parish priests.

DEVELOPMENT PLANS

Portugal had three principal goals in economically developing Mozambique and its other possessions after World War II: to realize the golden dream of obtaining great wealth from Africa; to justify continued retention of the colonies; and to settle Portuguese immigrants so as to relieve unemployment and to hold the territories in the teeth of burgeoning nationalism on the African continent. Much as British imperialists looked to colonies in Africa for Britain's rehabilitation after World War I, so now thirty years later Salazar spoke of the material and moral reserves of Africa. All colonial powers in the postwar decades either felt compelled to vindicate their imperial holdings by social and economic improvements or to prepare them for independence and continued economic exploitation without political domination. Long overdue schemes for bridge and road building, ports and irrigation development and health education programmes were hastily initiated or completed in much of colonial Africa. Portugal followed suit but with projects designed to integrate the colonies and the metropole and to stimulate production of vital commodities for home markets.

Coupled with building an economic infrastructure were settlement programmes for Portuguese colonization. The British and French encouraged emigration to Africa to exploit their colonial territories and to lessen population pressures, particularly during economic depressions. In addition, the Portuguese from mid-seventeenth century had backed the establishment of settlements to defend Mozambique's gold and strategic coastal bases against European and African enemies. Government sponsored emigration was also intended as a sign to Mozambican whites once the war began in the north that Lisbon meant to holdfast to the province. The first six-year development plan (1953-1958) contained provisions for emigration and in 1961, the same year Lisbon scrapped the *Estatuto Indígena,* the government set up a Provincial Settlement Board in Mozambique and Angola. The boards were empowered to supervise immigration and the relocation of African villages. Later, they sought to encourage Portuguese soldiers to become residents of the colony after military service as a further means to use the settler population as a civilian occupation force.

Immigration into Mozambique dramatically increased after the second World War. In 1937, there were 1,882 Portuguese immigrants to Mozambique. The figure jumped to 6,450 in 1955 and 10,319 by the end of the decade. The greatest inflow took place in 1965 with 11,276 and thereafter the numbers gradually tapered off to around seven thousand in 1969. Soon after, the number of colonists disembarking in Mozambique declined to less than 1,000. During the same years Portuguese emigration to Angola was two or three times as many. The table below shows the growth of the white population in Mozambique since 1930:[7]

WHITE POPULATION IN MOZAMBIQUE

1930	19,800
1940	27,400
1950	48,200
1960	97,200
1970	150,000 (estimated)
1973	200,000 (estimated)

Guerrilla advances into central Mozambique and the fall of the Caetano regime in April 1974 precipitated a headlong flight of Europeans from the colony.

Hamstrung by the rigid economic orthodoxy of the early Salazar years and a depleted treasury, Portugal confined development projects to minor schemes until after the war when it became progressively more ambitious and more lenient toward select foreign investment. Lisbon launched the first National Development Plan in 1953. It was followed by a second Six Year Plan (1959-1964) and a third (1968-1973) after a transition plan from 1965 to 1967. Under each plan, increasingly greater expenditures came from the National Treasury in the form of long-term loans. Marshall aid from the United States was used to build and modernize harbours, airports and railways in Mozambique. A solid financial commitment was made to economic development in the *ultramar* with the founding of a national Development Bank in 1959 to grant and loan funds for agricultural and industrial projects. Metropolitan and local banks (in Mozambique the Banco Nacional Ultramarino) threw off some of their previous reservations on lending in the colonies and provided about 30 per cent of the funds in the 1968-1973 plan. Early in the 1950s the government relaxed some restrictions on foreign investment to speed the economic potential of the colonies and to forge political links with Western governments through financial association with their investors. After the 1965 investment law, companies in nonstrategic fields could be 100 per cent foreign financed. By the third six-year plan participation of non-Portuguese firms reached 34 per cent.

All the plans were consistent in earmarking major investment sums for transportation, hydroelectric power, communications, mining and manufacturing. Agriculture, forestry and livestock also received sizeable support in Mozambique, but health, education and housing got considerably smaller allocations. The third six-year plan called for $585 million to be spent in Mozambique compared with $863 million in Angola. Although the plans increased Mozambique's agricultural and mining production and its exports, the rise was not sufficient to offset the province's deficit trade balance which was usually compensated by three 'invisible' revenue sources: transit trade through its ports (in spite of the 1966 closing of the oil-pipeline from Beira to Rhodesia); wages of migratory workers; and tourism. The tonnage handled by

Lourenço Marques's port, for example, rose from 4,134,285 tons in 1955 to 13,665,799 tons in 1970. According to official figures some 500,000 tourists visited Mozambique during 1971, most of them from South Africa and Rhodesia.[8]

At no time in Mozambique's colonial history was the tempo of commerce and industry so accelerated as the last twenty years of Portuguese rule. Portuguese and foreign capital built new railways and spur lines, irrigated dry lands, drained some sub-coastal marshes *(machongos)* south of Inhambane where African maize cooperatives were begun, erected hydroelectric stations, improved airfields at Beira and Lourenço Marques, constructed facilities at Beira, raised an oil refinery in Lourenço Marques and boosted coal output at Moatize from less than 200,000 tons annually to over 350,000. Still, industry by the end of the national war for independence only employed about 4 per cent of the work force and accounted for less than 10 per cent of the GNP.[9]

Up the Limpopo about 60 miles from its mouth, European engineers and African labourers constructed a dam that furnished a year-round water supply and irrigated nearly one hundred thousand acres. It also served as a bridge for a railway connecting Rhodesia with the Lourenço Marques port which diverted some of the heavy traffic from the overloaded line and docks of Beira. First proposed in 1925 and pigeonholed until 1950, the Limpopo scheme also envisioned the settlement of Portuguese farmers in a *colonato* at Chamusca (formerly Guíja). Owing to adequate irrigation and immensely rich black silt, the land favoured intensive cultivation of market garden produce, wheat, rice, beans, cotton and grazing for dairy cattle. Crops found an available market in Rhodesia as well as Mozambique. For the Portuguese settler and his family, the government provided free passage, a home, land, seed, tools and a clothing and food allowance for the first year. Despite the elaborate and expensive preparations, some Portuguese returned home or looked for less arduous work in the provincial cities or in South Africa. A much smaller number of Africans were resettled in the European villages where the government attempted to recreate rural Portugal with white-walled houses and red-tiled roofs. A great many more Africans were resettled nearby the white *colonato*. Beginning in 1960, a few African farmers were considered sufficiently evolved to be allowed to settle in the Portuguese villages. The next year 97 assimilated African families, or fivefold the previous year, were relocated in the Portuguese section. More were moved as the Portuguese immigrant population expanded. One goal of the Limpopo *colonato* was for the Portuguese peasant to set an example of industriousness and private land ownerships. Nationalists contended that the government's aim was to make the African peasant politically conservative and to deflect him from radical causes to change the political and economic order.[10]

Another goal of Limpopo colonization was to augment white agricultural settlement so disadvantaged in comparison with Angola by higher travel fares, smaller regions of temperate climate and the divided administation of the chartered companies. Since Freire de Andrada complained 'only men without brains or capital go to Portuguese East Africa,' it had been the Mozambique government's policy to exclude poor immigrants until the 1950s when it realized their value to development and to defence, and planned *colonatos*.

At the confluence of the Revuè and Sussunaenga rivers just below the Rhodesian escarpment in Vila Pery district, the government began *colonatos* for Portuguese farmers and agricultural schemes for Africans. As part of the giant Cabora Bassa Dam project in Tete district, it intended to resettle Africans and establish white settlements, although not to the unrealistic figure of one million immigrants as one official with more *loucura* than *siso* reported.[11] Further down the Revuè are located dams and a hydroelectric system, part of which were completed in 1953 to be the first in the province.

Partially eclipsed in Lisbon's propaganda utterances during the 1970s by the Cabora Bassa project, the development of the Limpopo remained a showpiece of Lusitanian enterprise. It 'honoured' Portugal as an engineering feat and as a living example of the spiritual ideal of racial integration. It also helped stiffen the resolve of African nationalists who viewed it and other settlement proposals as evidence of Portugal's determination to stay in Mozambique by settling its sons and daughters.

Initially, the private sector trailed behind the public but once enlivened it grew at a quick rate. The number of investment licenses rose from 7 in 1947 to 752 in 1959. At the outset of the Angolan war Mozambique underwent a temporary economic slump with the flight of some capital, but by 1965 and the new investment law, economic growth acquired a momemtum of its own that was undiminished until the opening months of 1974. Manufacturing industries and processing plants for textiles, paper pulp, matches, fertilizer, cement, beer, soap, tiles, sugar, cashew nuts and sisal reflected a visible growth in private enterprise and government efforts to diversify development. Most private undertakings were put up near Lourenço Marques, Beira, Vila Pery and Nampula; the remoter regions were left agricultural. Internationally known names—Firestone, Nestlé, Sumitomo—appeared in the provincial language, and other foreign firms quietly backed mineral exploitation, oil surveys of the promising southern coast and large construction projects. Placing most factories and plants in urban centres denied the 94 per cent rural population employment opportunities and quickened the drift to the towns—a common phenomenon in Africa.

The social effects of economic development coupled with the disruption of the war and the dislocation of the resettlement villages cannot yet be calculated. Increased demand for cheap labour to keep pace with public projects and private enterprise intensified labour shortages and led to excesses in coercing workers until the war in the north dictated a policy to win African loyalty. War costs prohibited the channelling of all the government's revenues from new industries into social services. Tax breaks to foreign capital to foster investment and favourable political ties for Lisbon also reduced the sources of tax funds. Rampant inflation further robbed the meagre gains of the urban worker who had begun to benefit from minimum wage laws. Since much of Lisbon's expenditures were aimed at projects from which the European commercial sector derived immediate advantage, the great majority of Africans reaped but little from the development of an economic infrastructure. What advances in the African standard of living occurred never matched those in the European community. On balance, however, the gains of the post-World War II era stand out from the centuries of underdevelopment. The output of goods and services multiplied and with them Portugal's sense of accomplishment and faith that given time the expansion of social services would bind Mozambique to Portugal.

REFORMS BEFORE THE STORM

Taking note of anti-colonial trends, Portugal not only altered the designation of its territories from colonies to overseas provinces and spent large sums on a development apparatus but also instituted reforms and recast laws directly affecting black Mozambicans. One of the earliest reforms involved African cotton growers in the north. Cotton cultivation had passed to the hands of African growers under the direction and control of concession companies after its failure as a large-scale European enterprise begun following World War I. In 1926, Lisbon granted concessions to companies for the purpose of stepping up cotton production and cutting Portugal's deficit trade balance caused by importing foreign cotton for its textile mills. Tonnage rose but was still short of satisfying the corresponding growth of Portugal's textile industry. The government intervened directly in 1938 and set up a Cotton Export Board (Junta de Exportação de Algodão) whose tough controls substantially raised Mozambique's cotton output from 15,000 tons in 1938 to 23,000 in 1942 — a figure representing 75 per cent of cotton grown in the *ultramar*. By requiring each African male to cultivate 2.5 acres of land, the government and the twelve concession companies boosted tonnage but 'this had the boomerang effect of reducing the planting of his other normal crops.'[12] As with the British, so with the Portuguese 'when they say Christ. . . they mean cotton.'

Malnutrition and famine stalked through the land, and criticism forced the government toward reform. When it renewed the concessions for ten years in 1946, the government laid down regulations requiring the holders to insure planting of equivalent amounts of land for food. Any improvement was slight; for Bishop Resende in the 1950s, as previously noted, reproached the government and the concession companies for a system that made the grower assume all the risks for a good or bad harvest. Yet the company assigned the acreage, time for planting and harvesting, and supervised the work and care of the cotton. Marvin Harris, an anthropologist from Columbia University who visited Mozambique, wrote that the 519,000 officially listed cotton sellers in 1956 got an average of $11.17 for an entire year of work which involved the labour of their families, making the true cotton force about 1 million workers.[13] A former peasant from Niassa district told

Eduardo Mondlane, assassinated President of the Mozambican liberation front, that: 'We were forced to produce cotton. The people didn't want to: they knew cotton is the mother of poverty, but the company was protected by the government.'[14] Legislation from Lisbon abolished the concessions in 1966. Mondlane believed the concession system lasted until guerrilla advances compelled the companies to close down.

Toward the late 1950s enlightened officials in Lisbon pressed for reform and achieved a milestone of sorts when Portugal ratified two international labour codes. Against the vested interests in exploiting African labour, such liberalizing influences alone would not have been fruitful in reforming practices overseas. The winds that bent Portugal's policy first blew from the Angolan revolt after which Adriano Moreira, the progressive Overseas Minister, was able to announce the repeal of the 1954 *Estatuto Indígena das Provincias de Guiné, Angola e Moçambique.* At the stroke of a pen 'uncivilized' Africans became in theory Portuguese citizens as the legal distinction between *indígena* and *não-indígena*, which had existed in Mozambique since 1907, was erased. To black Mozambicans it was another case of *plus ça change, plus c'est la meme chose,* for they still lacked political rights. Suffrage continued to be determined by the same qualifications — literacy, property tax and property ownership.

The next year brought a far more fundamental change. In 1962 Moreira, by now held by some ultra-conservatives to be a Communist, broke with the past in the significant field of African labour. The step was not without preparation — Moreira and other enlightened individuals had been influential in securing Portugal's signature on both the International Labour Code of 1955 and the Abolition of Forced Labour Convention of 1957 — but it was still a long and sweeping one. The 1962 Rural Labour Code superseded the 1928 Labour Code by freeing Africans from the obligation to work. It had been preceded three years before in Mozambique by the colonial government's termination of direct administrative recruiting for public projects. Right after the start of the Angolan revolution, the Republic of Ghana filed a complaint against Portugal to the International Labour Organization for violation of the Abolition of Forced Labour Convention. Eager to assuage potential discontent in Africa and to present a reformist image to a critical world alarmed by counter-atrocities committed by vengeful

Angolan whites against unarmed Africans, Portugal issued the new labour code which laid down provisions outlawing forced labour, recruitment of labour by authorities for private concerns and penalties for unfulfilled contracts.

Lacking the immediacy of the situation in Angola, Lisbon did not institute the watchdog agency of the new code, the Instituto de Trabalho, Previdência e Acção Social (Insitute of Labour, Welfare and Social Action), in Mozambique until 1964. Far-reaching and genuine as the new code was, it had to work against the flywheel of inertia and corruption. Despite the high-mindedness of a few Lisbon reformers and zealousness of a handful of top officials in Mozambique, scepticism lingered about lower echelon officials—the nemesis of so much legislation.[15] Given the slow turnover of administrative personnel, absence of trade unions and want of inspectors to enforce the new measure, the scepticism was well-founded.

Lisbon pressed ahead with other legislation. The Overseas Organic Law of 1963 was an attempt to turn international criticism from Portugal's firm control over its colonies and to appease restive white separatists in Lourenço Marques and Beira. By proclaiming an end to 'administrative integration' and providing for a slightly expanded say by a nearly totally elected Legislative Council in provincial budgetary decisions, the government hoped for the illusion of increased autonomy in Mozambique. Its philosophical basis represented a subtle return to the pre-Salazar concept of decentralized administration, but it weakened neither Lisbon's authority over political or military decisions nor its resolve to retain Mozambique. The law stressed the 'total respect for Portuguese unity.'[16] For Africans, the positive changes were nil. The law bolstered the confidence and political influence of the European population, most of whom opposed African freedoms or independence. Educational and property qualifications precluded the great bulk of black Mozambicans from voting either directly or indirectly through membership in one of the 'organic' groups based on occupation, let alone participating in the 27-seat Legislative Council. The intent of the law was not to do otherwise, for as Marcelo Caetano, Salazar's successor, wrote the decade before: 'Thus Portugal cannot accept in absolute terms the principle 'paramountcy of native interests. . . . ' '[17] Since most Africans lived in the regedorías (administratively grouped villages), they were also ineligible for voting or holding office in the newly implemented municipal elections. No change in the *circunscrição* or *posto* colonial apparatus meant no change in African political rights.

EDUCATION AND HEALTH

Judged by a past barren of concern for health service and educational programmes, efforts in these fields were gradually but significantly widened in the post-World War II period until the Angolan fighting impelled Lisbon to escalate its social reforms to gain African acquiescence, if not loyalty, before an anticipated outbreak of war in the east African colony. Measured on almost any yardstick, Portuguese educational and medical advances in Mozambique had lagged behind even the minimal programmes of the British, French and South Africans in other parts of the continent. It was a lag determined by Portugal's poverty, lack of concern for such activities in the metropole and in the case of education a deliberate policy so as to avert an educated protest.

Education in Mozambique never enjoyed a high priority no matter what has been said about its integral part in Portugal's *missão civilizadora*. A small amount of learning took place around forts and mission stations from soldiers and priests before nineteenth-century liberal governments twice authorized state provisions for education. These two decrees were virtually dead letters in Mozambique as student enrollment in government schools was 146 out of 1,195 pupils in 1900. Catholic and Protestant missionaries enrolled just over 600 and the rest attended municipal or private schools. From the onset of missionary and state education endeavours, a dual system developed — missionary schools in rural regions and government and private (in Greek, Indian, Chinese and Islamic communities) in urban centres.

As in so much else, the imperialists of the late nineteenth century rejected the liberal ideas of education for Africans. With his customary scorn for liberal schemes, Mousinho de Albuquerque wrote of his brand of education '. . . what we have to do in order to educate and civilize the *indígena* is to develop in a practical way his aptitudes for manual labour and take advantage of him for the exploitation of the province.'[18] Such attitudes from this worthy captain of the renascent Portuguese empire were widely shared in Mozambique's settler community and hardly conducive to a generous state programme for African education. What little education that was disseminated came from the efforts of dedicated missionaries.

Protestant missionaries, who permanently entered the colony in 1879, taught in the Mozambican vernaculars and accounted for some limited literacy in the extreme south of the country and on the eastern edge of Lake Malawi where they established a few schools, small hospitals and dispensaries. Anglican missionaries influenced a corner in north-eastern Mozambique; Methodists settled around the town of Inhambane; and the Swiss Mission set up educational and health facilities in the Lourenço Marques (now Maputo) district. Later, the Nazarenes were allowed to put up small posts, but most foreign missionaries admitted were Catholic.

The Republic initially opened the doors to foreign non-Catholic missions, seized Portuguese Church property and withdrew funds from Portuguese missions; but vehement charges that the Protestant foreigners denationalized the African population and subverted Portuguese sovereignty led to a 1921 decree banning the use of African languages for instruction. This was aimed at the Protestant missionaries. Two years later, the colonial government informed Lisbon of its fears of a growing foreign missionary presence and asked that Portuguese missions be established close by alien posts to counteract the 'bad influence.' Latter-day Republican officials and New State policy reversed the original easy access for non-Portuguese churchmen. By 1936, there were 115 non-Catholic missionaries and 19 mission stations. They provided education for 4,945 African pupils. Their Catholic counterparts taught 42,793 students and state and private schools accounted for 12,211 of the over 700,000 school-age children at the time.[19]

A report of the African Education Commission, which the Phelps-Stokes Fund financed, noted in 1925 that two-thirds of the schools were in the southernmost section where only 10 per cent of the population lived. It took to task the government for the dearth of education in the densely populated districts of Zambézia and Mozambique, and also the Mozambique Company's policy of exclusion toward non-Portuguese missionaries concluding that: 'The failure to formulate and execute sound policies for the development of the Native people is evidenced by the almost negligible provision for Native education . . .'[20] On the positive side, the report observed on the part of the understaffed Portuguese missionaries a genuine concern for the welfare of their charges.

Once again the New State carried the reversals of the late Republic governments a further step toward the past. The 1930 Colonial Act recognized Portuguese Catholic missions as 'instruments of colonization and national influence'. Next, it completed this return to a former order in 1940 when Salazar signed The Concordat and the Missionary Agreement with the Vatican. Confiscated missionary property was handed back and the Portuguese mission and education programmes, defined as 'institutions of imperial utility', were placed under the thumb of the government. Harkening back to Moushino de Albuquerque's thoughts on African education, article 68 of the Missionary Statute, implementing the Agreement, set forth the educational mission of Portuguese Catholic churchmen as 'perfect nationalization and moral uplife of the natives and the acquisiton of habits and aptitudes for work . . .'[21]

A separate and vastly unequal educational system had emerged before World War II, and the period afterwards brought scant departure from the inequalities. For the European or assimilated child, schooling paralleled that in Portugal, but for the black Mozambican the government stipulated a programme of *ensino de adaptação* (education for adapting), after 1956 termed *ensino rudimentar* (rudimentary education). After four years of primary instruction in Portuguese language and culture, the African student theoretically could proceed to secondary technical or academic schools. Before the opening of hostilities in the north, Lisbon pushed ahead mainly in the field of primary education, although much of the instruction was of poor calibre as it was carried out by graduates of the same course with negligible additional training. In 1961, elementary agricultural instruction was begun in Mozambique. As a result of the enlarged educational effort after 1955, the estimated literacy rate of the entire population crept from 1 or 2 per cent to between 4 and 6 per cent by 1967.[22] During the late 1950s the government increased technical and vocational training for Africans but straight academic education at the *liceu* stood beyond the reach of all but a few African students. High tuition rates and strict entrance requirements barred most black Mozambicans, some of whom gained admission to secondary institutions in South Africa and Rhodesia. Government figures for 1964-5 placed the number of students in mission and state primary schools at 426,904 and a further 20,553 in secondary schools, advanced commercial training or university level institutions.[23] In 1967, it was estimated that only 30 per cent of the populations of Mozambique, Angola and Guinea-Bissau spoke Portuguese.[24]

The University of Lourenço Marques, the first higher education institution in the colony, opened on a limited basis in 1963 with courses in agriculture, engineering, medicine, education and veterinary science. Of the nearly 300 students only five were African. Over the next ten years the enrollment tripled but the disproportionate white-black ratio stayed about constant. A select few Africans were sent to Portugal to complete their university work. Five years after its founding the university could grant final degrees, but it never offered degree programmes in the humanities or social sciences. They would not only siphon off manpower from critically needed skills but also raise the student's political consciousness. Although the government considerably expanded primary education and introduced more vocational courses, it was hesitant to create an intellectual elite similar to the one which played a leading role in the doom of the British and French colonial empires. The lesson had not gone unobserved.

Treatment of tropical diseases has been a point of pride to the Portuguese.[25] Arguing that their conquest of Goa and long contact with Indian physicians enhanced their knowledge of tropical medicine, they boasted of contributions to African health. As evidence of their well-established interest in tropical disease and cures, they pointed with pride to the founding of a medical school in Luanda in 1791 and the setting up of the Institute of Tropical Medicine, which was the first of its kind, in Lisbon in 1902.

In reality, the lengthy neglect that so characterized other Portuguese endeavours in Mozambique was also typical in the case of disease prevention, health centres and medical services. Not until the 1950s were large-scale immunization campaigns initiated against smallpox and typhoid fever that reduced the incidence of attacks but failed to eradicate them. Widespread malnutrition, need for sanitary conditions in rural areas and suburban slums and effective control of malaria, bilharzia, yaws, tuberculosis and hepatitis vied unsuccessfully for funds against construction schemes in the three major development plans. Yet there were greater strides made than in any previous period. The government established the Medical Institute of Mozambique in 1955 for research on endemic diseases of the territory. Early in 1964, Lisbon reorganized the Overseas Health Service so as to build more hospitals and extend medical and health services into remote regions by boosting the number of dispensaries, maternity centres and sending out mobile teams to small villages. In that year Mozambique had 415 doctors, or one for every 11,680 persons as compared to one per 20,000 in tropical Africa as a whole. Two-thirds of them, however, were concentrated in the three districts of Lourenço Marques (Maputo), Beira and Vila Pery. Many Africans in the north and north-west zones had never seen a doctor or received medical attention when the nationalists struck.

A century before, when British humanitarian indignation was at its height, Portuguese authorities intended reforms 'for the Englishman to see' (*para o ingles ver*). The priorities were radically changed in the 1950s and 1960s. African nationalism rising in the continent and its potential stirrings in the colony prompted an updating of the old saying and a departure from the old-style colonial rule. Seeking to offer attractive alternatives to black nationalism Portugal, as one modern authority observed, now instituted reforms 'for the black man to see' (*para o preto ver*).[26] Making the most of the calm before the storm the Portuguese introduced a few 'safe' Africans into the top levels of government. Two African Catholic priests joined the Legislative Council and Nampula had a black mayor by the early 1960s. The pressure of the war for national liberation further Africanized the colonial bureaucracy while not compromising Lisbon's control.

But as always, Portugal's ambitious plans for Mozambique exceeded its limited material and technical resources. A nation with the highest illiteracy rate in western Europe demonstrated a want of attention to education for its own masses and was ill-prepared to undertake a giant educational programme in the twilight of its colonialism. Then, too, there was the bridgeless gap between Lisbon's theories of material and educational ·progress for black Mozambicans and the practices of local whites. As might be imagined the perpetuation of Lisbon's sovereignty, bought at the expense of economic and political equality for blacks, was viewed by conservative whites with a basilisk eye. A cynic could add that the Lusitanian mission of cultural homogenization broke down not with the Africans alone but also with the settler community. They feared that an educated African population could become future competitors for jobs and economic opportunities, if not future subversives.

WHITE OPPOSITION

Settler resistance—characterized by *separatismo* and perhaps a form of nationalism—to Lisbon's interference and burdensome regulations declared itself in the manifold opposition of the *prazo* holders and slave traders before the expression of local grievances to policies of Republic and New State. Rebellious whites sometimes ignored Lisbon and at other times conspired and revolted against its taxes, officials and humanitarian impositions. When a liberal revolution rocked Portugal in 1820, the repercussions were felt in the city of Mozambique and on the lower Zambezi where near-anarchy prevailed in a burst of enthusiasm for independence from the metropole. Political deportees from Portugal formed masonic lodges and created a liberal climate on Mozambique Island before the government reasserted control in 1824.[27] The 1836 abolition of slave trading aroused separatists feelings among the slaving interests who favoured union with independent Brazil rather than subservience to the metropole's growing liberalism.

As the slave trade subsided but before the final collapse of *muzungo* pitched resistance, the whites of Beira and Lourenço Marques became disturbed about local issues that merged with the political crosscurrents sweeping Portugal. The swirl of liberalism, republicanism, monarchism, clericalism and anti-clericalism ripped across Portugal and unsettled Portuguese communities in Africa. *O Progresso*, the province's first privately published paper, in its initial issue of 9 April 1869 pulsed with liberal and republican spirit, exalting the virtues of a free press, 'the most precious and important of the liberties'. On the question of slavery and forced labour, however, settlers at variance with liberal ideals upbraided Lisbon for its misguided humanitarianism. Plantation owners and land company agents rallied to a conservative position at what they perceived as the ruinous policy of the liberal regimes in Lisbon. When slavery was abolished in 1878, the new labour code guaranteed the African 'absolute liberty to work or not to work'.

Terrible working conditions and poor wages (when they were not defrauded out of them) could scarcely be expected to entice sufficient black Mozambicans away from the mines and farms of South Africa and Rhodesia or village life into the colony's economy. The Mozambique whites blamed the government for stagnant commerce, uncultivated land and financial loss. So when the Enes-spirited labour code of 1899 repealed the former law and shackled Africans with a 'moral and legal' obligation to work, the settlers jubilated thinking that prosperity was at hand. Soon white farmers were again made unhappy when the government dragooned much of the black male population to build railways to the industrial heartland at the turn of the century, and when it signed agreements allowing for the wholesale recruitment of mine workers.

Inflamed with republican ideas, freedom of the press and criticism of the local government a small group in Lourenço Marques headed by Clemente Nunes de Carvalho e Silva, an indefatigable crusader, launched five weekly papers starting in 1900. Each in turn was suppressed by local authorities until the Governor-General of the colony, Azevedo Coutinho, banned the last sheet, *Progresso de Lourenço Marques*, in 1906.[28]

The fall of the monarchy and the freedom that it ushered in were widely applauded in Mozambique by settlers and *assimilados* who were stimulated with ideas of liberty and emancipation from Lisbon's tentacles. Economic difficulties and political disillusionment made for a short rejoicing. Unanimity in political sentiment was not achieved, however, by the death of the monarchy nor by change in Lisbon politics. Settler opinion was too varied for uniformity. Seen through the eyes of local authorities, Mozambican politics were marked by intrigues against officialdom and rivalry between contending groups that immersed the colonial government in petty squabbles.[29]

Toward the close of the Republican period conservative officials inspired by Colonial Minister João Belo reasserted themselves and began a clamp down. In 1925 the *Emancipador*, a paper of leftist views, printed articles on syndicalism and the cause of the proletariat. When the government closed its offices, the radical organ was distributed surreptitiously until at least October 1926, five months after the *coup* against the Republic. *O Radical*, an organ of local interest and of strong Republican persuasion was published from 1925 to 1926 when the government suppressed it. African and

European editors and journalists staged a collective protest against Belo's censorious press law of 1926 in a single edition called *Imprensa de Lourenço Marques*.[30] Chaves de Almeida, the leader of the protest, was exiled from Mozambique to Portugal for two years. His stand for a free press did not bind his Portuguese patriotism, however, for he, as described above, championed the 1930 Colonial Act to eliminate the British-financed Mozambique Company from the colony. One group of white rebels undertook but failed in 1931 to incite a company of African troops in Inhambane to revolt against Lisbon's dictatorial authority in the colony. After stifling the plot, the government deported 23 Europeans.[31]

The Republican tempestuousness that so animated white and *assimilado* Angolan politics never reached the same intensity in Mozambique where fewer Portuguese, greater distance from Portugal and the colony's special problems generated more interest in local issues. These were expressed in such moderate papers as *Notícias* and the *Lourenço Marques Guardian* (English owned and bilingual in Portuguese and English). The themes of white protest usually involved the foreign-backed chartered companies, mounting Indian immigration and the labour convention with South Africa.

The advent of the New State further dampened criticism as it imposed a curtain of silence on European and African protest alike. Not only was the radical press muzzled but moderate criticism was muted in all papers. By 1935, every edition of the province's papers and journals had been seen by the censor ('Visado pela Commissão de Censura') before printing. White and black police informers, deportation and imprisonment silenced outspoken settler dissent. Salazar would not brook any challenge to his goal of political and economic integration of the colonies with the metropole nor the primacy of Portugal's interest over those of Mozambican Portuguese.

After World War II, an anti-Salazarist opposition surfaced in Portugal and participated in the national elections until the rigged defeat of the last serious presidential candidate Air Force General Humberto Delgado in 1958. Opposition to Salazar's presidential choice, Admiral Américo Tómas, was strong in Mozambique where Delgado's middle-of-the-road liberalism fanned the existing feelings of political and economic autonomy from Lisbon. Despite official secrecy of the election returns, it was reported in Mozambique that Delgado received 65 per cent of the vote, winning a majority in all urban areas except Lourenço Marques over the only legally recognized party, the União Nacional.[32] Doubtful as the high figures might be, the New State recognized that settler discontent ran deep and took steps to secure its hold by suppressing Delgado's movement everywhere and dispatching units of the state secret police, Polícia Internacional e de Defesa do Estado, commonly called PIDE, to Mozambique.[33]

After failing at the polls, the democratic opposition in Portugal turned to subversive means to overthrow the Salazar regime until Delgado's body was unearthed from a shallow grave in Spain. Against the New State an underground movement, the Movimento Nacional Independente, hatched a tragicomic series of left-handed plots, aborted military *coups* and the flamboyant seizure of the *Santa Maria*. All these activities failed to shake the regime, but the example of resistance reinvigorated a small white opposition in Mozambique.

Following the 1949 elections, the police had uncovered in Mozambique an underground movement comprised of some prominent liberals in the European community, *mestiços* and Africans. This discovery appears to have dampened what skimpy white resistance existed. It was Delgado's challenge that enlivened a small opposition, however harebrained it may have been. Ten years after the first publicized discovery, the police cracked an anti-Salazarist pack when it tried to organize a boycott to the official reception of the incoming Governor-General by fluttering handbills from Lourenço Marques rooftops. Reportedly 16 members were arrested and António de Figueiredo, then a bank employee and later a free-lance journalist, was exiled to Lisbon where he escaped to London. In exile, he kept up the struggle in the international press.[34] Except for Figueiredo the movement seems to have been more anti-Salazar and separatist than pro-black or pro-African independence. The Mozambican Democrats wanted a suspension of police state controls, amnesty for political prisoners and 'revocation . . . of all legislation regulating commerce, agriculture or industry.'[35] The post-war emphasis on binding Mozambique's development to Portugal's economy and the special tariff and tax privileges granted to Lisbon-based firms in the colony embittered the resident businessmen. Some entertained strong separatist leanings leading to a commonwealth arrangement with Portugal, and others favoured closer ties to the modern economy of South Africa. Lisbon hoped to answer these desires for more autonomy by the 1963 Overseas Organic Law that widened the base and powers of the Legislative Council.

Still another section of Mozambican Portuguese changed the aims of the Associação dos Naturais de Moçambique from solely a defender of the rights of native-born whites to an organization to combat racial discrimination, to promote social integration and to obtain greater independence. The association also provided a few scholarships for African education. Membership was opened to Africans and purportedly 2,000 black Mozambicans joined to swell the overall membership to 10,000. Apparently alarmed by its 'political activity', the authorities forbade the election of officers in 1960 and placed the association under direct government administration.

There existed a stubborn settler mentality held by many who, whether native born or immigrants, regarded Mozambique as a white man's colony, a land of opportunity for Europeans alone, and saw the African as an exploitable resource. Their rags-to-riches success stories in the adopted land were celebrated in the local press and consecrated in the establishment of the Old Colonial Club in Lourenço Marques. They demanded that the black Mozambican forsake his civilization and embrace the cultural ideals and social mannerisms of the dominant group. When the African did assimilate, he was still scorned for putting on airs and graces, for always being a 'native'. Many with the settler outlook were at least sentimentally loyal to Portugal and others wanted a white republic. It was from such groups that the government could depend for demonstrators to protest the American stand in the UN at the start of the fighting in Angola. When the United States voted for a Security Council debate, an estimated 6,000 (some Africans participated in the parade) took to the capital's streets to vent their disapproval.[36]

One liberal section of whites organized the Movimento Democrático de Moçambique (MDM) which petitioned Salazar shortly after the Angolan revolt erupted. To avoid a war and black revenge in Mozambique, they sought an end to forced labour, extension of civil liberties and education to Africans and integration of black Mozambicans into the political leadership. In April 1961, the police arrested seven members of MDM for circulating anti-Salazarist petitions . Five months later some MDM pamphlets called upon Portuguese soldiers to revolt against the government and set up an independent Mozambique with African majority rule.[37] Petitions also circulated in Beira and Lourenço Marques listing numerous suggested economic changes between colony and metropole and expressing willingness to share equal citizenship rights with Africans. The government ignored the small group of lawyers, doctors and businessmen, and answered the appeal of the larger European constituency who now in their hour of crisis cried out for Portuguese ties and for a white citadel defended by Portugal.

Dissent with the government's political policies and military conduct was kept under wraps during the war by tight censorship, PIDE surveillance and the fear that it might weaken the defences of the colony. The full spectrum of white opinion was to be publicly cast into sharp relief when after the 'captain's' *coup* in April 1974, it became apparent that the soldiers' government intended to pull-out of Mozambique.

Dramatic as were the economic and political changes of the post-war years when viewed against previous decades of exploitation, oppression and neglect, they were too little and far too late to stave off African nationalist attacks. To the African, progress was still at a snail's pace. The independence of neighbouring states—Zaire, Malawi, Tanzania—made Portugal's hold an anachronism. Yet Lisbon's resolve to weather an anti-colonial hurricane was everywhere in evidence. But the times were against Portugal in Mozambique, and no policy or action could stay the rising nationalist tide.

NATIONALISM: PROTEST AND PARTIES

Mozambican resistance to Portugal's nineteenth-century colonial expansion had been a growing reality. Rarely unified for long and seldom without pro-Portuguese collaborators or neutral bystanders, the spirit of resistance lived on in some form and was embodied by some Mozambicans; it endured conquest, civilizing missions and campaigns to win African loyalty; it changed in the twentieth century with the changing circumstances of Portuguese rule; and it assumed different forms and degrees of intensity. And it triumphed. Military invasions, indigenous conquest polities and exploitive economic penetration for millennia by African and non-African instilled a spirit of bellicose resistance, a martial resilience, in the fibre of many of Mozambique's ethnic groups that cannot be solely attributed to the barbarous acts of the Portuguese alone. Nor could the Portuguese for long subdue this resistance. The Makonde, Shona and Ngoni as well as other groups have long nurtured military traditions that are still in living memory. Oral accounts of yesteryears' battles have been passed in fireside stories from grandfathers to grandsons. Modern nationalist leaders recount with undisguised pride the encounters of traditional warfare and assert the historic continuum between them and modern guerrilla operations. Strikes and riots of black Mozambicans served as links in this chain of opposition. Even if myth, it was a factor in the nationalist's war for liberation and exerts an influence in contemporary Mozambican politics.[1]

Not all resistance to Portugal was warlike. Much of it was stoic endurance and simple survival in the face of oppression. It found expression in Chopi songs of ridicule and hostility for the Portuguese, Makonde wood carvings of contempt for the religion of their oppressors, the flight of males to work in South Africa and Rhodesia, the sabotaging of cotton plants, the isolated slaying of a white *patrão*, the protests and petitions of black and *mestiço* associations, the strikes of African wage earners and the prose and poetry of black and brown intellectuals. Like nationalist development in the other parts of the continent, the Mozambican variety at different stages of its growth was the product of influences from Europe, America, the Caribbean, Africa itself and finally Asia. It is a fascinating, although only partially known, story of courage, resourcefulness, frustration, rashness, squabbles and dignity. It is not easy to form a clear picture of what was going on in Mozambican resistance circles; the veils of secrecy and censorship distort and obscure our image. What follows in this chapter is a barebones sketch of the evolution of Mozambican African nationalism.

EARLY PROTEST

Before the conclusion of the final pacification campaigns, a handful of educated African and *mestiço* writers began a protest of the pen rather than the sword. Not as prolific nor as rich as the Angolan *assimilado* newspaper protest which it resembles, the Mozambican literary response was still significant in helping to make the transition from primary or traditional resistance in the countryside to secondary or political opposition in urban centres. More settlers, Protestant missionaries and white restiveness helped make Angolan African politics more vociferous and turbulent at an earlier date than black Mozambican dissent. One of many fascinating Mozambican episodes in early literate protest was the role of Alfredo de Aguiar, a *mestiço* who came to the east African colony in 1879 as an officer in an Angolan battalion. He brought with him some of the protesting talents of the Angolan *assimilado* journalists and, in so doing, played a small part in the transference of ideas that took place between men of colour at the close of the nineteenth and beginning of the twentieth centuries. Irreverent and rebellious, Aguiar founded and edited at least three different papers critical of Portuguese rule. The first was started in 1885 on Mozambique Island, and the last and most successful, *Clamor Africano*, was published in Lourenço Marques from 1886 to 1894. Through the pages of his papers, he attacked Portugal in inflammatory language for slavery, forced labour and the lack of African education and job opportunities. His efforts at reform incurred official wrath, censorship and threats to his safety.

Another paper of vitriol, the semi-weekly *O Africano*, appeared in 1911 in both Portuguese and Shangana in an effort to maintain Mozambican dialects and reach a wider readership. It was distributed to many of the workers bound for South African mines. The editor José Albasini, an African who along with his brother João, is usually associated with the more well-known publication *O Brado Africano*. *O Africano*'s anti-government attacks and outspoken disillusionment with the achievements of the Republic led to its suppression in 1920.[2] Both in style and content, the first literary expressions of Mozambican nationalism contained much of the same polemical arguments and heated criticism of Portuguese republican and anti-monarchical sentiments of the times.

Less vigorous protest came from Rui de Noronha, a poet of mixed Indian and African blood, whose verse of melancholy despair for the plight of black Mozambicans in the first decades of this century was to become characteristic of some poems a generation later. Conscious of his mixed parentage, he was drawn toward his African heritage. His poems evoked traditional life and ceremonies but envisioned none of the political revolt so typical of Mozambican poets of a later day. His was a literary revolt.[3]

Early Mozambican nationalism also had an organizational side. With the 1911 Republican constitution came fewer restraints on associations, opinions or the press which fostered African and Portuguese political formations. Africans and *mestiços* founded societies in Tete, Inhambane, Beira and Lourenço Marques which had the common goal of redressing wrongs but had no common front or unity. Splintered by personality squabbles and ideological conflicts, the associations were small, powerless and often organizations only in name.[4] One of the principal associations was the Grémio Africano (African guild) comprised of *assimilados* who pinned their hopes on advancement within the colonial system, and displayed a deep loyalty to the Republic even after enthusiasm waned among Mozambican Portuguese. The Republic's ideals held out hope of progress, and the Grémio Africano's organ *O Brado Africano* endorsed them when it began publication in 1918. Edited by the Albasini brothers, the paper fought discrimination, forced labour and inequality. Its tone and message belied Portugal's assertion of African satisfaction with colonial rule.

Conditions becoming worse with the onset of the New State, *O Brado Africano* adopted an increasingly militant editorial posture that reflected not only a bitter disenchantment with Portugal's broken promises of education and civilizing mission but also with the promises themselves. In a fiery editorial called 'Enough', it poured scorn on Portugal's colonial mission and hinted of violence unless reforms were made.

> We do not aspire to the comforts you surround yourselves with, thanks to our strength. We do not aspire to your refined education . . . even less do we aspire to a life dominated by the idea of robbing your brother . . . We aspire to our 'savage state' which, however, fills your mouths and your pockets . . . We repeat that we do not want hunger or thirst or poverty or a law of discrimination based on colour . . . We will learn to use the scalpel . . .[5]

This high watermark of invective was preceded and followed by difficulties with the government. When the authorities briefly suppressed *O Brado Africano* for two months in 1932-3, the enterprising José Albasini resurrected the name of Aguiar's sheet and temporarily printed *Clamor Africano*. Then later in the thirties, the government took over and supervised African and *mestiço* associations and their publications, attempting to make them mirrors of official policy. *O Brado Africano* became a regime-sponsored paper.

The press failed as an effective instrument for redress of wrongs and for African *mestiço* advancement against growing exploitation and tightening government control. The promising start of the late nineteenth century and Republican period died as censorship throttled what was considered a threat to European hegemony.

As a Mozambican of the period whose revolutionary career belongs more to the history of Malawi (then Nyasaland) than the country of his birth, Charles Domingo warrants only brief mention here. Domingo when a youth was brought in 1881 from Quelimane to Livingstonia, the Scottish mission in Nyasaland. There he developed into an early defender of African culture, exponent of independent African churches and colleague of John Chilembwe, who later led the famous 1915 rising in Nyasaland. Although Domingo did not take part in the actual rising, his radical preaching fanned the discontent that culminated in the revolt. His independent church suffered in the British government's general reprisal against separatist churches after the rising, but not before his activities had served the cause of African resistance to European colonialism.

PROTEST ABROAD

Outside Mozambique, *assimilados* established association in Lisbon as well as Angola and the islands of São Tome and Príncipe. As early as 1910, *assimilados* living in Lisbon began gathering into unstable and short-lived groups that dissolved with divisions over issues and personalities and regrouped in new organizations. In Europe, they were influenced by talk of democracy and the right to territorial self-determination during World War I. They also became caught up in the whirl of heady racial doctrines of voluntary African exiles in London and Paris. From the United States, the robust racial pride of Marcus Garvey's movement merged with the pan-Negro and pan-African currents flowing between Africa, the New World and London since at least 1900.[6]

In Portugal, the *assimilado* associations embraced similar ideas as their provincial counterparts. Benefiting from greater freedom in Portugal, they adopted more extreme programmes and actions in publicizing goals and grievances to gain support of international associations. Yet they declared in speech and in publication that their ultimate programmes — promotion of African rights and their social and economic progress — were not radical nor contrary to the principles of the Republic to which they paid frequent and public loyalty. Nor did they advocate the separation of the colonies from Portugal.

After the war, two principal associations emerged to attract *assimilado* members from the wreckage of early movements. The first, Liga Africana (1910), was most well-known for its connections with the W. E. B. DuBois Pan-African conference movement and hosted the second part of the 1923 meeting in Lisbon.[7] As for the plight of Africans living in Portuguese colonies nothing official was reported at that conference and the two sessions focused on black American problems and the worldwide pan-African movement. The results of the Liga Africana's overall participation in the Pan-African Congresses were also negligible.

The second important association, the Partido Nacional Africano, organized in 1921, shared similar aims as the Liga Africana but evidenced an affinity for Garvey's brand of fierce race pride and pan-Negro nationalism. Using its freedom in Portugal, the Partido Nacional Africano published programmes for democratic and economic promotion of African rights, and it petitioned and sent representatives to the International Labour Organization of the League of Nations to protest forced labour in Portuguese Africa. While at the height of its activity from 1923 to 1925, the PNA's preoccupation with labour conditions also compelled it to vindicate black people before the distorted image of whites. Little of permanence was accomplished for all its pleading on behalf of the African masses. Repression in Portugal at the end of the 1920s left its only functioning office in Geneva where it lingered on into the next decade.

When the Republic foundered, the *assimilado* groups in the metropole and the colonies were dragged down in the authoritarian whirlpool only to resurface as thoroughly infiltrated appendages of the New State. Formed in 1931, the Movimento Nacionalista Africano, subservient to and regulated by the government, postured as an African federation in Portugal. Under the aegis of the New State, it represented a coalition of the Partido Nacional Africano and the Liga Africana.[8]

Meanwhile events followed a similar trajectory in Mozambique where the Associação Africana, a less accommodating outgrowth of the Grémio Africano, raised official alarms by demanding guarantees for African lands and an end to discriminatory labour practices. The government purged the Associação Africana of radical inclinations by making the leadership subservient to its will. Soon after the government had succeeded in turning around some of the leaders, a more militant faction withdrew to form the Instituto Negrófilo in the late 1930s. The rump of the Associação Africana that remained tended to-attract a *mestiço* membership. Comprised mainly of Africans, the Instituto Negrófilo also suffered from a purging of its leadership. It was renamed the Centro Associativo dos Negros de Moçambique. Emasculated by the New State's repressions, these organizations publicly confined themselves to social events, sporting pursuits, addresses by colonial officials and some gentle prods for African advancements within the colonial framework. Such organizations by their very existence alone, however, provided an environment for self-definition and political awakening, if not for insurrection. In the eyes of the colonial government, they were always suspect. The Centro Associativo was banned in 1965 for subversion and terrorism, and its president Domingos Arouca, one of Mozambiques few black lawyers of the time, was imprisoned in Portugal until near the conclusion of the liberation war.

The protesting associations of the 1890–1930s never evolved into progenitors of nationalistic-minded political parties like similar organizations in British and French territories. Instead, the government repressed them. Part of the explanation why the New State silenced dissident voices lies in Portugal's historical lack of democracy and parliamentary politics. Furthermore, the difficulty with which the Portuguese pacified resistance in Mozambique also conditioned them to crush any potential challengers. Mistakenly, Portugal took the surface tranquility that resulted as a sign of acceptance of its rule, if not loyalty. Bitten by an imperial bug, the Portuguese were blind to the depths of Mozambican aspirations for freedom and self-fulfillment and the spreading reaction to the colonial virus.

RE-EMERGING POLITICAL AGITATION

Mozambique's rising political consciousness after World War II owed part of its inspiration to a cultural revival that accompanied organizational and violent expressions of its re-emergence. This cultural renaissance sprang, as did the associational and newspaper protest, from black and *mestiço* intellectuals alienated from the white colonial society. Pressures on Africans to assimilate Portuguese culture and social standards provoked a search for genuine African-ness among black Mozambicans. Their counter-barrage, suffused with angry revolt, fired literary salvos against Portuguese economic and cultural imperialism. Although their traditional societies possessed rich oral traditions, black Mozambicans lacked a fully developed literary heritage of their own and looked to those confronted by similar colonial situations. Influences came from French territories in West Africa, the United States and the Caribbean where black poets using the poetic theme of *négritude* (an amorphous philosophy that pits itself against everything white) examined the internal conflicts of living in a world dominated by white values and racial inequalities.

Not surprisingly, Mozambican artists and writers living in urban areas were best placed to experience the contradictions between Lisbon's policy of equality and integration and the local practices of intolerance and forced labour. Through the mediums of poetry, short stories and paintings they cried out against colonialism and bitterly lamented the sufferings of their people. The most effective and best known of the postwar poets were José Craveirinha and Noémia de Sousa. A journalist Craveirinha, the son of an African woman and a swarthy European father from Portugal's southern province of Algarve, experienced the limbo status of European education and African appearance as few others. He dwelled on the endless drudgery of the African worker, extolled the beauty of Negroid characteristics, celebrated the 'primitiveness' of Africa and rebuked the mechanized and soulless European civilization. Craveirinha was also capable of angry revolt. One of his most widely quoted poems, 'Grito Negro' ('Black Cry'), metaphorically employed the word *coal* to call attention to the African's colour, exploitation and consuming combustibility once 'ignited':

> I am coal
> And you burn me, boss
> To serve you for ever as powering fuel
> But not for ever, boss
> . . . .
> I am coal
> I do have to burn
> Consume everything with my combustive might
> Yes!
> I am your coal, boss.[9]

Noémia de Sousa the poetess, also known by her African name Vera Micaia, sought for African roots and a reaffirmation of them in the face of the dominate white civilization. In 'Deixa passar neu povo' ('Let My People Go'), she transcended the borders of Mozambique to seek unity with suffering Africans everywhere. This poem revealed the influence of the black American spiritual called by the same name and interpreted by Paul Robeson and Marian Anderson.[10] As a result of a companion's arrest and deportation to São Tomé following the dock strikes in 1947, she was moved to call for revolt in her writings.

Another poet Marcelino dos Santos, a *mestiço* from the coastal town of Lumbo opposite Mozambique Island, was one of several writers who expressed angry revolt against exploitation characteristic of the first phase of *négritude*. In the work 'Xangano, filho pobre' ('Xangano, the indigent Child'), the 'poor son of a rich land' endures the present in hope that 'once again I shall be king'.

Writing often under his African name of Kalungano, dos Santos manifested a typical concern of *négritude* poets for a non-Occidental aesthetic value system and for an identification with pre-colonial Africa because of alienation in the modern European world.

Short-story writer Luís Bernardo Honwana employed prose to the same end as contemporary poets. Accustomed to government surveillance, he skillfully guided his reader, sometimes by parables, to arrive at a condemnation of Portuguese rule. Without preaching a message, Honwana in *Nós Matámos o Cão-Tinhoso* recreates the passive and tenacious Mozambican.[11] The painters José Craveirinha, the nephew of the poet, and Vicente Gowena Malangatana protested on canvas. Their works showed the influence of traditional carvings and myths. Drawing inspiration from the pre-colonial past, they challenged Lisbon's cherished thought of contented and 'lusitanified' Africans.

Many elusive moods of *négritude* — rage, rebellion, racial affirmation, an assertive rejoinder to European smug superiority — throb through the writings and paintings of Mozambican intellectuals and artists. But the movement, led by those unable to escape their European education, furnished only brief sanctuary for a few alienated Africans and *mestiços*, for neither the offer of its shadowy 'marginality' nor its unrealizable goal of a return to a pristine African state could for long sustain an ongoing opposition to Portuguese rule. Mozambique's intellectual and artistic revolt, in comparison to Angola's 'Vamos decobrir Angola' ('Let us discover Angola'), was never allowed to blossom, for it was cut short by the official reaction to the insurgency in the north. Following the onset of fighting, Craveirinha and Honwana were imprisoned, and Malangatana and others were closely watched by the authorities after 1965. Noémia de Sousa left Mozambique for Paris where she stopped writing poetry. Only Marcelino dos Santos, who had travelled in Europe, lived among leftist intellectuals in Paris and discovered Marxism, joined the revolutionary ranks.

Scorned in part by revolutionaries who considered their poems 'a style of eloquent self-pity . . . alien to the African reaction',[12] the cultural movement, as similar intellectual responses elsewhere, has also been recognized by its detractors as a necessary phase in the development of national consciousness.[13] Its suppression also served a purpose, too, in that it became obvious Portugal would refuse to recognize even literary deviation from the Lusitanian fold despite all the government propaganda of culture assimilation entailing the interpenetration of Mozambican and Portuguese worlds. Although narrowly confined to urban educated Mozambicans in a country predominately rural and illiterate, its chief value lay in awakening aspirations of a few. Cultural nationalism influenced a 'slightly younger generation of intellectuals' who carried their opposition into political movements. In brief, the cultural revolt accompanied and inspired other forms of rebellion.

Riots, strikes and local demonstrations made up another type of protest and growing national consciousness in the postwar period. Set in the context of colonialism, severe police repression and cheap or forced labour, African strikes and labour disputes assumed a form of political opposition. African nationalists reported the occurrence of docker's strikes on Lourenço Marques's wharfs during the 1930s. In 1947, the capital's docks, known by ship captains for their fast turn-around time and gruelling working conditions for the black stevedores, were again the scene of labour unrest which apparently spilled over to nearby agricultural workers. The racial and political overtones surfaced the next year when a planned disturbance took place in Lourenço Marques. Although quashed before it became widespread, the abortive rising resulted in about 200 arrests, some of whom were later jailed or transported to São Tomé.[14] Another strike in 1956 at the Lourenço Marques docks reportedly cost 49 workers their lives. A rash of strikes broke out spontaneously on the docks of Lourenço Marques, Beira and Nacala in 1963, but ended in failure and death.[15]

Despite Portuguese efforts to insulate Africans from news of independence and nationalism by prohibiting them to listen to non-Portuguese radio stations and forbidding them to read papers other than the now government-controlled *O Brado Africano*, a number of small local parties, espousing nationalistic programmes, came into existence in the 1950s and 1960s. The organizers had their political consciousness raised by Nkrumah in Ghana, Nyerere in Tanzania, Congolese independence, the African fight against formation of the Central African Federation and the dramatic visit of the Mozambican Eduardo Mondlane (then employed by the United Nations) to the land of his birth in 1961. In the former district of Manica e Sofala, the União Progressiva de Moçambique, formed in 1953 or 1954, demanded independence and claimed contact with one of Angola's principal movements, the Movimento Popular de Libertação de Angola (MPLA). The Partido Socialista Católico was also established in the Inhambane area. Reportedly, the Núcleo Negrófico staged a protest in 1953 resulting in imprisonment or death of its leaders.[16] An *assimilado*, Hlomulo Chitofo Gwambe later claimed that he returned from six years of working in Rhodesia to found the Partido da Unidade Nacional in 1960, somewhere 200 miles north of Lourenço Marques.

Evidence of these and other shadowy groups comes from petitions to the United Nations and Brazilian publications. Their effectiveness in weakening Portuguese resolve to hang on to Mozambique was nil, but some of their participants were involved later in the formation of more significant groups. As for the parties themselves, they were extirpated by the New State which, unlike even the repressive South African regime of the same period, never allowed independently organized African political groups or trade unions. Their manifestos and petitions advocated a peaceful transference of Mozambique to African rule. Soon the realization dawned that peaceful dissent would not bring independence.

Discontent also manifested itself among secondary school students in Lourenço Marques. Influenced by the cultural movement together with returning students from South Africa, secondary pupils formed the Núcleo dos Estudantes Africanos Secundários de Moçambique (NESAM) in 1949. Linked to the Centro Associativo dos Negros de Moçambique, NESAM's small membership of relatively privileged youth discussed nationalist ideas, declared their distinctiveness from European culture and rejected the assimilation process. They printed for a short time the magazine *Alvor* ('Dawn'), and maintained contact with former students, which later purportedly facilitated a rudimentary underground network of communication to other areas of the country for FRELIMO (Front for the Liberation of Mozambique).[17] Its activities raised suspicions, and in 1964 PIDE suppressed the student organization. Some members made good their escape to foreign countries, but others were arrested or returned to the Portuguese authorities by the co-operating police forces of Rhodesia and South Africa. In 1963, onetime members of NESAM organized the União Nacional dos Estudantes do Moçambique (UNEMO). This Mozambican student union established groups in the United States, Europe and Africa with the mission of furthering the struggle by publicizing its goals.

Colonial students in the metropole also played a part in the early formation of a Mozambican resistance just as had the voluntary African and mestiço exiles participated in assimilado associations during the interwar years. A handful of students from civil service fathers and assimilado families were sent to Portugal beginning in the late 1940s to be trained for positions in the colonial administration. This limited programme of university education backfired in that many of the future leaders of nationalist movements came from the student elite educated in Lisbon or Coimbra in the 1950s. From Mozambique came Mondlane, one of the founders of NESAM, and dos Santos. While in Lisbon, Mondlane kept company with Agostinho Neto, subsequent President of the MPLA and Amilcar Cabral, later assassinated Secretary-General of the Partido Africano de Independência da Guiné e Cabo Verde (PAIGC). Alienated from the society around them, the African students gathered together or with faculty members and liberal Portuguese to discuss Portugal's colonial policies. Official harassment created a poor environment for study, and led Mondlane, who had a scholarship from the Phelps-Stokes Foundation, to continue his studies in the United States in 1951. A later group of students, among them dos Santos , fled to France and Switzerland, overcome with frustration in being unable to effect change and fear of reprisal after hostilities opened in Angola. Before their flight, some of them had established in 1951 the Centro de Estudos Africanos. Ostensibly a cultural association, the Africans examined the role of culture in liberation and other nationalistic theories until its dissolution in 1965. The students also made contact with sailors from Portugal's African territories through the Club dos Maritimos. The political atmosphere generated by the anti-Salazarist opposition stimulated discussions and broadened the political sophistication of the African students.

As in so much else, Mozambican Africans suffered in numerical comparison to the Anglophone and Francophone African student population in Europe. Of Mozambique's prominent nationalist leadership only a bare handful of the top layer has undergone university training. Mondlane left Lisbon before intellectual radicalism against the New State peaked in the late fifties, and his successor, Samora Machel, attended no university. Hence FRELIMO's direction came from Mozambicans with little elite

European education and experiences. This may explain the lack of
a split between intellectuals and less-well educated as occurred in
the early Angolan nationalist leadership, producing seemingly
irreconcilable differences.

Many other nationalists, such as Paulo José Gumane, travelled
outside the country for work and came into contact with some
nationalist thought in the then more politically tolerant South
Africa and Rhodesia. While in Cape Town, Gumane joined first
the African National Congress and then the Pan-Africanist Congress. As branch secretary of the Laundry and Dry Cleaner
Workers' Union, he became involved in political organizing and
participated in the Defiance Campaign of 1952.[18] According
to nationalist accounts two other Mozambicans in South
Africa — Tomas Betulane Nhantumbo and Diniz Mengame — tried
to organize their countrymen working in the mines into the Partido
de Libertação de Moçambique from 1956 to 1957. Their efforts
reportedly brought them into collision with the police who turned
the two over to the Portuguese in 1962. Mondlane may not have
overemphasized too much the unifying force of work south of the
border when he wrote: 'Mozambican unity was born out of toiling
together in the deep, hot, narrow and dust-ridden shafts of the
gold, diamond and coal mines of the Transvaal and Orange Free
State.'[19] When the South African government cracked down hard
on African politics following the Sharpeville shooting in March
1960, a number of Mozambican activists journeyed to neighbouring
territories to set up parties in exile.

It remains to examine the Mozambican countryside for signs of
agitation and proto-nationalism. Nationalist documents avow that
'between 1918 and 1964, a number of minor, local tribal uprisings
took place in various parts of Mocambique.'[20] As of yet other
evidence of unrest in rural areas is slender, but the postwar decades
did see the formation of co-operative markets by farmers. Holding
monopoly buying powers over the African farmer, Portuguese and
Asian merchants paid penny-cheap prices to the unorganized pro-
ducers of cotton, rice or cashews. Collective action was needed to
expand production and inch up prices. One fleeting co-operative was
avowedly set up by the soft-spoken Gumane and his reluctant father
in the Inhambane district in 1960. This activity brought young
Gumane into conflict with the authorities, who co-operated with
the commercial interests, and forced him to flee to South Africa.[21]

In the north among the Makonde people, a more throughgoing co-operative system was established in the 1950s. Lazaro Kavandame, who later was in FRELIMO's Central Committee before deserting to the Portuguese, founded and operated a co-operative movement which soon ran afoul of the colonial authorities. The concession companies protested to the government, and it financially harassed the co-operatives. The colonial authorities distrusted any African organization and especially one that smacked of collectivism. A small amount of Communist literature found in the territory contributed to the alarm,.as did the appearance of Egyptian President Abdul Gamal Nasser's picture in northern coastal communities.

The Makonde were among the last ethnic groups to be 'pacified' in Mozambique. In their modern history, they also suffered some dislocation during the First World War, endured the Niassa Company's exploitive administration until 1926 and thereafter experienced more remote Portuguese rule and assimilation plans than groups to the south. With the coming of Tanzania's independence the Makonde, who span the Mozambican-Tanzanian border, showed signs of growing restiveness and new aspirations of which Kavandame's co-operative was one manifestation. Another sign of incipient political awakening was the organization of a Makonde party, the União Makonde de Moçambique, which in 1961 formed part of the Mozambique African National Union. The Portuguese crushed this agitation with heavy African casualties in what became known as the Mueda massacre.

Many references have been made to this dramatic event. Still there remains confusion about the facts, conflicting accounts, suppression and bludgeoning polemics. In the months preceding the demonstration at the town of Mueda in Cabo Delgado district, a number of local African leaders worked for liberalization of Portuguese rule and higher pay for labourers. The Portuguese arrested some of the spokesmen—Tiago Muller, Faustino Vanomba and Kibiriti Diwane—and the local administrator invited nearby villagers to air their grievances at Mueda where the district governor and a company of soldiers had been assembled. According to nationalist accounts, several thousand people gathered on 16 June - 1960 for the discussion, and rioted when the authorities arrested outspoken demonstrators. During the ensuing fray the troops opened fire reportedly killing over 500 Africans.[22] No out-

sider observed the incident, and some scepticism existed surrounding the reports and the number of victims. But subsequent
reports from foreign observers of other mass killings, especially the
internationally publicized destruction of the village of Wiriyamu in
1972, lend in retrospect substance to nationalist charges.

Taking place two months after the Sharpeville massacre of over
60 African demonstrators against the pass laws in South Africa, it
marked in the southern tip of the continent the beginning of a
determined counterthrust to the advances of African independence.
The Mueda massacre was a visible sign, although others probably
occurred previously, that the military had begun to strengthen
police repression. Whether Portuguese authorities were influenced
by the South African shootings is a point of speculation and
interest. Certainly the Portuguese had grown uneasy with decolonization to the north. The PIDE had demonstrated their apprehension by arresting anyone suspected of rebellion or subversion.
Taking place even before the Angolan flare-up and its aftermath of
murdering white counterattacks on Africans in Luanda's *muceques*
('slums'), Mueda also underlined the ruthlessness of the Portuguese
response to African aspirations. The incident strengthened the conclusion of the Mozambican nationalists that parties would have to
be formed in neighbouring states and armed rebellion would have
to be used to gain independence. Not all these lessons crystallized
immediately, but Mueda served as a bloody reminder to nationalists
of the dangers of wrongheaded actions. Mueda acted as a catalyst
from which the chemistry of Mozambican nationalism hardened to
a new form of resistance. The revolution was sealed with the blood
of martyrs, most of them humble peasants.

FORMATION AND VICISSITUDES OF A NATIONAL FRONT

Given the extent of repression within Mozambique, the nationalists
could only form viable political organizations beyond the borders of
the country. Participants of previous parties, co-operatives or small
upheavals, if not silenced, either journeyed to nearby states to
organize political groups or acted as cadres for exile movements,
particularly FRELIMO, once formed. Rooted in centuries-old
resistance, Mozambican nationalism first budded in foreign soil.

Workers and exiles mostly from south and central Mozambique

established the União Nacional Democrática de Moçambique (UDENAMO) in Bulawayo, Rhodesia on 2 October 1960. Active in its formation were David Mabunda, Uria Simango (a Protestant pastor from the Beira region), and Gwambe, the President. Gumane, the soft-spoken school teacher from Inhambane, joined UDENAMO in Dar es Salaam. In February 1961, the Mozambique African National Union (MANU) emerged in Mombasa, Kenya from a Makonde self-help and cultural association, the Tanganyika Mozambique Makonde Union, which had been founded in 1957 by Mozambican plantation and dock workers in Kenya, Tanzania and Zanzibar. The President, Matthew Mmole, Secretary-General Lawrence M. Millinga and other leaders were English-speaking.[23] MANU drew inspiration and support from the governing national unions in Tanzania and Kenya. A third smaller party, União Africana de Moçambique Independente (UNAMI), was organized in Malawi by Mozambicans from Tete district. It was led by José Baltazar de Costa Chagong'a, a former medical orderly and political organizer from the town of Moatize. These three loosely organized groups, which had only a limited following in Mozambique, represented indirectly the aspirations of many more Mozambicans unaware of their existence.

Tanzanian independence in December 1961 influenced all three parties to move their headquarters to Dar es Salaam where they received strong pressure to merge from newly arrived Mozambican refugees fleeing redoubled Portuguese security measures after the rebellion in Angola. Such state leaders as Kwame Nkrumah of Ghana and Julius Nyerere of Tanzania also pressured for a merger. One future FRELIMO leader took an active role in laying the groundwork for unification. Dos Santos, then Secretary-General of the recently formed Conferência das Organizações Nacionalistas das Colónias Portuguêsas (CONCP), which was created to coordinate African movements in Portuguese territories, was influential in getting the council of CONCP to urge UDENAMO and MANU to 'come together'. Delegates from the two organizations met in March 1962 and laid plans for eventual unification. In mid-June at the Conference of Freedom Fighters at Winneba, Ghana, the host President Nkrumah exerted pressure on the representatives of the Mozambican groups. Meanwhile the Tanganyika African National Union, which granted sanctuary to the exile parties, pushed for amalgamation. Finally, the parties formed a front. Out of a conference in Dar es Salaam during 20–5 June emerged FRELIMO from a coalescence of UDENAMO, MANU, and UNAMI. The next year the Organization of African Unity (OAU) recognized it as the sole recipient of aid to Mozambican groups. The front's leadership included organizers of the former organisation.

Former UDENAMO members occupied several key posts: Mabunda became Secretary-General; Gumane assumed the position of Deputy Secretary-General; and Simango became the Vice President. From MANU came the treasurer, Mmole. Dos Santos was elected Secretary of External Affairs because of his years in European exile and his links with *mestiço* intellectuals from other Portuguese territories with whom he helped establish CONCP. Other members of the front's leadership had recently journeyed from Mozambique where they were more familiar with the political ground than the longtime exiles. Some had participated in mutual aid associations. These included: Silveiro Rafael Nungu and Samuel Dhlakama from the Beira region: Mateus Muthemba and Shaffrudin Khan from southern Mozambique; and Jonas Namashulua and Kavandame from the northern peasant co-operatives. Khan in time became FRELIMO's representative first in Cairo and then the United States. Nungu, one-time Secretary for Administration was implicated with Kavandame in Mondlane's death and executed by FRELIMO in June 1969.

The selection of a president for the fragile front, already beset with the jockeying of ambitious men, was a tricky business. Anyone too closely associated with the previous movements or the merger wranglings would be certain to encounter opposition or unable to command widespread allegiance. The presidency fell to Eduardo Chivambo Mondlane who had flown from the United States to take part in the consolidation conference. References have been made to Mondlane's being 'hand picked' by Nyerere for the tightrope-walking job as head of a fraction-formed movement.[24] True, Mondlane, while working as a research officer at the United Nations, had favourably impressed Nyerere who later called him to Tanzania. But others did likewise. When visiting Mozambique in 1961 under the auspices of a UN passport, Mondlane later recalled: '. . . thousands of people asked me to organize a national movement'.[25] While there, many Mozambicans, including Samora Machel who became President after Mondlane's assassination, told the young UN officer that conditions within the country were ripe for revolt. Chagong'a the leader of UNAMI, on his arrival in Dar es Salaam in 1961, wrote urging Mondlane to create a united movement. The delegates to the unification conference selected Mondlane who they perceived as educated, sophisticated and without prior political attachments except a distant connection with UDENAMO.

At the time of the formation, Mondlane was a professor of anthropology at Syracuse University in New York and outwardly an unlikely candidate to head a national liberation front and a guerrilla movement. A booming friendly voice, amiable smile, and academic air, Mondlane was a man of iron will, who became a hard-core revolutionary of radical thought. Coming from the relatively privileged few Africans educated abroad, he could have accepted offers from Moreira and others to join the Portuguese administration in a plush job or have taken a position at a university in Portugal. It is almost a historical corollary now that youths from the pampered classes can be a society's bitterest critics and even subversive of its foundations. Mondlane was not from a 'pampered' class, but his educational advances far surpassed the vast majority of Mozambican youth. Experiences in his own life and influences of his kinsmen, however, disposed him to a revolutionary course in life.

Born in 1920 in the southern district of Gaza, he came from a traditional Thonga background. His father was a minor chief who along with Mondlane's uncle was occasionally at odds with the colonial administration. Gazaland had only been 'pacified' from the resistance of Gungunyane and his military heir Maguiguana a quarter of a century before Mondlane's birth. Their resistance left a marked impact on the region for over a generation. Mondlane's response to his insurgent heritage appeared early in his life.

Until ten years old, he tended the family livestock. At the urging of his mother (his father's third wife), he attended a government and then a Swiss mission school where he met Henri-Philippe Junod, who like his distinguished father, did extensive ethnological field work in southern Mozambique. At an American Methodist agricultural school, he learned English. Being beyond the legal African age for continuing his studies in Mozambique, he enrolled in a Swiss secondary school in the Transvaal. Four years later he obtained a scholarship that enabled him to register at the Witwatersrand University, but when Dr D. F. Malan's Nationalist government came to power, he was dismissed from the university for being a 'foreign native'. Back in Lourenço Marques, the police arrested and questioned Mondlane for his activities in NESAM. The colonial authorities presumably decided that Mondlane's transgressions were minor and his usefulness to the administration still redeemable, for it recommended that his education be continued in Portugal to cure his 'embryonic spirit of black nationalism'. Police surveillance in Lisbon convinced Mondlane to finish his studies in the United States; he graduated from Oberlin College in 1953 with a BA and earned a PhD at Northwestern University. After a year spent in research at Harvard University, Mondlane accepted a position at the United Nations where he remained until 1961. That September he took an assistant professorship at Syracuse University so as to disengage himself from the international organization. From his teaching post, he wrote articles and spoke out several times at various places in the United States about conditions in Mozambique and Portuguese colonial policy before taking part in the creation of FRELIMO.

In September 1962, three months after the founding meeting, FRELIMO held in Dar es Salaam its first party congress. FRELIMO's programme recognized the obstacles of negotiating a peaceful independence for Mozambique when it declared its aim of establishing an 'efficient organization of the struggle of the Mozambican people for national liberation.'[26] Along with condemning Portuguese colonialism, the congress in a series of resolutions called for development of an organizational structure, unity among Mozambicans, mobilization of the people by training cadres and promoting education, co-operation with other African nationalist movements, organization of propaganda and gathering of diplomatic support. Consolidation and unity proved to be FRELIMO's greatest hurdle from the start of the front. Mondlane's departure to complete the final year of his teaching contract helped open the door to factionalism. During his year in the United States, he garnered important private American support, but also during his absence the unity of the front was severely tested.

Soon after formation of FRELIMO, personal, regional, ethnic and ideological rivalries burgeoned and led to several splinter groups. Some of the factionalism was attributed to Mondlane's allegedly pro-American sympathies as evidenced by his education and his white American wife (Janet, née Johnson). He was also charged with being too moderate and a puppet of the Central Intelligence Agency by a few shrill detractors. A brief summary of Mondlane's political ideas — ideas that guided FRELIMO after his death — will clarify his methods and goals, and throw light on the accusations.

In FRELIMO's struggle, Mondlane sought to forge as wide a coalition of nations against Portugal as possible. Pragmatically, he reasoned that aid and diplomatic supports from the West were as useful as that from the East. FRELIMO sometimes held, however, that aid carried an ideological commitment. In 1973, it refused an offer of assistance from West Germany because of that country's military support of Portugal through NATO. Before Lisbon's pressure curtailed its aid, the Ford Foundation funded the Mozambique Institute, a nursing and primary teacher training school in Dar es Salaam for Mozambican students. The United States gave no overt assistance to FRELIMO, but its Agency for International Development provided a few scholarships for Mozambicans to study in America. Anonymous private contributors, many of them friends of Mondlane, financed or secured money for FRELIMO's health, publicity and educational projects, while military equipment and training came from Algeria, Russia and China.[27] This policy of aid-seeking, although pragmatic and imitative of earlier African independence drives in British-, French- and Belgian-controlled territories, ultimately contributed to factionalism, for divergent groups each accused the other of pro-Western, pro-Soviet or pro-Chinese sympathies. Other reasons for cleavages were the stresses and strains of exile politics among a heterogeneous leadership of varied ethnic, language, religious, social and educational backgrounds who had little political experience.

As the conflict intensified, the political ideas of Mondlane and the younger nationalists radicalized. He identified FRELIMO's efforts with those of similar liberation movements around the world fighting against colonialism and imperialism. His conception of society in an independent Mozambique was also revolutionized. Mondlane and the young revolutionaries opposed the exploitation of chiefs and traditional leaders as much as that of the Portuguese concession companies. They no longer thought of only an anti-colonial war for independence but a restructuring of society to insure political and economic equality with an end to 'the ex ploitation of man by man'. At the root of his revolutionary philosophy lay the goal of rebuilding Mozambican society, using the intensive solidarity of the revolutionary struggle to transform it into a state free from foreign or traditional exploitation.[28]

Side by side with the far-reaching goals of his programme, Mondlane advocated multiracialism and war against Portuguese colonialism, not Portuguese people—something that contributed to his being labelled a moderate by racialist-minded critics. But Mondlane was not moderate nor pro-American. Shrewd revolutionary that he was, he pursued his goals in a practical manner. He, therefore, took aid from the West as well as the Communist bloc. One American journalist wrote that the Central Intelligence Agency 'has been supporting a rebel group led by a pro-West nationalist named Eduardo Mondlane.'[29] Knowing the record of the United States, it seems plausible that the CIA would secretly fund a rebel movement while the American government supplied material to Portugal. If any such aid was given to Mondlane, it achieved no softening of FRELIMO's goals or means used toward them, anymore than technical assistance and weapons from the East made FRELIMO a blind instrument of the Soviet Union or China. Machel, Mondlane's successor, continued the leftward movement of FRELIMO, decidedly modelling its programmes and actions on those of the People's Republic of China which he visited three times.[30] This revolutionizing of FRELIMO's platform catalyzed some of the factionalism within the party's top ranks between reformers and revolutionaries. Similar reformist-revolutionist conflicts blazed within nationalist ranks in Angola and Guinea-Bissau with even more murderous consequences in the case of the former country.

The first splinterings from FRELIMO occurred early in its history. When Mondlane returned to the United States for his last year of teaching, he left as his 'personal representative' the enigmatic figure of Leo Clinton Aldridge, Jr (alias Leo Milias) who served as Publicity Secretary. Born in Texas, Aldridge tried to pass himself off as a Mozambican of Zulu parentage. When denounced as an ambitious impostor, he expelled several ranking members including Gumane and Mabunda, both of whom he had arrested by the Tanganyikan police. The internal factions of the newly founded front enabled him to pull off these expulsions. During the fall of 1962, other FRELIMO members resigned either to reconstitute old parties or establish new ones. Amazingly Aldridge now Secretary of Defence and Security, lasted until August 1964 when he was exposed as a black American impostor and expelled by the Central Committee.[31] Revengefully, he accused Mondlane of being a CIA agent. It remains unclear to what extent Alridge generated factionalism or exploited its presence, but less uncertain are the results of the dissension.

Fragmentation of political entities in southern Africa politics is a phenomenon with roots in the pre-European past with succession disputes and an individual's rallying to a strong overlord in times of stress. Splintering within Mozambican ranks was as old as the resistance to Portuguese colonialism. During the national liberation war, the opportunism among the leaders of mini-parties and their want of maturity and resolve helps explain the *dementia emigrantis* that infected many who were refugees first and genuine revolutionaries last. The full role of PIDE in these fractures cannot be ascertained until its records are opened, but certainly it stood ready to encourage dissension within FRELIMO ranks. What splits took place in FRELIMO, however, occurred with much more devastating consequences to other nationalist causes which sometimes spawned a dizzying proliferation of groups and internecine quarrels.

Among the first to break ranks with FRELIMO was Gwambe, a founder of UDENAMO who ambitiously grasped for the presidency of the national front. The Tanganyikan authorities ejected him for being a Portuguese agent and later the Central Committee excluded him from the front. In Kampala, Uganda he established the Comité Secreto da Restauração da UDENAMO and later reformed it as UDENAMO-Monomotapa. Travelling to Cairo, Gumane and Mabunda, both of whom had been dismissed from the national front by Aldridge, formed UDENAMO-Moçambique, and Mmole reorganized MANU. Meeting in Kampala in May 1963, Mmole, Gwambe and Sebastene Sikauke of the Mozambican African National Congress (MANCO) merged into a front called the Frente Unida Anti-Imperialista Popular Africana de Moçambique (FUNIPAMO). They accused Mondlane of fostering tribalism and regionalism within the movement.[32] When some six more members of the FRELIMO Central Committee were read out of the party, they banded together in the Mozambique Revolutionary Council (MORECO) which joined UDENAMO-Moçambique in late 1964.

This fracturing alarmed African state leaders as well as some heads of the factions, for it undercut pan-African unity and weakened the struggle against the Portuguese. In February 1965, a serious attempt was made between UDENAMO-Moçambique and FRELIMO for unification, but disagreement over the number and power of central committee posts each movement would receive ended the talks and outraged Gumane at Mondlane's poor offer.[33] Under the auspices of Zambia's President Kenneth Kaunda, the representatives of the contending groups met in Lusaka in June 1965. These reunification talks partially foundered when Mondlane departed after the delegates of other organizations rejected his offer that they join FRELIMO as individuals and not groups. Thereupon the representatives of the remaining four parties—the two UDENAMO movements, MANCO and MANU—sank their differences and coalesced into the Comité Revolucionário de Moçambique (COREMO). The new organization established a headquarters in Lusaka with the Zambian government's permission and elected Gwambe as its first President. Within a year, the old charges of Gwambe's connection with the Portuguese resurfaced and he was expelled from COREMO. Gumane became president.

After its formation COREMO constituted a second, although smaller, movement engaged in limited political action and some guerrilla warfare in Mozambique. Gumane and COREMO spokesmen were more modest in their battle reports of Portuguese casualties than FRELIMO claims. By the same token, its success in gaining international aid and support also proved much more modest than its Tanzanian-based rival. Despite a determined effort at the Tenth Session of the OAU's African Liberation Committee (ALC) in 1967, COREMO failed to gain anything but *de facto* recognition of its activities. It was denied financial and material assistance and even permission to set up a branch office in Dar es Salaam where the ALC maintained its headquarters.

COREMO spokesmen reported a shooting incident in which FRELIMO guerrillas were said to have killed three members of one of their patrols in Tete in February 1972. Gumane complained of the 'massacre' to FRELIMO and President Kaunda. FRELIMO representatives in Zambia replied that African soldiers in the Portuguese army had shot the COREMO men.[34] Apparently no more incidents took place, which points more to the absence of

COREMO guerrilla operations than to the effectiveness of Gumane's warning to FRELIMO. The lack of OAU endorsement or of battlefield success did not prevent COREMO from getting an occasional favourable comment from a foreign journalist nor dim its hopes of emerging from relative obscurity in the topsy-turvy politics of southern Africa. By war's end COREMO, however, ceased to be a serious contender for power.

The formation of COREMO failed to stop the expulsions, cleavages and defections. Following his dislodgement from COREMO, Gwambe put together yet another group, Partido Popular de Moçambique (PAPOMO). Still another faction splintered off COREMO to become União Nacional Africana da Rombézia (UNAR) with a headquarters in Blantyre. This micro-party's unrealistic programme called for Malawi to control the territory between the Rovuma and Zambezi rivers in return for Portugal's domination of the southern two-thirds of Mozambique and support of the UNAR against FRELIMO. Malawi with its territorial aspirations over fellow Nyanja-speaking people in Zambia and Mozambique may have given some countenance to the plan.

The commencement of military action in Mozambique helped to obscure to outsiders the simmering conflicts which openly erupted after Mondlane's assassination in 1969. Even before his death there existed significant telltales that all was not well within FRELIMO. A series of still inadequately explained deaths of FRELIMO militants—Filipe Magaia, Paula Kankhomba and Jaime Siguake—happened between 1966 and 1968. Amid the murders, which could not be directly attributed to the Portuguese, speculation turned on the possibility of infighting within the FRELIMO hierarchy. Misgivings were confirmed when in 1968 a student revolt broke out at the Mozambique Institute and a dispute flared at the second party congress.

Founded in 1963, the Mozambique Institute in Tanzania prepared Mozambican students for higher education abroad and taught nursing and teaching skills for primary instruction. The institute was conceived as the apex of FRELIMO's educational system. On Mozambican soil, the front established mobile 'bush schools' to provide primary schooling for children and literacy campaigns for adults along with a programme of political education to spread FRELIMO doctrine. Headed by Mrs Mondlane who received an MA from Boston University, the Mozambique Institute enjoyed success in gaining aid, securing foreign instructors and placing students abroad. Dissatisfaction with the curriculum, progress of the war, Mrs Mondlane's control over the school and her alleged ties to the CIA, caused disagreements between students and staff. But the underlying conflict revolved around the unwillingness of the educated youths to participate in the war effort. Lured by examples of their privileged counterparts in independent Africa, they chose to snipe at the FRELIMO leadership. The public manifestation of the turmoil burst forth in March 1968 when the students, inflamed by Father Mateus Gwenjere, a young priest from central Mozambique, struck. A severe critic of Mondlane, he accused FRELIMO's president of being a 'traitor' because he 'moves too slowly and speaks too softly'.[35] Whipped up by Gwenjere, the students succeeded in closing the institute until the following January. The secondary school reopened down the coast at Bagamoyo to remove students from the 'temptations of city life'.

This was not Mondlane's first conflict with students. The year before he faced similar criticism from Mozambican students studying in the United States, some of whom proved reluctant to join the struggle. Mondlane censured them for allowing their 'egotistical tendencies' to obstruct their 'total participation in the struggle' by not returning to the war after their education, often arranged by FRELIMO. In May 1968, some of the students in UNEMO replied in a mimeographed paper calling Mondlane a 'puppet of American interests' and a failure.[36]

Also in May 1968, dissident elements (some sources say Makonde militants who bore a disproportionate share of the fighting) raided FRELIMO's main office in Dar es Salaam and stabbed one staff member to death. A partial explanation of some of this bitter dissent came to light at FRELIMO's second party congress in July 1968.

FRELIMO held its second party congress in Niassa district both to prove its occupation of Mozambican soil and to resolve internal pressures. In attendance were about 150 delegates from many parts of the country. Organizationally, the most important outcome was the expansion of the Central Committee from 24 members to 44 to provide representation for younger party militants who had achieved positions of responsibility in the course of the war. It was decided that between meetings of the Central Committee, which confined itself to legislative matters, the Executive Committee (comprised of the President, Vice-President and various department heads) would deal with urgent problems in managing the war and political affairs.

From Basil Davidson, a British journalist and historian who attended the congress as a sympathetic observer, it is learned that the congress revealed to the delegates a schism between the conservative Makonde leaders from Cabo Delgado and the more radical nationalists from that district and other areas. Since the political delegates from Cabo Delgado boycotted the congress, the showdown took place afterwards. At the southern Tanzanian town of Mtwara in August, the established Makonde leaders, led by the elderly Kavandame, challenged FRELIMO's increasingly revolutionary social programme and disclosed a scheme for a separatist movement. Ethnic separatism had long produced strong feelings among the older Makonde strongmen. It seems that Kavandame and the União Makonde de Moçambique only joined FRELIMO when they realized the need for wider-based support to fight Portuguese colonialism. Gradually, they became alarmed at FRELIMO's revolutionary development which undermined their original separatist and reformist programme.[37]

Threaded between the reformist-revolutionist discord was the fact that some Makonde resented bearing the burden of the fighting in the beginning stages of the war and sharing power with militants from other ethnic groups and regions. Educationally, southerners, who lived close to Portuguese and mission schools, enjoyed an edge over people from remoter regions. This advantage was reflected by their predominance in the top ranks of the front.

Young Makonde militants such as Alberto-Joaquim Chipande and Lourenço Raimundo rose in the FRELIMO hierarchy and were less concerned with the loss of power and status of traditional leaders. Their endorsement of FRELIMO's national and revolutionary programmes threatened the old guard. At the Mtwara meeting, Kavandame's hopes for a Biafran-type breakaway state evaporated when Tanzanian officials refused to grant support or financing as they had to Biafra after its secession from Nigeria. Provincial Secretary Kavandame temporarily accepted unity. Before his defection to the Portuguese, he had been removed from office on grounds of profiteering.

Signs of greater dissension higher up the leadership ladder came to light after Mondlane's death on 3 February 1969. That morning

Mondlane kept to his routine of going, when nagging paper work required concentration, to the seaside bungalow of a wealthy American friend Betty King to work free from the noise and congestion of FRELIMO's cramped office on Nkrumah Street. At his desk, he opened a Moscow-postmarked package containing a book which exploded killing Mondlane and nearly destroying the small building. Rumours and accusations flew as to the identity of the assassin. Three years later the Tanzanian police made public the results of their investigation with Interpol.[38] They reported that the bomb had been assembled in Lourenço Marques, probably with the help of the Portuguese, and carried to Dar es Salaam by two FRELIMO dissidents—Kavandame, who defected soon after the murder, and Silveirio Nungu, who was executed by FRELIMO. At the FRELIMO-hosted 'show trials' shortly before Mozambique's independence, Simango confessed that he and Nungu had knowingly transported the bomb from Tete to Mondlane.[39]

Mondlane's death, whatever the facts surrounding it, brought into the open wide splits within the top-rank and set-off a succession struggle of which the outcome has been easier to determine than the behind-the-scenes squabbles. Apparently, Vice-President Simango lacked the endorsement of the younger members and the military to assume automatically the presidency. A crucial meeting of the Central Committee in April to select a successor revealed deep divisions between militants and moderates, bureaucrats and soldiers. Consequently, Simango was forced to share power in the Council of the Presidency with dos Santos and the previously little-known Secretary of Defence, Samora Moisés Machel. A former medical student born in Gaza in 1933, Machel had been among the earliest recruits sent for guerrilla warfare training in Algeria. He replaced the first Secretary of Defence Filipe Magaia who was killed in October 1966. Machel was also Commander-in-Chief of the Armed Forces. This triumvirate dissolved in November 1969 with the expulsion of Simango and the ascendancy of Machel to the presidency. Dos Santos retained his post as Secretary of Political Affairs, and Mrs Mondlane stayed on at the Mozambique Institute.

Simango's ouster was sealed by his publication of a 13-page report in which he charged that FRELIMO was riven by 'sectarianism, regionalism and tribalism', causing fratricide quarrels. He accused Mrs Mondlane of being a 'source of massive corruption' and his fellow triumvirs of hatching murder plots.[40] In political philosophy, he associated himself with the conventional nationalism and elitism of Gwenjere and Kavandame, all of whom later confessed to being Portuguese agents. Unless his demands were met for the resignation and trial of Machel and dos Santos, he threatened to resign. Such bitter denunciations and a desperate threat indicated the deterioration of Simango's position, for he broke party regulations by issuing to the press his report of internal matters and foolishly challenging his associates to resign—something he must have known they would not do. If this confrontation was meant to rally adherents to his cause, it had little prospect of success. Simango's role in the party's functions had shrivelled as the military wing's strength mounted and as the movement evolved along a more radical path. Privately, he had complained of the absence of meaningful duties even before Mondlane's death. A few months after his open break with the leadership, he adopted an equally unsuccessful ultra-left appeal to curry Chinese favour at a meeting of the OAU's African Liberation Committee. After his ejection by an emergency meeting of the Executive Committee, Simango left Tanzania under police escort and subsequently persisted in his venomous triades against living and dead FRELIMO members. Finally, he joined COREMO, and Machel became President. Machel's triumph signalled not only the pre-eminence of the military in FRELIMO's operations in Mozambique but also the rise of the military activists within the party. The bureaucratic tail in Dar es Salaam would no longer wag the front.

Other departures followed.[41] In November 1969, Dr Miguel Murupa, Secretary of External Relations, defected to the Portuguese after falling out with FRELIMO earlier in the year. A personal appointee of Mondlane, a university graduate (Howard University) and a high office holder in the liberation front, Murupa's desertion was a much-celebrated *coup* for the Portuguese. Later, he held a press conference for their benefit testifying that FRELIMO had fallen under a 'communist takeover' and that 'no real nationalism existed in Mozambique but rather exasperation over racial inequalities and slowness with which Portuguese applied their principles of racial integration.'[42] The Portuguese treated him well. First he worked for the Psychological Warfare Department of the army, then Jardim's *Notícias da Beira* and finally *Voz Africana*.[43] As an associate editor of *Voz Africana*—a weekly catering to African readers—Murupa was not a perfect puppet.

Occasionally, Murupa and the paper criticized the government for not fulfilling its promises of health and education facilities for the African population.

Desertions also hit at FRELIMO's army. Guerrilla soldiers in small numbers deserted to the Portuguese, just as Portuguese troops crossed over to FRELIMO. Both antagonists publicized with relish the surrenders of their opponents, playing up the importance of the defections and their loss to the enemy. In 1971, the Portuguese exaggeratedly claimed 3,000 defectors 'came over to us'.[44] Two years later the Portuguese touted that two military com- manders—Jeremias de Lazaro of Doa camp in eastern Tete and Zeca Caliante of the southern Zambezi sector—had turned their coats.

Likewise ephemeral groups kept hiving off FRELIMO after Mondlane's death either to denounce the parent organization or announce a 'new commitment to the struggle', and then faded away quickly and quietly. Two such groups were: Mozambique Liber- ation Movement (MOLIMO) organized by Henriques Nyankale in mid-1970, and Mozambique United Front (FUMO) led by Mar- celino Nbule in June 1971.[45] Many of the former FRELIMO leader- ship came together in a hastily formed coalition (which will be noted in chapter 9) at the conclusion of the war in 1974.

The proliferation of tiny parties and disgruntled defectors had more to do with the enormous pressures and frustrations en- countered in exile politics and the harsh rigours of guerrilla warfare than the justice of the Porguguese cause. Similar fissiparous tendencies have marked southern Africa's history and plagued revolutionary movements there and around the world. FRELIMO's development from a conventional nationalist movement, frustrated in achieving a quick assumption of power, to a party bent on a Maoist social revolution generated factions which were embittered by ethnic and personality differences. There is little doubt the PIDE fanned this infighting with paid agents and informers.[46] The radicalization of the party's leadership, which accompanied the split-offs of moderate and conservative elements, was as important as the battles fought against the Portuguese army.[47] This revolutionizing process is more likely to affect the course of Mozambique's future than the skirmishes in the bush.

A detailed discussion of expulsions and discord obscures FRELIMO's unrivalled advances and growth in comparison with other movements in the Portuguese territories or southern Africa during the period. The political mobilization of the population within guerrilla-dominated zones and FRELIMO's growing sympathy throughout the country appears to have gone on unimpaired by discord at the party's top. That fractures existed within Mozambican nationalism is a fact of its history. Sympathizers in the United States and Britain, however, became outraged or concerned when factionalism was openly discussed at African studies conferences or in books such as Richard Gibson's *African Liberation Movements*.[48] Their fears of the possible debilitating effects of an untrammelled examination of Mozambique's independence struggle overcame their faith that the tree of liberty had taken firm root in African soil. No amount of study of disunity could minimize the fact that Mozambican nationalism developed into a political-military front that the Portuguese were unable to defeat in spite of greater resources and capitalization on the splits. That is the more important fact of Mozambique's independence history.

9

THE WAR FOR NATIONAL LIBERATION

Warfare between African and Portuguese was as old as the European presence in Mozambique. The conflict in pre-colonial Mozambique ebbed and flowed, diffused and crystallized over the centuries. Peace was rare. Despite Portuguese successes in enlisting African auxiliaries into their forces, past and modern, the century-old antagonism persisted and in itself shaped the determination of each to endure a protracted guerrilla war. Thus steeled, both sides drew strength of conviction and inspiration of ultimate victory from their historical struggle. Portugal's history in Mozambique was replete with the 'heroic' deeds of *conquistadores*, soldier-administrators and recently medal bedecked paratroopers. African nationalists for their part pointed with pride to the stubborn last-ditch stands of Gungunyane, Zambezi chiefs and the Barue royal houses, and it along with hopes of a brave, new Mozambique fostered a resolve to win the war of national liberation. Locked in a seemingly endless unconventional war, African guerrilla and Portuguese soldier were committed for historical as well as ideological convictions to defeat their opponent.

As in the old time campaigns, Lisbon successfully recruited large numbers of black fighting men into its ranks, and Africans again found their brothers pitted against them. What made this war fundamentally different from previous conflicts was the high degree of ideological commitment subscribed to by both sides. As a consequence, some Portuguese joined the Africans (not for the self serving reasons of the early *prazo senhors*) or sympathized with their revolutionary programme. Ironic though it appears, the revolutionary ideology of an African nationalist party influenced Portuguese army officers against their own government; it was not deflected by Lisbon's dream to Latinize black Mozambicans or to perpetuate the fiction of Mozambique as an overseas province of Portugal. The war for Mozambique's national liberation was then as much a struggle for the mind of the people as for the land itself. The result was a war of bitterness and cruelty where bombast often substituted for fact.

Facts about guerrilla conflicts are much like the encounters themselves—shadowy, hit-and-run and frequently inconclusive. The very nature of guerrilla warfare with its heavy reliance on propaganda infused with holy-cause ideology from incumbent, challenger and sympathizer makes for few reliable documents or dispassionate observers. A draconian Portuguese censorship over the domestic and foreign press cut down the outflow of factual information. Nationalists also muddied the picture by turning out communiqués proclaiming huge, one-sided defeats of the Portuguese in which the enemy lost hundreds of soldiers and tons of war equipment to the cost of a handful of guerrillas. Truth is, therefore, the first casualty of guerrilla warfare. The following overview is offered with few illusions to pinpoint accuracy.

Whereas in Angola the Portuguese were caught unprepared for the scale and carnage of the half expected rebellion, in Mozambique their forces awaited since the formation of FRELIMO an attack across the northern border. Even before the Angolan explosion a series of defensive and anti-subversive measures were undertaken, which were intensified after the tumult in the west African colony and the independence of Tanzania. PIDE arrested suspects and penetrated opposition groups. In May 1961, the police executed chief Zimtambira Chicusse from the Angonia region around Vila Coutinho. He had been under surveillance or in detention since 1955 for seditious statements and activities.[1] Once hostilities commenced in Mozambique, the police and army tightened security to a greater degree. The Centro Associativo dos Negros de Moçambique was banned, and its president, Arouca, was imprisoned for subversion in 1965. The next year Malangatana, Craveirinha, Honwana and Rui Nogar, a poet of European ancestry, were tried, given varying prison terms and closely watched upon release. Some thirty others were accused of involvement with FRELIMO and sentenced to terms ranging from six months to eight years. Unluckier victims of the security dragnet simply disappeared.

The army expanded its ranks from 4,000 soldiers to 35,000 between 1961 and 1964. The government trained whites in civil defence organizations, eased permits for arms purchase and issued anti-sabotage instructions before the upheaval in Angola.[2] Along the Tanzanian border, the expected place of attacks, the army built a network of landing strips, dug in mortar emplacements and patrolled the 500 mile frontier. But it had no armoured vehicles for road patrols and only five aircraft, none of which were helicopters, at the start of the war. Its two small gunboats could not halt infiltration along the Lake Malawi coast.

To separate the Makonde people from their kinsmen in Tanzania, the government forcefully resettled them away from lands adjacent to the border. Thousands of Makonde streamed into Tanzania with reports of hut burning and coercion. In 1965, there were 10,000 refugees, mostly Makonde, in Tanzania. By 1971, the figure increased to 55,000 and a further 5,000 Nyanja-speaking refugees in Zambia and Malawi.[3] The Mozambican Makonde, who swelled FRELIMO's ranks, had been without strong Portuguese influence or control; the first garrison of a few Portuguese soldiers was established in 1918 and civilian administration not until 1931. Only three years before the nationalist war, tax collection had been less than 5 per cent in the region. Knowledge of Tanzania's independence also contributed to a certain Makonde rebelliousness that was exacerbated by Portuguese defence measures.[4]

Lisbon attempted to awaken or reinforce black and white political and sentimental identification with Portugal. In July 1964, the Portuguese President Américo R. Tómas made a two-week, confetti-and-bunting tour which was greeted by large, officially-encouraged crowds of Africans and Europeans. At instances, Africans broke the police cordons to kiss the hand of the white uniformed figure whose cruise ship stopped along the coast for brief inland tours. Despite a certain chill in the northern regions around Vila Cabral, official sources commented that the tour 'showed the world that peace, progress and racial harmony exist in Mozambique.'[5] Less than two months later 'peace and racial harmony' were cast into doubt by the start of the war for national liberation.

THE WAR BEGINS

FRELIMO began military preparations in June 1963 by dispatching select recruits to Algeria and the United Arab Republic for training as guerrilla fighters and political cadres.[6] When FRELIMO opened hostilities, it had by its own estimates some 250 men in Mozambique. In August 1964, one month before the attack, a small band of marauders led by one time MANU leader Lucas

Fernandes struck a hunting party killing a Dutch priest from the Catholic mission at Nangolo and a few of his African companions. The action of the raïders, who were captured or killed by the army, alerted the government forces and probably precipitated FRELIMO's combat plans. For military and propaganda reasons, FRELIMO militants were ordered to hit some minor administrative positions on the Makonde plateau in Cabo Delgado district on September 25, 1964.

In spite of government preparations, the initial strikes enjoyed limited, local success, for the insurgents hit from within the country and not as expected from across the border. Using unconventional warfare tactics of ambushing patrols, sabotaging communications and hit-and-run raids on lightly defended posts and then fading into the inaccessible Makonde highlands, groups of ten to fifteen militants evaded pursuit and surveillance. Co-operation of the Makonde enabled FRELIMO bands to gain food and information about government countermanoeuvres.

The guerrilla's initial gains encouraged the FRELIMO high command to mount small-scale raids in Niassa district. Whether to achieve a diversion (as FRELIMO maintained) or from faulty judgment (as the Portuguese army claimed) the guerrillas also initiated campaigns in the districts of Zambézia and Tete in November. Both campaigns diverted some government troops from the northern areas, but proved premature and were aborted until later in the war. One FRELIMO document reflects expectations of a 'real national insurrection' with the commencement of fighting, but nothing approaching the scale of the Angolan rebellion materialized.[7] At the war's outset, FRELIMO had scant prospect of a military victory; its hope lay in a war of attrition to compel a negotiated independence from Lisbon. Want of a democratic society in Portugal ruled out the likelihood of open opposition to the war. Still, FRELIMO and nationalist movements in other Portuguese colonies fought with the goal of making the war so costly that eventually Portugal would withdraw — a goal made difficult by loans from the United States and West Germany and arms from NATO.[8] Portugal fought its own version of protracted warfare. Apart from the large, conventional sweeps to uproot the guerrillas, it tried to confine the insurgency to the remote, less profitable regions of the country, allowing life to proceed as normal in the European populated, wealthy zones. Had the Portuguese succeeded with a minimum of expenditure and casualties, the war could have remained undecided for much longer. But the expense in blood and treasure, not military defeat, cost Lisbon the war; its army was never destroyed on the battlefield, although some of its officers were converted to FRELIMO's revolutionary social goals for Portugal.

Taking advantage of its following among the Makonde, FRELIMO closed down the sisal plantations near Mocímba da Praia, which the army found too vulnerable and unprofitable to defend. But built-up, populated areas were avoided as the guerrillas attempted to consolidate their position in the backcountry while inflicting a few casualties and reducing their own. South and east of the Makonde plateau the guerrilla advance ran into one of the ethnic animosities that have plagued Mozambique's past anti-Portuguese fronts. The traditional hostility of the Makua to the Makonde was played upon by the Portuguese to hamper guerrilla infiltration below the Messalo River. It seems that FRELIMO achieved minor headway among them toward the end of the war, but in the main the Makua acted as buffer to guerrilla penetration.

During the first half of 1965 FRELIMO fighters, preceded by political cadres, gained a stronghold in the highlands of Niassa district among the Nyanja-speaking peoples, a majority who live in Malawi. Many of those who live in Mozambique along the Lake Malawi coast speak English and are Portestant, which is attributed to two Anglican missions established since the late nineteenth century at Messumba in Niassa and on Licoma Island, Malawi territory only three miles off the Niassa coastline. In the recent past, the British-financed Niassa Company further arrested Portuguese influence and administration in the northern tier of Mozambique. Like the Makonde, the Nyanja accounted for many of the men in the guerrilla forces. The Yao, who also live in Niassa, joined the ranks of the Portuguese army as Lisbon exploited their differences with the Makonde. They like the Makua bore an Islamic imprint. This heightened the irony that Catholic Portugal's African soldiers practiced the same religion of its greatest foes of bygone conflicts. Toward the conclusion of the war some of the anti-FRELIMO animosity among the Makua and Yao seems to have broken down but the degree is difficult to gauge.

Among a friendly population the guerrillas rapidly swept down the isolated and rugged terrain on the eastern bank of the lake, and temporarily threatened Nova Freixo, then a railhead for the only trans-country railway within hundreds of miles. The Portuguese counteroffensive pushed the guerrillas back northward but could not dislodge them from a rectangular zone of territory stretching the length of the lake, then to the town of Catur and up to the Tanzanian border. The Portuguese retained control of Vila Cabral, Catur and the small posts, but much of the countryside was liberated from their permanent military and administrative authority. By too rapidly advancing, the guerrillas overextended themselves and suffered one of their most serious reverses of the war. In the future 'politicization and mobilization,' which sometimes involved coercion or kidnapping of pro-government leaders and policemen, preceded military action by 50 miles or more.

During the summer of 1965, two small detchments moved from Malawi into the Zambézia district to strike at the tea-planting country between Milange and Tacune, but the Portuguese army and Malawi's President Kamuzu Banda stopped for a time subsequent attacks.[9] Soon after, COREMO infiltrated political cadres into the Tete district from their base in Zambia with the mission of training the population for a 'massive rising at a propitious time,' but their efforts came to naught. The Portuguese, who regarded COREMO as an inconsequential military threat, killed the movement's Secretary for External Affairs, Mazunzo Bobo, near the Malawi border in February 1968. COREMO's most publicized action occurred in January 1971 when its militants supposedly attacked the Mukangadzi settlement near the Cabora Bassa Dam. They caused damage and casualties, and the raiders captured six Portuguese agricultural experts (later reported killed) before making good their escape to Zambia. The use of Zambia as a guerrilla sanctuary and its alleged role in the kidnapping touched of a series of secret meetings between Lisbon and Lusaka officials, and a temporary stoppage of Zambia's badly needed maize shipments at Beira.[10] Except for periodic incursions, little of note was heard of COREMO's military campaigns after the Mukangadzi assault. On the diplomatic front, its president Gumane journeyed to the United States and other countries in fruitless attempts to gain recognition and overt aid.

THE LULL IN THE FIGHTING

By 1968, FRELIMO's quick advances appeared slowed. The leadership, particularly Mondlane, came under criticism for the seemingly faltering . war effort. The causes were numerous: Portuguese resistance stiffened; the government's resettlement programme withdrew some civilian support from the guerrillas; FRELIMO's drives had outstripped administration in rebel-held zones; and the controversy (discussed in chapter 8) within the nationalist command over a consolidation period versus a sustained offensive perhaps diverted attention. In all, the nationalists claimed 'liberation' of one-fifth of Mozambique and one million people from Portuguese control in 1968. Not surprisingly, Portuguese estimates were considerably lower, usually about 8 per cent of the land and 200,000 inhabitants. The FRELIMO dominated zones included one tract of territory about 100 miles in width down the coast of Lake Malawi in Niassa and another on the Makonde plateau reaching southward to the Montepuez River in Cabo Delgado. But whatever the exact extent of FRELIMO domination, certainly less than its comminiques indicated, it was enough to provoke the Portuguese army into atrocities and the use of napalm and herbicides against suspected insurgent villages and crops.[11]

Another part of the army's plans to stem the guerrilla tide was the resettlement of inhabitants in contested areas in *aldeamentos,* or fortified villages. Increased Portuguese troop strength accounts for still another means used to block the guerrillas. FRELIMO sources maintained that by 1968 the army numbered between 65,000 and 70,000 men against their 8,000 man guerrilla force organized in companies and battalions.[12] Both sets of figures seem high. Although Portugal did not divulge its troop figures then, it probably had no more than 50,000 soldiers pitted against 4,000 guerrillas in squad and platoon size units.

Faced with a military slowdown in Niassa and Cabo Delgado, the FRELIMO high command decided on two dramatic courses of action for 1968: it held its second party congress on Mozambican soil, and opened a new front in the Tete district. Fighting there began in March. Candid Portuguese army personnel later admitted that with their focus on Cabo Delgado and Niassa they had been caught napping in Tete. Before the shooting started, FRELIMO mobilizers actively worked with the Chewas who also span the

Malawi, Rhodesia and Zambia borders. The Chewa formed an important, although only one, segment of the guerrillas in Tete. Their heavy participation along with the Nyanja and Makonde, however, led some government military leaders to conclude incorrectly even late in the war that Portugal faced only three distinct 'tribal uprisings.'[13]

Just as Tete had been the scene of many bloody battles in the past, so it became again a bitter arena between nationalist and Portuguese forces. Tete's abundant coal and mineral wealth greatly enhanced the strategic value of the Zambezi River. Beginning in 1969, the construction of the giant hydroelectric and development scheme at Cabora Bassa Gorge added a paramount symbolic and propaganda reason for spreading the insurgency. An apparent stalemate in the north furnished another reason for a new battleground.

The mammoth scope of the project and the firm commitment to remain in Mozambique it entailed on the part of the Portuguese brought forth violent condemnations from nationalists. Nothing that the dam would 'hold more than water,' they considered it a bulwark of modern day colonialism. Echoing President Kaunda's denunciation of it as 'a crime against humanity,' the guerrillas determined to 'bust the dam.' The decision to attack the project involved not only a extension of the war to Tete but also a change in FRELIMO policy. At the start of the fighting, FRELIMO leaders planned to avoid destruction of development schemes that independent Mozambicans would inherit.[14] In 1968, the symbolic value of halting the Cabora Bassa Dam outweighed a doubtful heritage.

Assaults on the site itself met with costly failure, because of the strenuous Portuguese defence; they encircled the area with three protective rings of crack troops and reportedly over a million mines. During the summer of 1971, FRELIMO turned with more success to ambushing and mining the work site's approaches. These stepped-up efforts interrupted the 275 mile flow of concrete (for a time it had to be flown in) and other materials, but the work, carried on day and night, proceeded ahead of the announced schedule.

Besides the Tete offensive, 1968 also witnessed FRELIMO's second party congress. Held with advance publicity in a wooded section of Niassa the meeting was something of a propaganda *coup*, for it demonstrated possession of territory. The Portuguese searched in vain until a reconnaissance plane discovered the spot on the last day of the congress. By the time the bombers arrived the following day the delegates had scattered. This was to be one of FRELIMO's last bright spots in the next couple of years.

FRELIMO's fortunes fell to a low ebb in 1969 as a result of uncertainty in the leadership after Mondlane's assassination, a large Portuguese counter-offensive, the temporary diversion of insurgent attention to consolidation of gains in the northern districts and preparation for further penetration southward. The wavering policy within the FRELIMO top ranks helps to account for the guerrilla's decline on the battlefield during the late 1960's. Uncertainty and controversy on the correct course to victory centered not only on whether to consolidate positions or attack new targets but also arose from the decision on which front to advance — Tete or the north.[15] Once the Tete front was opened, the guerrillas encountered sharp losses in direct attacks on the dam site until a switch in tactics in September 1971. Ambushing convoys, mining roads and blowing up bridges raised the Portuguese price in blood and treasure but did not halt the dam's progress.

Another temporary, although overrated by the Portuguese army, setback to FRELIMO forces took place in summer 1970 when the Portuguese mounted the largest counter offensive of the war. The recently appointed commander of forces in Mozambique, Brigadier-General Kaulza de Arriaga, launched a 10,000 troop drive concentrated on guerrilla strongholds in the vicinity of Mueda on the Makonde plateau and in the north-eastern highlands of Niassa. Arriaga's campaign differed from previous search and destroy missions by the objective of seizing and holding terrain. Code named operation 'Gordian Knot,' the offensive scored tactical surprise and local success. Air bombardments and helicopter borne troops swooped down on poitions previously considered impenetrable. Elite units parading on June 10 in Lourenço Marques to celebrate the Day of Portugal were engaged in combat on the Rovuma frontier that same evening.

Portuguese forces closed the principal infiltration routes across the river, surrounded guerrilla camps as large as 600 occupants, reopened roads and captured caches of arms which they later displayed. Lasting into the rainy months of spring, the drive of 35,000 troops disrupted the guerrilla network and resettled several thousand Makonde in *aldeamentos.* Arriaga, who gained a hardliner's reputation among army officers (some whites came to view his policies as too soft), proclaimed a military triumph that needed only the 'accompanying psychological and social operations' to 'achieve final victory.' Continued guerrilla activity was disparagingly dismissed 'as limited acts of banditry.'

Two guerrilla advances threw doubts on the highly touted 'victory' of Gordian Knot. Small groups of militants pushed south of the Messalo River in Cabo Delgado with the intention of cutting the road connecting Vila de Montepuez and Porto Amélia in February 1971. Although the guerrillas were unable to cross the Messalo in force or cut the road, they demonstrated an aggressiveness out of tune with reports of their defeat. More alarming to the Portuguese was FRELIMO's crossing of the Zambezi in Tete, probably first done in November 1970.

It also seems Portuguese losses were greater than anticipated in the Gordian Knot offensive. Arriaga's campaign improved the army's position, but his predecessors had managed to contain the guerrillas with a minimum of casualties. In 1971, two large drives — *Garrote* and *Apio* — were deemed necessary in Cabo Delgado despite army claims of the previous year to have 'wiped out' FRELIMO. Aside from a few similar sweeps, Arriaga shifted from such conventional campaigns to smaller unit actions employing white and black shock troops and emphasizing measures to terrorize or to persuade the African population that their best interests rested with Portugal.

THE ARMY'S RESPONSE

To limit FRELIMO's contact with the African population, the army intensified the *aldeamento* project that had been begun at the start of the war. Copied from British regroupment efforts in Burma and Malaya and the American strategic hamlets in Vietnam, the *aldeamento* scheme was intended to prevent the rural population from being infiltrated, influenced or attacked by the guerrillas. Government officials endorsed the plan because it better enabled them to gain the loyalty of formerly scattered peopled by furnishing education, medical care, sanitation and agricultural aid. Plans for improved living conditions appeared to be genuine, if for no other reason than to placate potential subversives, but funds and staff were usually inadequate. Outside of the showplace *aldeamentos* such as Chiulugo, near Vila Cabral, few had running water and electricity.[16]

At first, the army organized *aldeamentos* in disputed areas. In the north, for example, the government in 1966 announced the resettlement of 250,000 people in 150 villages from the 50-mile strip of land between the mouths of the Montepuez and Messalo rivers and running 100 miles inland. Later in the war, the army anticipated FRELIMO's advances and removed African peasants from the insurgent path. As the guerrillas penetrated into the central region of the country in 1973, the Provincial Secretary of Agriculture announced that by 1976 in the southern district of Gaza 900 families would be settled in Macalauane *aldeamento* on the left bank of the Limpopo, opposite the *colonato* of white settlers.[17] The number of resettled Africans steadily rose with the widening political and military scope of the war. In mid-1973 Arriaga stated that one million people had been moved into 1,000 *aldeamentos*. According to the general, the government had planned to shift all Africans to specified areas within five or six years.

The new villages, some of which comprised 1,500-3,000 inhabitants as opposed to traditional groups of twenty to thirty villagers, were placed near patrolled roads. Unlike traditional groupings, the inhabitants of the resettlement villages were instructed to build their huts in straight rows for control and surveillance. Residents farmed and grazed animals outside the village during the day, but they had to return at night. Not only were the villagers required to report missing neighbours and strangers to the Portuguese, but also in many *aldeamentos* they served in the militia.

Encircled by trenches and barbed wire, the *aldeamentos* were subjected to both nationalist criticism as concentration camps and to guerrilla sieges. FRELIMO rocketings of the villages lowered Portuguese military prestige and nullified any social benefits provided. Critics considered the widespread implementation of resettlement but a short step from the *apartheid* system of South Africa's Bantu Homelands. Caught in the cross fire between soldier and guerrilla, some Africans may have willingly opted for the relative protection of fortified villages with the promises of amenities and education. But the great majority of Africans had little choice than be removed from their ancestral lands, for to have done otherwise they would have risked death in a designated free-fire zone. Once inside, the fortified compound life still held many uncertainties for the resident. Harassment, extortion and rape of women residents by soldiers were noted in FRELIMO bulletins. The resettlement fueled the confrontation between ruler and subject among rural people, some of whom had previously little contact with Portuguese domination.[18] Nor did the *aldeamento* programme halt the spread of the war.

An ambitious extension of the *aldeamento* policy was initiated by Arriaga in the village construction at Nangade on the Rovuma, about 75 miles from the Indian Ocean coast. Army engineers constructed with African labour a town for 2,500 Makonde people. They put up concrete buildings for a school, post office, store and market. Instead of villagers building their own dwellings of mud and wattle, the engineers erected concrete homes, for which the occupants were reportedly to pay a small down payment and monthly rent for twenty years. According to official Portuguese sources, Lisbon dispatched farming and fishing experts to teach modern methods to the townspeople. Arriaga envisioned a string of modern towns in this 'operation border' from Nangade to the port of Palma with a tarred road connecting them as the best means to stop infiltration from Tanzania.[19] But as with so many belatedly begun Portuguese programmes, time would not wait.

The much older programme for the enlargement of European settlement was heartily endorsed during the war but with poor results. Unlike Angola where the white settlers had spread throughout the territory, those in Mozambique had concentrated in a few centres mainly in the south. Whereas Mozambique's Portuguese were largely untouched by the fighting, the Angolan settlers in the northern coffee plantations played a crucial role in the defence of the colony during the early stage of the rebellion in 1961. The Angolan settler's tenacity in hanging on despite sometimes hopeless odds demonstrated their worth to a hard-pressed colonial regime.

In Mozambique, General Arriaga redoubled efforts to settle Portuguese colonists in the northern rural and frontier zones, to hold land and to block guerrilla infiltration. The programme's first batch of immigrants to settle at Montepuez in Cabo Delgado and Nova Madeira in Niassa arrived in February 1971. Most of the 178 settlers were teenagers from the island of Madeira. The typical settlers lacked agricultural training making them unlikely farmers and unprepared to backcountry hardships. To establish a kibbutz-type defence mentality the government granted large allotments of land, 250 acres for crops and 350 for grazing, and supplied seeds, equipment and an allowance. Despite the prohibitive costs of establishing *colonatos* (sometimes $20,000 per family), Lisbon pressed ahead. The war, opportunities in Angola and immigration to Europe, however, retarded settlement, but the Junta Provincial de Povoamento (Provincial Council for Settlement) in Mozambique declared that 'about 800 European colonists arrive every month for settlement in the *colonatos*.'[20] A South African newspaper gave a much more realistic but still too high figure of about 1,000 settlers a year.[21] Whatever the exact number of immigrants, many were subsequently lured to the province's cities or to South Africa by better living conditions and higher pay.

The government's counterinsurgency response also included the construction and resurfacing of a network of roads. All-weather roads are a must in anti-guerrilla campaigns for mobility to help offset the element of surprise. FRELIMO's extensive use of mines added another compelling reason for tarred roads. The Portuguese had had little difficulty in detecting the metal mines first deployed by the nationalists, but after 1968 the guerrillas' new Chinese-made plastic mines took heavy tolls in dead and maimed.[22] After experiments with mine triggering vehicles failed against delayed fuses, the government turned to asphalt roads as the most effective way of reducing casualties and restoring morale. Land-mines and booby traps continued, however, to raise havoc on unpaved roads and in the *mato* ('bush').

Poverty accounts for only one explanation why Mozambique was without even a rudimentary road system before the wartime pressures impelled Portuguese soldiers to build roads where rutted paths had crisscrossed the land. Since most of the large urban centres are on the Indian Ocean littoral, coastal shipping served the trade and communication needs making an elaborate road system unnecessary. Military and economic development considerations spurred a change in viewpoint.

Most of the new roads linked the coastal cities with each other and the interior towns. Lourenço Marques, Beira and Tete were connected by tarred roads and bridges over the Save and Zambezi to facilitate north-south traffic. Although the mileage of asphalt road doubled between 1964 and 1972, it still stood at only 14,000 miles. Railway track was laid for similar reasons as roads were built but in much shorter distances. One important line linked Malawi with Nacala, via Vila Cabral.

Since air power for supply and military strikes forms an essential weapon in a counterinsurgency arsenal, the Portuguese upgraded Mozambique's airfields from two international airports capable of receiving Boeing 737 jets (or their equivalent) to nine. Scores of airstrips were bulldozed at smaller towns and fortified bases throughout the country, some of which were vital for resupply in contested zones. Hard facts on the Portuguese air force are difficult to come by, but it was certainly smaller and more often grounded from shortages of replacement parts than the nationalists' communiqués report of massive air strikes.[23]

Another counterinsurgency effort included an intensification of the old tactic of divide and rule. Among the Makua-Lomwe people, the Portuguese propagandized that FRELIMO was a Makonde dominated movement and that 'the Maconde tribe is the enemy of the Macua tribe, and the Macuas should join forces with the Portuguese to fight against the Maconde.'[24] Guerrilla leaders were aware of the manoeuvres by Portuguese African agents 'to undermine national unity' by ethnic and regional appeals.[25] Despite such attempts some Makua did join FRELIMO.[26] The guerrillas in fact steadfastly maintained that they were a multiracial organization. They attracted some white deserters and promoted some Europeans to high positions in the party.

Finally, the government responded to FRELIMO's widening of the war by greater efforts to Africanize its armed forces. By 1967, the manpower needs demanded the use of considerable drafts of black Mozambicans into the Portuguese military and para-military forces. After the outbreak of the Angolan revolt in which about 400 whites lost their lives, there was some initial reluctance in Mozambique to expand the African corps despite its long roots in Portuguese military tradition. But immediate gains outweighed potential risks, for Portugal realized several advantages by Africanizing the army: it reduced white casualties which increasingly worried Lisbon; it vastly augmented the army's manpower pool; it scaled down costs in transportation and training; it was designed to defuse criticism of Portugal perpetuating a racial war; it decreased the number of Portuguese opponents by pitting one African against another (some white racial cynics caluclated that the war improved the demographic balance by killing off blacks); and it hoped to give Africans a stake in the Portuguese war effort. The use of black troops also preserved the legacy of enlisting Africans to inflict corporal punishment on other Africans.

Along with attempts at the politicization, or 'mentalization' *(mentalização)*, of his troops, Arriaga (the 'rebel basher') recruited large numbers of black soldiers for regular and elite units. By 1974, Africans made up 60 per cent of the 70,000 soldiers in Mozambique according to official statements. In regular units the actual percentage of African troops was probably about half the propaganda figure, but when militia, police and elite units are counted, the overall number approximated the 60 per cent officially stated. The crack outfits contained voluntary defectors, Makua and Yao recruits and men without ethnic affiliations in the war zones. The Portuguese formed three elite organizations: *Grupo Especial* (GE), *Grupo Especial Paraquedista* (GEP) and *flechas* ('arrows'). Comprised of 90 per cent African volunteers the units underwent at Dondo Base, near Beira, specialized training in various missions: the GEs, ethnically alike, returned home after commando courses to function locally as an irregular force; the GEPs received paratrooper training before being formed into ethnically diverse units to broaden their operating regions; and the *flechas* consisted of commando trained black soldiers who worked like the guerrillas in small, self-supporting groups for the Direcção Geral de Segurança (DGS), which was the new name for PIDE after 1968. Many of the *flechas* had FRELIMO backgrounds and reportedly treated the guerrillas and their civilian supporters with an especial vengeance. Reliable estimates placed the number of special forces stationed in the north at between 10,000 and 12,000 men in 1973.[27] The deployment of elite units multiplied the difficulties facing the guerrillas, although the special troops were not without defections to FRELIMO.

THE CAMEL'S HUMP: THE WAR SPREADS

In spite of the army's stiff response, FRELIMO guerrillas knifed deeper into Tete during the early 1970s. Machel, FRELIMO's president and military commander, summed up the importance of Tete in 1972 when he said: 'Tete is like the camel's hump—it is where their [Portuguese] strengths and reserves are concentrated.'[28] Shifting forces from Cabo Delgado and Niassa to the north-western district, the guerrillas outflanked the Portuguese in the north and beefed up their assaults in April 1971 to a point where Lisbon felt compelled to fuse the military and civilian power in Tete under a top army officer in order to better coordinate its defence.

In September 1971, the first insurgent landmine exploded on the Tete section of the road linking Salisbury and Blantyre. Strategically and more so psychologically, the incident and subsequent minings and ambushes demonstrated not only the limits of the government's counterinsurgency programme but also slashed the sole land route between the Republic of South Africa, the linchpin of white rule in the southern end of the continent, and its client state of Malawi. The guerrilla activities brought forth aggressive actions from the army: it undertook further resettlement of several thousand Africans and distributed leaflets showing and stating that it would shoot civilians crossing the Zambezi, holding them to be 'bandits.' A flood of 2,000 refugees crossed the Rhodesian frontier and 3,000 more moved into Malawi in December 1971, claiming to be victims of army atrocities. Inexorably, small groups of guerrillas pressed southward until they edged into Manica e Sofala (administrated as two districts—Vila Pery and Beira—after 1972) to begin hostilities in a fourth district in July 1972.

The Rhodesians, never impressed with Portuguese martial vigour since World War I, sounded alarm at the guerrilla advances toward their road and rail lifelines from Umtali across Mozambique to Beira. As in the times of the Mwene Mutapas, so in the present, a threat to central Mozambique was synonymous with a threat to the Rhodesian plateau. Because of mine-laying on the Salisbury-Blantyre road, the Rhodesian white-rebel government declared it 'unsafe' and took a more active interest in its neighbour's defences, committing troops and aircraft for specific missions. Contrary to Salisbury's denials, its troops operated in Mozambique on the minimum in hot pursuit actions since at least (and probably before) April 1971 when the first Rhodesian soldier was killed by a mine. Rhodesian apprehensions proved well founded, for in 1972 the insurgents expanded their activities to cut another artery.

Operating from bases in Malawi (President Banda denied the existence of FRELIMO staging points claiming that only unarmed Mozambicans were allowed transit through territory) the guerrillas repeatedly mined a 100-mile stretch of track on the railway between Beira and Tete. More importantly for Rhodesia, it came under direct assault in December 1972, when after four years of peace, African nationalists reattacked in the northeast corner. There was obvious coordination of tactics and strategic goals between FRELIMO and the Zimbabwe African National Union (ZANU) that became more apparent as the war continued.* FRELIMO's southerly advances naturally favoured the Rhodesian insurgents by lengthening the border of their sanctuary from which they struck.

Halfway through 1973 small advance groups of FRELIMO militants had fanned out to just north of the Púnguè which flows into the Indian Ocean at Beira, 60 miles above the Umtali-Beira rail and road connections. Soon afterwards, the guerrillas raided the periphery of the Gorongosa game reserve leading to the cancellation of safari parties from abroad and the departure of professional hunters for the Central African Republic. These minor incidents in the Gorongosa (northwest of Beira), one of Mozambique's most celebrated tourist attractions, had no strategic value, but they did demoralize the Portuguese population. The guerrillas quickening pace can be partly attributed to efforts to beat the plans for filling the lake behind Cabora Bassa in late 1974. Stretching from the dam to the Zambia-Rhodesia border, the artificial lake was expected to cut infiltration routes and hamper guerrilla operations south of the Zambezi.

The introduction of Chinese, Russian and Czech weapons, the help of Chinese guerrilla experts in FRELIMO's Tanzanian bases and the greater military sophistication of the guerrillas were apparent in the nationalists' advances. Popular local backing also assisted the guerrillas. Remembering their resistance to Portuguese occupation a century before, the people of the Zambezi region, and particularly the Shona, rallied to FRELIMO. Guerrillas continued to strike at night and to inflict maximum damage in sharp, violent fire-fights before melting into the *mato*. But under reportedly Chinese instruction they scaled down the size of units to six-man

---

*   Zimbabwe, derived from the ancient Karanga ruins, is the nationalist term for Rhodesia which they disapproved of having been taken from the name of Cecil Rhodes, in their view the arch-imperialist of southern Africa.

groups, the so-called 'tactics of the ants.' Smaller units multiplied the number of raids and diminished the groups vulnerability to retaliation and supply. The use of Soviet AK 47 assault rifles and 122-mm rocket launchers sometimes increased the firepower of the individual guerrilla fighter beyond the individual Portuguese soldier. The rocket shelling of such targets as Estima, a defence base about 20 miles from the Cabora Bassa Dam, caused concern in the summer of 1973 among candid Portuguese officers. That spring Soviet ground-to-air missiles fired by insurgents of the PAIGC downed their first Portuguese aircraft in Guinea-Bissau. When this was followed by more 'kills,' army officers voiced fear of similar missiles challenging the government's mastery of Mozambique's skies. At war's end, no ground to air missiles, however, had been fired in Mozambique, but FRELIMO reported the downing of enemy planes by sophisticated employment of conventional weapons from time to time.[29] The crippling of Portugal's rule came on the ground and not in the air.

Beginning 1974 with a propaganda and military bang, the guerrillas on New Year's Eve derailed a mail and passenger train on the Beira-Umtali line. The worst fears of the Rhodesians had been confirmed. Within the next three months, a chain of encounters substantiated the fact that the rail assault was not to be an isolated strike: the Beira-Tete line was hit repeatedly and guerrilla units began a hit-and-run shelling of the military base at Inhaminga, 90 miles north of Beira on the road to Malawi. But for an entirely new twist in guerrilla tactics, the Portuguese population may have remained satisfied with the army's efforts to contain these latest flare-ups. Now for the first time the guerrillas raided for psychological reasons a white-owned farm killing one European. This raid was followed by other attacks on Europeans and white farms around the towns of Vila Pery and Vila de Manica. Attacks on whites in rural areas had been a part of Rhodesian guerrilla operations since the early 1960s, but similar assaults in Mozambique represented a *volte-face* (if in fact the guerrillas were responsible) in FRELIMO actions and doctrine.[30] Up to this point the nationalist declared a war on 'Portuguese colonialism and not against the Portuguese people.' By this FRELIMO had dispelled charges of 'black racism,' and reassured settlers of their acceptance in an African controlled independent Mozambique.

The deaths of less than a half-dozen settlers provoked two days of angry white demonstrations in Beira against the army and Lisbon's handling of the war. Shortly afterwards, railway workers halted work to protest the lack of safety on the Beira-Tete line following the death of a conductor at the hands of the guerrillas. Estimates of mounting guerrilla strength further unnerved a rattled civilian population. By spring 1974, FRELIMO was to have had within the country 10,000 full-time fighters in a force of 25,000 party activists. This represented an increase of 2,000-4,000 fighters over the past two years. All the more alarming to civilian and military personnel was the widely held counterinsurgency yardstick in Mozambique that the 'front of subversion' was usually 50 to 100 miles ahead of the observable guerrilla actions. Frightened farmers cabled Caetano to complain about the want of security. In response, Lisbon dispatched General Francisco da Costa Gomes, Commander-in-Chief of the Armed Forces, to bolster confidence in the army and Portugal's steadfastness to retain Mozambique. Lisbon also promised more troops. Yet Portuguese forces held all the urban areas, and FRELIMO never reached the third and final stage of guerrilla warfare—the employment of regular troops and conventional tactics in set-piece battles as in the last phases of the Cambodian and Vietnamese wars. But the psychological damage of FRELIMO's campaign and the army's *coup* in the metropole shattered former illusions of Lisbon's ability to prosecute the war to a victorious conclusion.

THE NON-SHOOTING WAR

Both the Portuguese and the nationalists embarked on social, economic and political programmes to win the 'hearts and minds' of the people (or in Lisbon's case at least the neutrality of black Mozambicans) and to convince outsiders of the righteousness of their cause. Both made appeals at the United Nations and enlisted smpathetic journalists to buttress their case and criticize that of their enemy's.

With *de facto* control over bush and forest areas in the northern districts, FRELIMO assumed the functions of a provisional government. On the Makonde tablelands and in the lacustrine corner of Niassa, the void left by the retreating Portuguese required FRELIMO to institute an administrative apparatus and basic services to the inhabitants. Here FRELIMO set up village committees to perform administrative and judicial functions. The nationalist established schools for primary education and adult literacy, and set up health facilities—the first ever in some areas. Treatment of the seriously wounded, who survived the rigours of the march, took place at Américo Boavida Hospital (named for a dead Angolan revolutionary) in Mtwara, Tanzania. The Italian hospital, St Maria Nuova, at Reggio Emilia assisted with medical supplies and orthopaedic equipment; the West Germans treated certain critically wounded Portuguese soldiers. By mid-1974, FRELIMO put the number of its primary schools at 200 and open-air clinics at 150.[31] The 'bush schools,' kept mobile to escape bombing, taught the three Rs and Portuguese as a *lingua franca* to facilitate communication among Mozambicans and to eliminate potential ethnic squabbles over language. FRELIMO avowedly viewed education as one of the principal goals of its programme, but progress was slow. Local party administrators and field commanders were often semi-literate.[32] Advanced education and training was carried out in Tanzania and abroad. Nationalist cadres undertook an intensive programme of political education to spread the goals of independence and restructuring society along collectivist lines.

Under first Mondlane and then Machel, FRELIMO doctrine held the war to be an opportunity to reconstruct Mozambique away from traditional chiefly rule, colonial domination and individual gain toward a society of party government and collective endeavour. FRELIMO leaders looked to China and Tanzania for models and inspriation. In the economic sphere, the nationalists organized agricultural cooperatives to expand food production for the local population and a self-sufficient guerrilla force, to open a small export trade to Tanzania and to help shape a collective society. Enough pragmatism existed in the programme, however, for private tillage of individual *shambas,* or plots, so as to stimulate production and personal initiative. African farmers traded their produce at markets for tools, cloth and personal.items. FRELIMO reported that by 1968 peasants in the nationalist dominated zones had begun to export cashews, sesame seeds and Makonde wood carvings to Tanzania. Export was said to have reached 222 tons of cashew nuts and 500 tons of sesame seeds from the harvest in 1973.

The party carried out a vigorous foreign policy to attract aid and recognition in addition to efforts to achieve self-sufficiency. It approached progressive or socialist governments and groups. China and the Soviet bloc supplied weapons and training. Financial and material support from such countries as Sweden, Denmark and the Netherlands, donors such as the Rowntree Foundation in Britain and international organizations such as the World Council of Churches, although earmarked for noncombatant use, provided much-needed assistance as well as recognition in the West. To sum up: the nationalists operated their zone as a proto-independent state with external trade, diplomatic relations and services to the inhabitants.

Portuguese officials ridiculed as propaganda the idea of FRELIMO occupied territory, not to mention the state responsibilities in them, just as the nationalist scoffed at the notion of conditions for the African population being ameliorated in government areas. They went so far as to maintain that western journalists had been duped into thinking that FRELIMO's villages in southern Tanzania were actually in Mozambique.[33] But these slurs did little to cast doubt on the authenticity of the reports, some of which were made by perceptive, if not always non-aligned, observers.[34] Still, nationalist accomplishments in 'liberated' zones remained modest—the lack of enough trained school teachers, any doctors and many basic medical and educational supplies—except when compared with past neglect. Then, too, the nationalist zones were not free from bombing or heliborne raids. Although the Portuguese had to supply them by air for fear of ambushes and mines, they preserved their presence in disputed zones by occupying fortified posts.

Within the Portuguese controlled region, possibly the greatest changes occurred in the economic development of Mozambique's resources. By 1967, the slump following the outbreak of fighting in Angola had passed, and Lisbon's development loans became successively more generous. Soldiers' spending and foreign investment along with the increasingly profitable mainstays of Mozambique's revenue—transit shipment, migrant labour earnings and tourism—pumped large sums into an expanding and developing economy. Mozambique's annual growth rate during the war was nine per cent, which compared favourably to the three to six per cent rates in half of the African countries over the same period.[35]

Government-contracted surveyors searched for exploitable natural wealth in many areas heretofore unsurveyed. Oil prospecting along the coast proved disappointing but a vast deposit of natural gas was discovered in 1965 at Panda, 125 miles north of the capital. Several minerals were located and some mined in Tete demonstrating Mozambique's endowment to be worthwhile, although not as bountiful as Angola's. The construction of roads opened the interior to commerce. Roads, bridges and the Massingir irrigation dam (scheduled for completion in 1976 on the Elefantes River, a tributary of the Limpopo) were important segments of development, but the chief project was the Cabora Bassa Dam.*

Portuguese planners envisioned as early as 1957 the Cabora Bassa Dam as the cornerstone of Mozambique's economic development. As the fifth largest dam in the world, its enormous electrical power (3,600,000 kilowatts) could be used to mine the rich iron ores in Tete. Its power grid includes the countries in southern Africa, among which the industrialized Republic of South Africa was intended to benefit most by a lion's share of cheap electricity. Rhodesia and Malawi's bauxite mining also stand to gain from a ready, inexpensive source of power. Plans also called for irrigation, agricultural development and European and African settlements, similar to the Limpopo project. Overly exuberant officials once ventured the preposterous figure (perhaps to dampen fears among whites of a Lisbon pullout or a disproportionate advantage going to South Africa) of one million Portuguese immigrants for colonization of the Zambezi Valley. The prediction caused outraged concern among nationalists and their sympathizers. Realistically, Portugal with its small population (8.6 million in the 1971 census) never could have afforded such a massive population haemorrhage to Mozambique, let alone induced or financed that many Portuguese to settle in Africa. Resettlement of about 25,000 Africans in the path of the lake behind the dam did take place.

Yet another proposal envisioned waterborne transportation on the Zambezi from the Indian Ocean to Tete town, a distance of 260 miles, and shipping from Cabora Bassa to the Zambia-Rhodesia frontier, a further distance of 190 miles. Additional dams and locks below Cabora Bassa would be required to complete the long-dreamed-of navigation of the Zambezi, but then barges could carry downstream the copper, fluorspar, manganese, vanadium, nickel, chromium, asbestos and sizeable amounts of cokeable coal of the

---

* Cabora Bassa means in the local dialect 'the work is done' or 'no more work'. The gorge and rapids acted as a natural barrier ending the labour of boatmen from the coast. Only porterage moved trade goods further inland.

region. With characteristic Latin hyperbole, the Portuguese spoke of it as the Ruhr of Africa.

The dam phase of the project, scheduled for completion in 1975, was a product of international capital and technical expertize under Portuguese direction. ZAMCO, the international consortium, was heavily financed by South African funds. European and South African engineers, who were housed in a specifically constructed community at Songo, supervised the building of the dam walls and installing of the three generators. Equipment and material bears many Western trademarks. FRELIMO appeals to the United States and European governments to restrict their citizens from participation, however, met with a degree of success. American, Italian, Swedish and German firms dropped contracts for material. Yet Czechoslovakia, a state within the Russian orbit, sold trucks and tractors for the project.[36]

The economic development of Rhodesia, Zambia and Malawi enhanced Mozambique's importance as the historic gateway to the landlocked interior. Beira suffered a decline (the only port blockaded by a small British squadron) because of the imposition of United Nations' sanctions against Rhodesia after its Unilateral Declaration of Independence (UDI) from Britain in 1965. Other Mozambican ports took up the slack, and Portuguese officials falsified documents on goods to and from Rhodesia which enabled Beira to keep serving the rebel regime. So significant had the revenues from transit trade become that the Portuguese initiated planning of a port at Dobela Point, south of the capital, which could compete with the South African port at Richard's Bay for the iron ore and coal of Swaziland and South Africa.

Portuguese development policies emphasized the European-dominated enterprises. The African farmer got less in the way of support. This same pattern of industry over agriculture characterized a dozen or more independent African states, but in colonial Mozambique it added to African grievances. Higher minimum wages and wider employment raised the living standard of those who obtained jobs in the cities or on building sites. But their gains were offset to a large degree by increased local defence taxes and inflation caused by shortages in consumer goods after Lisbon reversed its policy of economic integration with the African territories. Despite its worsening military situation, Lisbon continued to spend heavily for projects, and encouraged foreign corporations to establish companies and franchises. It is as if the development so long overdue in Mozambique was used to compensate for military setbacks and to win what the army was incapable of.

On the civilian 'front', Lisbon moved to correct long-standing abuses and yet kept a tight rein on African or anti-metropolitan white dissent. In brief, Portugal adhered to a policy of carrot and stick. As in the case of military preparations, some reforms were begun before the start of the war. Two early reforms were the repeal of the Native Code of 1954 and the introduction of the Rural Labour Code of 1962 which have been mentioned in chapter 7. Literacy qualifications and property rights still denied the great majority of the African population the right to vote. In the October 1969 election, only 82,539 voters cast ballots, less than one per cent of the total population. During the same election, the government disqualified seven candidates of the opposition Democratic Movement. As predicted the União Nacional, a branch of the metropolitan party of the same name, won by a landslide. In the March 1973 election, only 109,171 ballots were cast to elect 20 of the 50 representatives to the newly expanded local Legislative Assembly; the remaining 30 were elected by official organizations such as chiefs and business groups.

As for implementation of the Rural Labour Code, the other prewar reform, it is difficult to judge the degree of effectiveness. Forced labour gangs on roads were no longer seen (except in war zones for military projects), the wholesale complicity of administrators in securing workers for private companies appeared ended and large companies, open to easy inspection, stopped forcibly recruiting their manpower. The fairness of labour dealings between employer and worker in the backcountry remained open to doubt. Centuries of slavery, forced work and contract labour were not easily swept away by the stroke of a pen in far-off Lisbon. The relationship between European and African was still very much one of master to servant. To make the professed racial tolerance of Mozambique a reality, Lisbon changed in 1971 the laws of cafes, restaurants and hotels to eliminate discriminatory clauses. Economic segregation, however, sufficed to exclude all but a few Africans from patronage of even lower-class white establishments.

Other reforms included an extension of education, sanitation and health facilities from what they had been before the fighting.

Running water, electricity and army-taught schooling in some *aldeamentos* was one manifestation of concern for African loyalty. Another was the mobile health units from the Psycho-Social Service that dispensed innoculations, treated minor ailments and supplied information on prevention of disease before moving to the next village. Education plays a recognized importance in protracted guerrilla warfare. Cognizant that it must improve the daily lot of Africans and persuade them of their membership in a larger Portuguese family, Lisbon expanded African education, especially primary and technical schooling, from the prewar level. Primary schooling accounted for 87 per cent of the total 1972 enrollment of 650,751 pupils. The goal of education stayed the same: 'inculcation of Portuguese values and promotion among African schoolchildren of a conscious identification with Portugal'.[37] History, geography and pictures in the textbooks focused on Portugal rather than Mozambique. Portugal's educational efforts bore meagre fruit. According to the Lourenço Marques newspaper *Notícias*, only 30 per cent of Mozambique's children attended school in 1972, which was a better record than some independent African states but not one commensurate with a civilizing mission. Literacy was put at seven per cent.[38]

Social programmes were, however, handicapped by the escalating costs of counterinsurgency borne by Mozambique. The colony's defence costs doubled between 1960 and 1970 to 28 per cent of the government's expenditure. Taxes were imposed or increased on a wide variety of items and services including newspapers, entertainment, government documents and imported goods as the war dragged on. War expenditures for Mozambique stood at 838 million *escudos* in 1967. In 1972, they had risen to 1,303 million (about $40 million). The projected figure for 1973 reached 2,204 million (about $70 million), or nearly double that of the previous year. Most of the vast increase went to the army.[39]

As evidence of success in restoring its opponents to the Lusitanian fold and as part of its public campaign of benignancy, the authorities released 'rehabilitated' prisoners from time to time on national holidays. On 9 July 1972 the government announced the release of 1,500 political prisoners (scepticism lingers on the number actually set free) in celebration of Mozambique's change in status from 'province' to 'state' of Portugal. Mozambique's most well-known prisoner, Dr Domingos Arouca, was announced freed from a metropolitan prison to a fixed residence in Inhambane in June 1973. The police arrested Arouca in 1965 on charges of being a FRELIMO agent and communicating with Mondlane. At the time of his arrest, he was the head of the Centro Associativo dos Negros de Moçambique which was suppressed with the removal of its president. Sentenced to a four-year term in prison, Arouca was further detained at the end of the period until Caetano abolished arbitrary prolongation of imprisonment.

Along with its 'carrot' reforms Lisbon did not neglect the 'stick' to preserve its control over the African population. The *aldeamento* scheme represented one instrument of control; others were censorship, informers and mass arrests of suspected *turras* ('terrorists') and saboteurs. Sabotage had presented a constant threat since the beginning of the Angolan war but more so after the mysterious case of the *Angoche*. The *Angoche*, a Portuguese coastal steamer, was found damaged, abandoned and adrift off the northern coast. FRELIMO spokesmen did not claim credit for the gutted ship and missing crew. At first, Portuguese authorities suspected sabotage by the Armed Revolutionary Action, a leftist underground group in Portugal, but later they explained that an explosion in a packing case caused the damage. A suspicion of sabotage lingered, however.

Periodic arrests were carried out against suspected FRELIMO agents. Most individual and mass arrests in war zones went unreported.[40] In June 1972, South African newspapers reported the arrest for planning sabotage of 1,800 African workers in government buildings in Lourenço Marques and a sugar plantation in Xinavane, some 60 miles north of the capital. This was the largest mass arrest ever recorded by the foreign press. The next June another sweep of 200 Africans was made by authorities in Mozambique. After interrogation many of those arrested were purportedly released by the DGS. Amnesty International, a European-based organization concerned with the fate of political prisoners, criticized Mozambique's authorities, however, for the use of torture and indefinite imprisonment without trial of some of the arrested.[41]

Military tribunals from time to time publicly tried and sentenced 'terrorists' for subversive activities. Although the sentences given in public were not particularly harsh—something that contributed to the attitude of Portuguese sympathizers that the government was benign to its opponents—they served as warnings to potential detractors. A military court in Lourenço Marques in March 1967 sentenced 28 Africans to four years imprisonment for subversion.* Three months later, a military tribunal sentenced Methodist Reverend Jaconias Massango to three years confinement for recruiting FRELIMO members and spreading propaganda in Swaziland. In spite of their military air and greater efficiency over civilian courts, tribunals were not noted for stiff penalties. Once in prison, whatever the process—military or civilian court or uncharged—the African prisoner, however, was unsure of release upon completion of his term.

The government crackdown on 'threats to the survival of the state' pressed most severely but not exclusively on Africans. In September 1972, the University of Lourenço Marques's Student Association was banned and seven members placed in detention for a year in an undisclosed part of the country. Originally formed as a sports group in 1968, the Student Association moved into the political realm with clandestine meetings on opposition to the war and the distribution of anti-war pamphlets and posters. Three of its members evaded the draft before the suppression of the organization. To mute settler and international criticism, Lisbon passed reforms in other areas.

Portugal's sovereignty over its African possessions underwent constitutional and economic modification in the early 1970s. White businessmen displayed restiveness over Lisbon's domination of the provincial economy and government at a time which coincided with Portugal's efforts to project internationally a liberalizing image. Grants of some political autonomy to Mozambique's settlers was also motivated in part to prepare Portugal's legal position for association with the European Economic Community. Proof of a European economy was a prerequisite for Common Market association, which Portugal obtained in 1972.

Under the Caetano government, two broad policy changes took place which constituted departures from Salazarist doctrine. In July 1972, a year and a half after Caetano introduced his constitutional reforms to the National Assembly, Mozambique· and Angola officially became 'states' within the Portuguese nation. The new Organic Law for the Overseas Territories gave limited autonomy to provincial governments 'without affecting the unity of the nation'. Mozambique's Legislative Council of 27 seats, largely appointed by the Governor-General, was expanded to a Legislative Assembly of

---

*   Lucas Fernandes, described as the most important, received a sentence of eight years.

50 members, 20 elected by an educationally restricted franchise and 30 selected by 'safe' traditional authorities, employers, official workers' organizations and the Church. In the March 1973 elections, Lisbon electorally arranged and calculatedly appointed a narrow non-white majority (18 Africans, 3 *mestiços*, 3 Indians, 1 Chinese and 1 Goan) of 26 representatives. Subject to Lisbon's veto, the local assemblies had the right to legislate and control finances. But the Governor-General, named by Lisbon, still retained control over defence and foreign relations and the prerogative to veto legislation. Caetano's call for 'autonomous regions' aroused concern among right-wing politicians in Portugal who viewed the reforms as a prelude to independence while not satisfying extreme white separatism in Mozambique.

The other break with former New State policy reversed the plan for economic integration of Portugal and its African territories. In 1963, Salazar had backed a ten-year programme for gradual elimination of tariffs and establishment of a common currency. Over the years, Mozambique and Angola had piled up massive debts to Portugal by purchasing goods with provincial *escudos*. By early 1972, when Lisbon announced its economic reforms, the two territories had amassed debts of ten billion *escudos* ($367 million) or five per cent of Portugal's annual GNP. A complex series of decree-laws provided loans for the debts and instituted a new payment mechanism placing Portugal on virtually the same footing as a foreign country. Mozambique was required to pay for Portuguese goods and services in either metropolitan or foreign currency, not territorial *escudos*.

In abandoning strict controls over Mozambique's expenditures with the metropole, Lisbon went a long way in dissolving some of the classic economic ties between colony and mother country. Previously, the New State had forced Mozambique and other of its possessions to purchase certain goods (wine, textiles, olive oil, leather products) from the metropole, barred local businessmen from setting up competing industries and restricted foreign investment that might deprive Lisbon of future profits. Mozambique business circles complained about the privileged status of large Lisbon-based companies in tariff exemptions and in withdrawing earnings from the country. After introduction of the reformed payment scheme, Mozambique still had colossal balance-of-payment problems.[42] The shortages of imported goods due to import restriction on items from Portugal contributed to inflation, but stimulated local industry to produce some consumer goods. The economic sufferings weighed heaviest on those at the bottom of the monetary scale, the Africans, while they shared not at all in the white autonomy.

There was a certain irrelevance to Lisbon's eleventh-hour tinkerings while other events were occurring that made Portugal's domination of Mozambique impossible in any form.

MASSACRES AND MISSIONARIES

Wars infused with ideological hatreds, racism and colonialism could almost be expected to generate the conditions in which atrocities take place. Examples abound of massacres and torturings of helpless civilians during the Algerian, Vietnamese and Middle Eastern conflicts. Where the Mozambique war differed from similar wars was in the frequency of reported massacres and the prominent role of missionaries in their reportage. Historically, missionaries have played only a small part in shaping Mozambique's past. Whether foreign or Portuguese, their numbers were always minuscule and their endeavours, evil or good, have rarely stood out. Aside from the sixteenth-century accounts of dos Santos, the evangelism of Gonçalo da Silveira and the anthropoligical studies of father and son Junod, missionary names and undertakings have not left a deep historical mark. Their predominant part in the allegations of massacres during the war for independence was beyond what one could anticipate from their antecedents.

Anyone pursuing a factual retelling of the major reported massacres in Mozambique would be confronted by contradictory and fragmentary information that was so much a part of the liberation war. That which follows is only a sifting and summary of the published material available.

The squall of massacre charges first clouded the horizon when the White Fathers announced in May 1971 the intended departure of 37 missionaries from central Mozambique. Founded in 1869 in Algeria by French Cardinal Lavigérie, a crusader against slavery, the White Fathers had operated schools and small hospitals in Mozambique since 1945. Confrontations with the government during the mid-1960s over Portuguese treatment of Africans resulted in the expulsion of six members of the Catholic order. But the voluntary leave taking of the entire mission was calculated to protest publicly four principle criticisms of state and church behaviour in Mozambique: injustices and police brutality; seizure of African land; acquiescence of the local Church hierarchy; and Vatican silence because of Portugal's 1940 Missionary Agreement with Rome.[43]

It surfaced shortly after the announced withdrawal that the White Fathers had had a long-standing feud with high Church authorities for not joining or forwarding to the government their protests against army and DGS atrocities. They further took to task the church hierarchy for not appointing an African bishop to one of the nine dioceses. For their part, Portuguese church spokesmen levelled charges of complicity with FRELIMO at the White Fathers. The government contended that they had overstepped their spiritual and religious bounds by entering the political realm. The split opened between church and state by the White Father's attack was widened after their departure by the liberal bishop of Nampula, Manuel Vieira Pinto, who rebuked the church's collusion with the government. Once out of Mozambique, some White Fathers listed specific charges to the press of personally witnessed torture and murder of African civilians and by so doing added their voices to a fusillade of massacre accusations.

No sooner had the furore over the White Fathers' pullout subsided than news came to light of killings, near the town of Mucumbura in remote southern Tete, close to the Rhodesian border. According to the testimonies of two Spanish priests of the Burgos Order (so named because the Spanish Institute for Foreign Missions was located in Burgos before moving to Madrid), some 30 villagers had been murdered by Portuguese and Rhodesian troops in early May 1971 for their alleged part in FRELIMO's mine-planting that killed fellow soldiers the month before. Fathers Martin Hernandez Robles and Juan Valverde Leon's attempts to publish their accounts of murders and statements by army and DGS officials ('terrorism must be fought with terrorism') met with slow progress in the narrowly-read church magazines. From May to November, they purportedly gathered further documentation of other atrocities which they later released to the press.

While in Rhodesia during January 1972 to visit missionaries there (the Portuguese maintained they had fled), the two priests were arrested and interrogated before being returned to authorities in Mozambique where they were to spend nearly two years in Machava Prison awaiting military trial on charges of high treason for aiding FRELIMO guerrillas. The trial was halted when accounts of a large-scale massacre at the village of Wiriyamu in Tete appeared on the front pages of several European newspapers in July 1973. Apparently, the Portuguese authorities decided to grant amnesty to Fathers Valverde and Hernandez in hopes of quietening the case in view of the storm brewing over the Wiriyamu incident. Besides, the government charge sheet against the two priests contained implicit acknowledgement of civilian killings at Mocumbura. Their case would have raised more questions and suspicions about army practices in Mozambique, and at that moment there were far too many queries and doubts.

Concurrently with the arrest and imprisonment of the Spanish missionaries, two Portuguese priests incurred the government's wrath. From his pulpit in Macuti parish, a suburb of Beira, Father Joaquim Teles Sampaio accused the army in January 1972 of killing unarmed villagers in Tete and Cabo Delgado districts. In the same month, Sampaio and Father Fernando Marques Mendes stopped a troop of the Moçidade Portuguêsa, the national youth movement, from carrying the Portuguese flag into church so as to make the distinction between church and state to African members of the congregation. Such actions brought them into conflict with the government. They were arrested for making seditious statements and 'crimes against the state' and detained for a year before their trial.[44] As the first official airing of possible army misconduct, the case aroused interest. The calls of Jorge Jardim's *Noticias da Beira* for stiff punishment reflected popular white feeling.

Before the military tribunal in January 1973, the Bishop of Tete, Felix Niza Ribeiro, revealed knowledge of atrocities committed by Portuguese soldiers, and Father Valverde, another defence witness, testified to the Mocumbura killings as well as to similar slayings in Muculala village in Cabo Delgado in November 1971. As a consequence of their strong defence, the Macuti priests were given suspended sentences, small fines and set free. Angry demonstrators, who were as enraged at the army's failure to stop the spread of the war as at the military court's lenient sentence, protested in Beira's main streets.

Still another internationally reported confrontation between church and state began when in June 1972 the police swooped down on the Presbyterian Church of Mozambique arresting about 30 clergymen and what most reports gave as several hundred members. The Mozambique Presbyterian Church, which was founded in 1887 by a Swiss minister Paul Berthoud, maintained ties with the Swiss Presbyterian Church and the 40 Swiss missionaries in the country, but had its autonomy under an African pastor Zedequias Manganhela.

The imprisonment of Manganhela and another African clergyman, José Sidumo, ended in tragedy when after six months the Portuguese alleged their suicide by hanging. The government argued that their deaths had been an outcome of 'isolation and pressure of interrogation'.[45] Neither had been formally charged nor had the original mass arrests been officially explained beyond rumours in the press about complicity with FRELIMO. Reprisal against the World Council of Churches for its grant of $200,000 to the chief African Liberation movements, including FRELIMO, and for the allegations of the White Fathers were considered motives.[46]

Much of the missionary controversy and talk of massacres in the bush might have remained the knowledge of a narrow circle but for the publication in *The Times* (London) on July 10, 1973 of an article by Father Adrian Hastings describing a massacre at the village of Wiriyamu (the Portuguese referred to it as Wiliamo), 19 miles south of Tete town. Hastings, an ecumenically-minded Catholic priest, gathered his information from the Burgos Fathers whom he had visited in Spain the previous month. From some of the fathers formerly stationed at the San Pedro Mission in Mozambique, he learned of a large massacre of African civilians at Wiriyamu and surrounding villages. The Burgos Fathers listed the names of 86 victims, but estimated 400 villagers slaughtered (some mutilated and violated first) on December 16, 1972 by GEPs transported by helicpoter to the site. The delay in its revelation to the press, where it received wide coverage for over a month, was explained by Burgos Fathers as a fruitless hope that appeals to Portuguese church and civil authorities would lead to a Lisbon-sponsored investigation and thus not endanger the Burgos mission with the government by public disclosure.[47]

Not surprisingly, the Portuguese charged that the article in *The*

Times was timed to embarrass and disrupt Caetano's state visit to Britain to help mark the 600-year anniversary of the Anglo-Portuguese alliance. An uproar was in fact touched off in Britain by news of the massacre. The Labour Party's moves in the House of Commons to halt Caetano's visit failed; but protest marches and rallies punctuated the heavily-guarded tour. American and European press attention was sustained by reports of other atrocities, testimonies by alleged survivors, tours of select journalists to the Wiriyamu region, and the expulsion of British newspaperman Peter Pringle for spending too much time at the San Pedro mission.

Newspaper stories and Hastings's appearance before the United Nations Decolonization Committee tarnished Lisbon's reputation — the worst incident since the slaughter of Africans in the aftermath of the 1961 Angolan uprising — and moved it to undertake an investigation. Lisbon barred the UN investigators from Mozambique, but its Commission of Inquiry conducted investigations in Europe and Tanzania and predictably found the allegations of massacre to be true. The Portuguese National Defence Department issued in August a statement acknowledging that 'contrary to expressed orders . . . isolated units carried out acts of unjustified violence at another point of the region'.[48] Also in August, London's *Daily Telegraph's* reporter Bruce Loudon wrote that Portuguese investigators at Chawola, a village close by Wiriyamu, found 'unnecessary civilian deaths' in a Portuguese assault. The army explained that many of the 53 dead at Chawola had been used as protective shields by the guerrillas against advancing government troops.[49]

Unidentified Portuguese officers doubted the death of 400 people around Wiriyamu because most villages in that area had 60 to 70 inhabitants, but admitted that GEP units had killed 'three or four here, three or four there'. These sources stated that many of the atrocities were committed by African troops, some of them ex-guerrillas, in retaliation for FRELIMO killings and kidnappings. Missionary accounts of Portuguese murders also contained references to selective FRELIMO attacks on pro-government chiefs, headmen and African police officers but not on the scale of the army killings.[50] Missionaries pointed out that the military command knew of the army atrocities and did not prosecute the offenders. Portuguese charges that foreign missionaries had assisted

COLONIALISM AND NATIONALISM 217

FRELIMO were partially borne out when Burgos Father José Maria Lechundi admitted sending young Africans to join the guerrillas.

Lisbon stated its intention of instituting discipline proceedings to try offenders for the 'unnecessary deaths' at Chawola, but little came of it. The government dismissed Colonel Armindo Videira, the hard-nosed Governor and Military Commander of Tete district, and separated his joint civilian-military post into two positions as it had been before the merger in mid-1971 when FRELIMO stepped up attacks in Tete. In January 1974, the Portuguese accused FRELIMO of massacring 20 villagers at Nhacambo, 50 miles northwest of Tete. Although the alleged murders drew negligible press coverage, they did provoke FRELIMO spokesmen in Dar es Salaam to denounce the Portuguese claims as heavy-handed propaganda to discredit the nationalists.

After the Lisbon *coup,* Dutch missionaries of the Sacred Heart reported that Portuguese soldiers had systematically executed and buried in mass graves nearly 200 Africans from January to March 1974 around Inhaminga. The Dutch missionaries stated the slayings were in retaliation for FRELIMO attacks in the area. The government expelled in April the Portuguese Bishop of Nampula, Manuel Vieira Pinto, and nine Italian missionaries for their criticism of the army's atrocities. Pinto was called by angry Europeans the 'FRELIMO bishop' because of his sympathy for the guerrillas. These expulsions temporarily strained relations between Lisbon and the Vatican until the army *coup* and the collapse of Portugal's military position in Mozambique.

The final casualty of Wiriyamu may have been General Arriaga. Whether Arriaga's tour of duty in Mozambique was truly completed after three and a half years or abruptly terminated without an extension granted as a consequence of Wiriyamu is unknown. It is generally known that Arriaga, an uncompromising hardliner, conducted counterinsurgency strategy with a strong measure of 'punishment and reduction' against civilians among whom the guerrillas operated.

Excesses against the African population, however, have been perpetrated long before Arriaga or the national war of liberation. Four hundred and one years before Wiriyamu (1571), for example, another Portuguese military expedition, frustrated with its progress, suspicious of the indigenous people and equally inflamed with sublime faith in the righteousness of its cause, ran amok in a civilian community. Francisco Barreto had encamped along the Zambezi some 125 miles down river from Wiriyamu's future site. He was on a holy crusade to avenge what was believed the Muslim-instigated death of the Jesuit missionary, Gonçalo da Silveira, at the hands of Mutapa Nogomo. Struck by fever and blinded by hatred of another faith, Barreto's men butchered a community of about 50 Muslims. Like so much else in Mozambique's past, massacres and missionaries reoccurred in its contemporary history.

THE LAST PHASE OF PORTUGUESE RULE

Difficult problems, old and new, hit and broke Portugal's fast-slipping grip on Mozambique from the start of 1974. FRELIMO's seemingly unstoppable southward spread into the narrow waist of the country, cutting repeatedly Rhodesia's lifeline to Beira, bombarding with rocket fire Portuguese military installations such as at Inhaminga and putting to flight hundreds of whites in the Vila Pery and Vila de Manica area, evaporated illusions of containing the guerrillas, let alone of a military victory. The deteriorating military situation in Mozambique prompted the Caetano government to nod approval in February to the formation of Grupo Unido de Moçambique (GUMO)—a multiracial lobby that advocated an autonomous Mozambique with political and economic ties to Lisbon. Further recognition of military decline in high government circles also came two months before the *coup* with Caetano's approval for publication of General António de Spínola's *Portugal and the Future*. Recently returned from his position as Commander-in-Chief and Governor of Guinea-Bissau (1968-73), Spínola (who had the writing assistance of top soldiers, businessmen and political scientists) admitted the futility of Portugal's exertions for victory and recommended self-determination for Mozambique, Angola and Guinea-Bissau (formerly Portuguese Guiné) within the framework of a Lusitanian Federation as equal partners with Portugal. The monocled counterinsurgency officer's dovish ideas of scuttle kicked up a controversy leading to his ousting as Deputy Chief of Staff of the Armed Forces (a position created for him) and an abortive *coup* of 300 soldiers that was a prelude to the military takeover six weeks later.

On 25 April 1974 army units in Portugal led by field-grade

officers, deeply disenchanted with the unwinnable African wars and imbued with revolutionary doctrine gained from their guerrilla opponents, nearly bloodlessly seized key buildings and ministries in Lisbon.[51] Caetano, Tómas and other members of the authoritarian regime were flown to Madeira Island. A proclamation from the Armed Forces Movement (Movimento das Forças Armadas), which masterminded the *coup*, pledged 'the restitution to the Portuguese people of the civil liberties of which they have been deprived', and denounced the Salazar-Caetano regime for being 'unable to define a concrete and purposeful overseas policy leading to peace among Portuguese of all races and creeds.'[52] War weariness, hatred of the dictatorship and social and economic hardships in Portugal sharpened by the war undermined the stability of the 48-year old authoritarian regime creating the climate for a military *coup* to end the wars.

Of the three wars, it was the collapsing military position in Mozambique that revealed to the army their inability to contain the guerrillas in remote regions and to protect the white population.[53] The other fronts offered no such revelation. In Angola the badly splintered nationalist movements had ceased to engage wholeheartedly the Portuguese forces. The stalemate favoured the Portuguese, for the guerrilla movements were confined to inhospitable terrain far from vital European areas. Although militarily more successful, the PAIGC's 1973 bid for international recognition of its independent status in liberated zones of Guinea-Bissau — a poor West African wedge of territory with a scant 2,000 Portuguese colonists — did not tip the military or diplomatic balance against Lisbon anymore than the guerrilla movement's *de facto* control over wide areas had. Fighting there had reached a standoff, neither side could force a decision. Portugal's retention of the coastal zone and beleaguered interior bases which was predicated on the 'domino theory'; that is, if Guinea-Bissau went Mozambique and Angola would follow, was unjeopardized by recognition of PAIGC independence claims by over 70 nations. Although FRELIMO still relied on unconventional tactics of raids and sabotage, it inexorably drove deep into Mozambique, hundreds of miles from its secured areas in the north or its Zambian sanctuaries, and convinced many in the army and white population that it was unrestrainable. Its growing strength among African peoples in the central part of the country despite massacres, intimidations and resettlement schemes, offered no prospect of reversing the tide.

Headed by Spinola, the new government wanted a cease-fire and negotiations on the political future of Mozambique and other Portuguese territories. Spinola personally desired a federal system and the participation of FRELIMO as one party of several in a general election in Mozambique. Meanwhile, the army continued its bombing raids. FRELIMO's answer was to continue the war through the spring and summer. By doing so, it buttressed its bargaining position and expanded its influence in the south and in the Zambézia district; but the attacks may have exacerbated the exodus of settlers who began leaving the country for Portugal or South Africa at the rate of 1,000 a week from early May. The shortage of farmers, technicians, doctors and engineers was to become a front-rank problem for the FRELIMO provisional government. Even after the opening of the first round of cease-fire talks between Machel and Mario Soares, the new Portuguese Foreign Minister, in Lusaka the first week in June, FRELIMO poured guerrillas into the middle section of the country, as one army officer put it, 'like fleas through a rug'. Caught off guard by the suddenness of the *coup*, FRELIMO strove to consolidate its position. In July, FRELIMO opened a front in the Zambézia district and captured its first town, Murrumbala, which is located near the Malawi border. Settlers fled in droves to Quelimane. Army morale plummeted. Most soldiers, black and white, saw the *coup* and the negotiations as a step toward eventual withdrawal. Breakdowns in discipline occurred everywhere. In Niassa district, the army played soccer and drank with the guerrillas. Troops at Vila Gouveia would not go into action. By mid-summer, an undeclared truce had been established since most troops refused to fight.

The civilian 'front' likewise spun toward chaos. Black dockers struck for higher wages; white railway employees protested the lack of army protection. Farmers ceased planting. Lawlessness haunted the backcountry. Disbanded militia and mobs of hungry, tattered men roamed the countryside burning, looting and settling old scores with former white employers. Alarmed by approaching anarchy and the loss of skilled workers, FRELIMO de-escalated the fighting, handed over wrongdoers to the Portuguese and assured settlers of their safety and future in an African-ruled but multiracial Mozambique.

The *coup* had immediate repercussions in Mozambique's politics where Lisbon's new policies of negotiation were interpreted as tantamount to a surrender. The government released some 2,000 political prisoners, mostly black; it recalled the Governor-General, Manuel Pimental dos Santos, fearing his leadership in a white separatist movement; and it disbanded the DGS, relegating it to a branch in the army and arresting those secret police unable to escape to Rhodesia and South Africa. Later, many DGS men were set free in spite of liberal opposition.

Basking in the sunshine of political tolerance, the first since the fall of the Republic, Mozambique mushroomed with parties and political activity. Crowds of blacks and whites numbering in the thousands thronged the main streets of Lourenço Marques and Beira. On successive days, either groups demonstrating for or against a black independent Mozambique held their rallies. In the capital's African suburb of Xipamanine, the soccer stadium was filled with eager listeners who were aroused by FRELIMO sympathizers or advocates of some form of limited independence. Newspapers carried a spate of proclamations stating support for or opposition to various groups and ideas. Young whites from the University and liberals called for reform, peace, a multiracial society, co-operation with FRELIMO and a majority (African) governed Mozambique. Working and lower-class whites staged counter-demonstrations demanding that Mozambique be kept Portuguese. Some reactionary elements beat up liberals and others made thuggish threats. Reminiscent of the French population in Algeria during its independence turmoil, their slogans were 'out with the traitors' and 'Mozambique is our life'.

Soon the moderate GUMO, which had been formed before the *coup* with the blessings of Caetano, was joined by a plethora of other groups that were more political lobbies than organized parties. Over 200 small groups sprung up, many of which later merged with larger and more important associations. Of the numerous movements that emerged in post-*coup* Mozambique, the Front for Independence and Continuity with the West (FICO, which in Portuguese means 'I am staying') rose to draw support from settlers who were determined to perpetuate white supremacy. They stood for a white autonomous state. Ominously reminiscent of the settler-military OAS in Algeria, FICO attracted 5,000 Europeans to its first rally in the capital. Two weeks later it drew less than 1,000 to a second rally. The movement for white independence à la Rhodesia was clearly not viable in Mozambique which lacked both a settler-controlled administration and internal security force.

More to the centre of the political spectrum, GUMO with its programme of multiracial autonomy and links with Portugal was outpaced by events once the nationalists rejected Spinola's pet plan for referendum on a Lusitanian Federation. The captains and majors in the Armed Forces Movement pressed for grants of independence to the African colonies and the old guard officers reluctantly agreed. More and more GUMO's programme appeared irrelevant, if not colonialist.

A small but influential pressure group, the Mozambican Democrats, comprised of white liberals from the professional classes and university students, supported FRELIMO and worked for its acceptance among the white population. They held familiarization talks about FRELIMO to inform Africans in the south whose understanding of the movement had been inhibited by censorship and police informers. In addition, the Mozambican Democrats compiled dossiers on DGS men and acted as the prime mover for their roundup. Approximately 120 of the 200–300 DGS agents were detained in Machava Prison.

Much of the African population rallied to FRELIMO either by showing their sympathy for the liberation front or by establishing organizations that endorsed FRELIMO. Suppressed nine years before, the Centro Associativo dos Negros de Moçambique was reconstituted with a headquarters in Xipamanine and worked on behalf of FRELIMO among the 800,000 Africans around the capital. Other Africans publicly declaring their faith in a multiracial, independent Mozambique but opposing FRELIMO hegemony were less visible but present. Elements within the Makua, the largest ethnic group in the country, sought to take advantage of the rivalry with the Makonde. A group of four traditional chiefs claiming to speak for all the Makua stated in the Lourenço Marques paper Noticias their opposition to FRELIMO and their endorsement of a federal system in Mozambique after independence. Their self-claimed right to speak for all Makuas was disputed by others of the same ethnic group who acclaimed FRELIMO.[54] Another group, the Commercial, Agricultural and Industrial Association of Niassa, demanded that the Makua be taken into account in Mozambique's political solution.[55] Judging by the fiery reaction of FRELIMO the most worrisome from its viewpoint of the Makua organizations was the Mozambique Common front (FRECOMO) led by Joana Simião, onetime secretary of GUMO. FRELIMO radio in Dar es Salaam broadcasted a steady stream of abuse aimed at the group and its leader, calling her a 'Portuguese stooge' and a 'CIA agent'. Five of these microgroups, including FRECOMO and its Simião, coalesced into the Partido de Coligação Nacional de Moçambique (PCN) in Beira in late August 1974. Its Executive Commission was formed by some ex-FRELIMO members: Simango became President; Gumane assumed the Vice Presidency; and Gwenjere took over as National Advisor. Against Lisbon's exclusive talks with FRELIMO, the PCN proposed 'a democratic process in which all the people can express themselves freely. . . .'[56]

During the prolonged negotiations between FRELIMO and Lisbon over the summer of 1974, the name of Jorge Jardim, wealthy Beira businessman and Malawi's consul in that city, frequently cropped up in connection with a Mozambican UDI like that of Rhodesia. Rumour was that Jardim had the unquestioned loyalty of a thousand crack paratroopers—mainly made up of former FRELIMO guerrillas—in a phantom force which stealthily slipped across the Rhodesian frontier to attack FRELIMO. Rumour was wrong. Jardim had during the war subsidized and trained, with the assistance of his daughters, *flechas* in parachuting and airborne operations. Shortly after the *coup,* Jardim entered the Malawi embassy in Lisbon and from there secretly slipped to Malawi where his presence aroused considerable uneasiness for Mozambique's territorial integrity in government and FRELIMO circles. Banned from Mozambique and his financial assets frozen in Beira, Jardim shadowly centred in every likely right-wing plot conjured up by disgruntled whites or apprehensive Portuguese authorities. Toward the end of the summer, Jardim was reportedly financing a white-officered black force of former *flechas.*[57] Also in August, Colonel 'Mad Mike' Hoare—the British soldier of fortune who commanded white mercenaries in the Congo during the early 1960s—arrived in Malawi and Rhodesia. The *Rhodesian Herald* carried advertisements urging former members of No. 5 Commando 'to report for a reunion'. A delegation of the 'mercs' was in fact held which did nothing to allay fear of their intervention into Mozambique. Amid speculation of 'another Congo' in

Mozambique, right-wing extremists struck in Lourenço Marques.

On 8 September 1974, the day after Soares and Machel signed an accord in Lusaka, the self-styled Dragons of Death (probably made up of ex-servicemen) disrupted the offices of the Liberal *Noticias* and blew up an arsenal on the capital's outskirts. FICO members seized unopposed the radio station and appealed in the name of the Free Mozambique Movement for assistance from journalists, ex-commandos and all opposed to the 'sellout' to FRELIMO. They enjoyed some conservative African support from Simango, Kavandame, Gwenjere, Simião and others hostile to FRELIMO. Three days later the army, reinforced by units from the military's headquarters at Nampula, reasserted control, and the rebellion folded. In its wake, widespread looting and rioting erupted in the African suburbs in protest to the white revolt. The death toll was estimated at 87, mostly Africans. Gradually the African townships quieted, but not before hundreds of whites fled to South Africa fearful of a bloodbath. The prospects for a 'white revolution', never bright in Mozambique, flickered out.

The agreement that precipitated the rebellion called for independence on 25 June 1975 — the 13th anniversary of FRELIMO's founding — a multiracial society, a transitional government with a prime minister, six of the nine ministers appointed by FRELIMO and acceptance by the nationalists of financial obligations incurred by Portugal if deemed in the country's interest.[58] The war had ended.

10

THE FUTURE AGAINST THE PAST

The period from the installation of the transition government on 20 September 1974 to independence was in keeping with Mozambique's turbulent and event-filled history. Street fighting erupted in Maputo (formerly Lourenço Marques) at the end of October after a trivial spark between a Portuguese commando and an African youth ignited the tensions among Europeans and Africans. Black and white civilians became involved before Portuguese and FRELIMO troops, acting once again in a peace-keeping role, restored order. The death toll stood at 49, again mostly African.

This shoot-out marred an otherwise peaceful transition. Despite disquieting incidents of gun-toting guerrillas at roadblocks demanding money, wine and cigarettes,[1] FRELIMO's takeover was disciplined and reasonably efficient. Working together with the Portuguese, FRELIMO police 'nipped in the bud' two reported 'reactionary plots' by uncovering caches of arms and arresting white and black suspects in Nampula and the capital. The FRELIMO-dominated interim government averted strikes on the docks and mines by appeals to the workers for reconstruction of the country.[2] Judging by FRELIMO policies and actions, it remains, however, to instill a work ethic among Mozambican labourers who for so long regarded labour as of little benefit to themselves.

Fears of a violent independence celebration proved unfounded. No attempted *coup* took place. Strict security measures were in evidence but did not dampen the festivities of parades, speeches and street camaraderie. To show its displeasure at their support for the former Portuguese government's war efforts, FRELIMO refused invitations to the United States, France, West Germany, Rhodesia, and South Africa for the independence-day ceremonies. Fifty invited delegations from nations around the world witnessed the midnight flag raising at the crowded Machava stadium in the capital.

Some whites greeted the transition government by continuing their old pursuits of business and pleasure as usual but with a feeling of impermanence and uncertainty. The October race riot caused many more to flee. Between September and April, a further 52,000 left the country making the Portuguese population only 100,000, half of what it had been two years before.[3] A few promised to return once the political situation stabilized. But European departures did not stop after independence on 25 June 1975. Estimates placed the white population at between 50 and 60,000 in early 1976, when the government nationalized private homes, seized unoccupied homes vacated by whites and criticized Asian and Europeans for racism. The new government's revolutionary economic programmes fell hardest on the Portuguese settlers, the most privileged group under colonialism, and increased white feelings of being a persecuted minority.[4]

Pressing problems beset the interim government. Floods in the Limpopo Valley left homeless some 80,000 and caused near famine among a further 250,000. The impending return of war refugees, number about 110,000 from Tanzania, Malawi and Zambia, added to the plight of resettling many thousands of *aldeamento* inhabitants. Worse, the white flight of administrators, technicians, auto mechanics, telephone operators, school teachers and, most critically, doctors boded ill for the immediate future of the Mozambican economy and welfare.

During the transition, FRELIMO's activities centred on consolidating its power, especially in the south, by rounding up political dissidents and by politicizing the population. Following in the Maoist tradition, FRELIMO posted newspapers and political messages on notice boards at public places. Political education replaced religion in the schools. FRELIMO's army maintained its dominant role as a political instrument, but the party also enlisted civilians.[5] Political groups were established in towns and villages. White volunteers in wealthy suburbs took part along with Africans in *grupos dinamizadores* ('activating groups') to assist FRELIMO's politicization. They conducted *mentalização* programmes and literacy classes throughout the country but mainly in the towns.[6] When politically advanced enough, the *grupos* are to be transformed into political committees.

Such participation by whites helped to reduce the fear of a reactionary settler bid for power and temporarily improved race relations. President Machel, who delayed his return to Mozambique until near the day of independence, voiced concern about renewed violence and stated that the party's goal was to 'forge a Mozambican mentality from the Rovuma to the Maputo without distinction as to race, ethnic group or religion'.[7] Multiracialism, eradication of tribalism and women's liberation are also hopes of the new society.* The prominent role of women in the liberation was as combatants or support forces should accord them similar status in peacetime.[8] But the long-standing subservient view of women as well as traditional ethnic distinctions will require modification in the years ahead.

In Chinese fashion, FRELIMO paraded before independence on two occasions former members, PIDE agents and 'reactionaries' before large crowds at its Nachingwea training camp in southern Tanzania. Among the 250 self-confessed enemies were Simango, Gumane, Gwenjere and Joana Simião. Machel hosted the ceremonies for 'political education'. He observed: 'There are no revolutions without traitors. But we will not kill them; we will learn from them.'[9] The object was humiliation and rehabilitation of the 'traitors' in 'mental decolonization' agricultural co-operatives. It served, too, as a lesson to potential deviants from the party line.

ECONOMIC INDEPENDENCE

FRELIMO's blueprint for development involves a one-party state and an austere society with a revolutionary imprint. Prostitution was outlawed, and its practitioners sent to the countryside to work the land in 're-education farms'.[10] Luxury goods stopped being imported. The party leadership laid down repeated commandments against private gain, profiteering and the 'economic sabotage of capitalism'. It seeks to eliminate most private enterprise by freezing bank accounts, fixing mortician fees and nationalizing the services of doctors, lawyers and private missionary schools so as to provide equality of treatment and service. Similarly, the government took over the broadcasting system and the exportation of cashews — a product Mozambique ranked first in world production under colonial rule. So far the government, however, has moved cautiously against small businesses.

Striking or 'instigating disinterest in work' are considered counter-revolutionary. The penalty is internment in a mental decolonization camp to bring about a change in attitude by ideo-

---

* See Appendix II for a statement of many FRELIMO goals.

logical persuasion and hard work. In a similar vein, FRELIMO moved against elitism by sending secondary school and university students into the fields to work. But it backed off earlier pronouncements to rid the army of elitism by continuing its rankless character. Now there are provisions for three grades in the People's Forces for the Liberation of Mozambique.[11] In spite of these instances of well-advised pragmaticism, FRELIMO seems to be consistent in its demands for revolutionary morality. Purges have been carried out since independence in both the party and the army for 'corruption, dishonesty, immorality and indiscipline'.[12] These purges reportedly brought about a revolt among some 400 dissident soldiers and police which jolted the capital for two days in late 1975. When the shooting subsided, the Machel government was in firm control but warned the population to be alert for subversives.[13]

The raising of a Spartan Marxist state and the avoidance of neo-colonial domination by big financial interests are viewed as two sides of the same coin. While striving to preserve the indigenous character of its revolution, the People's Republic of Mozambique has embarked on a course similar to Maoist China's self-help and self-dependence. Nevertheless, Communist countries have been to date the chief aid donors. With 40 per cent of its GNP derived out of port dues and transit fees from the Republic of South Africa and Rhodesia, the way of self-reliance will be difficult. An interruption of Mozambique's co-operation, however, would be harmful to all. On the one hand, the Transvaal mines rely on at least 200,000 Mozambican labourers a year and Rhodesia depends on transit across Mozambique. On the other, Mozambique's colonially-shaped economy, which is deeply intertwined with its white-ruled neighbours, would suffer severe dislocation, if a sudden break occurred. South Africa and Rhodesia use Mozambique's railways. They furnished free-spending tourists before the Lisbon *coup*. Under Portuguese arrangements, South Africa paid remittances to Lisbon on 60 per cent of the miners' wages after the first year in gold at the official rate of $42 an ounce. Portugal in turn reaped a handsome profit in sales of the gold on the free market. Independent Mozambique plans to maintain the arrangement with some guarantees for workers' rights and safety. Likewise, it still intends to sell cotton, tea, sugar and most of all hydroelectric power from Cabora Bassa while demanding changes in the white regimes' racial policies. Economic relations continue with Pretoria and Salisbury despite the absence of formal diplomatic links. In the long haul, FRELIMO hopes for a measure of economic independence with its mineral wealth and agricultural potential.[14] So also, it strives for greater economic integration with the governments of Zambia and Tanzania. The first step in that direction was the establishment in September 1975 of a Permanent Commission of Co-operation, 'whose main function is to make the economies of Mozambique and Tanzania complementary.'[15]

The first step of this independent economy demands a self-sufficient food supply. Stimulated by Tanzania's *ujamaa* villages and 'self-reliance' programme, plans appeared for communal farms and co-operative work places during the war. It was announced just prior to independence that 250 of the 953 *aldeamentos* would be turned into rural communes. By collectivization, the party seeks to end capitalism and *a exploração do homem pelo homen* ('the exploitation of man by man') but emphasizes that everyone will work. Hence FRELIMO intends to effect a social revolution with the equal distribution of goods and glorification of manual labour for all.[16]

Wrapped in the future is the unlikely prospect that goals radicalized during the independence war could mellow with the exercise of power, although the methods to achieve them will, it seems, remain pragmatic. Economic realities will take priority over ideological goals. Since its evolution from a conventional nationalist movement, FRELIMO has viewed its efforts as part of the world-wide class struggle. But its Marxist parlance is more often than not realistic in its aims and methods of salvaging a war-ravaged country and a debt-ridden treasury. President Machel soberly warned soon after independence that 'we will not be prey to adventurism'.[17] Scarcity of resources and investment capital compels the government, as in other underdeveloped nations, to establish priorities and strict allocation of the means required to realize them, if diversification and development are to be achieved. Against a background of underdevelopment · and the rising expectations of rich and poor for improved social services and consumer goods is the recognition that only a strong government with central controls can divert foreign imports and local resources toward developing and broadening the economy and away from consumption of luxury items. This vigorous government planning diverges from the practice of private enterprise to produce economic development. Such state intervention leads some in the West to be unsympathetic with the methods of the FRELIMO government for economic independence and prosperity.

FOREIGN ENTANGLEMENTS AND CHANGE

It will take more than an all-encompassing ideology and abundant dedication if Mozambique is ever to cease being a cockpit of contending disasters. It will take a peaceful and constructive resolution of the southern African problem, where the Portuguese pullout is the most significant transformation since the breakup of the white-dominated Central African Federation (the Rhodesias and Nyasaland) in 1963. FRELIMO's decision during 1975–7 to send about 300 troops to aid the like-minded MPLA in the post-independence Angolan conflict is an indication of the changed realities of southern Africa. Another indication is a reported FRELIMO 'recruiting drive' in Swaziland, a tiny monarchist, capitalist and landlocked state which shares borders with Mozambique and South Africa.[18] Up to now Pretoria's clientage of Swaziland has seemed secure from challenges by its neighbours.

The question that preoccupied foreign observers during the transition months and after was an independent Mozambique's relations with the neighbouring white regimes of Rhodesia and South Africa. Mozambique's geographic location and revolutionary government make it a key to the austral African cauldron. Salisbury and Pretoria worried that Mozambique would become hammer instead of anvil, the springboard of guerrilla invasion instead of the historically invaded.

FRELIMO allows ZANU guerrillas the use of sanctuaries near the Rhodesian border. Machel pledged support to the Zimbabwe nationalists, sought compensation from other states for the closing of Mozambique's ports to Rhodesian traffic and alerted Mozambicans for volunteer service in Zimbabwean ranks. Rhodesia's vulnerability and dependence on communication across Mozambique lend it most likely to nationalist attack. By early 1976, there had been several clashes between Rhodesian forces and guerrillas along the border near the town of Umtali. Uncertain at this date is the degree of Mozambican participation, if any. Peace and trade benefit Mozambique more than war and economic disruption. While almost simultaneously vowing solidarity with Zimbabwe guerrillas, FRELIMO has shown much interest in a peaceful solution to majority rule in Rhodesia. Machel, along with Zambia's President Kaunda and Tanzania's President Nyerere, has pushed for unity among Zimbabwe nationalists and for a settlement with the Rhodesian government. For the short run, South Africa's military strength and Mozambique's economic reliance guarantee Pretoria peace from raids across its north-eastern border. For the long run, the future remained hard to discern.

The People's Republic of Mozambique in time will not resemble Portugal's former colony which Lisbon so hoped to pattern after the metropole. A new ideology of transformation has descended. The FRELIMO government substituted African names for Portuguese: Lourenço Marques was changed to Maputo, João Belo became Xai Xai and Porto Amélia is now Pemba. Street names changed, and statues of Portuguese heroes were dismantled to gather dust in museums. Next FRELIMO banned manifestations of foreign culture to include infant baptism, night clubs and foreign dances.[19] These changes and restrictions have as much to do with African nationalism cleansing its colonial legacies as with revolutionary puritanism. Seen from the future, Portugal's impact, apart from language, will be perhaps as slight as Rome's influence on ancient Britain—a few roads, bridges and buildings. At Machel's independence-day speech, he reiterated his theme that 'we are engaged in a Revolution whose advance depends on the creation of a new man with a new mentality.'[20]

Outsiders wondered about the difficulties of fulfilling newly awakened aspirations of a decent standard of living while pursuing goals of an ascetic Marxist economy. Just as crucial is whether the revolutionary participation of the anti-colonial war can be extended into the arduous period of post-colonial reconstruction. The nub of the problem centres on checking the formation of a bureaucratic elite, a 'new class', and securing mass involvement in decision-making. Failure to obtain voluntary participation of the people and most of all the army could result in political instability. At this juncture, FRELIMO's control has been institutionalized in many areas of Mozambican life, but whether the revolution can be institutionalized only time will tell. Independent Mozambique faces a formidable gauntlet of problems that will test FRELIMO solutions.

American and Russian naval strategists talked about bases on Mozambique's coast along the oil lanes to the Persian Gulf and about its several large ports on the Indian Ocean. To date Soviet pressure to establish bases on Mozambique's coast has been resented and resisted by FRELIMO, which has the goal of 'transforming of the Indian Ocean into a denuclearized and peaceful zone'.[21] If the past is any mirror of the future, then the future may see a partial return of Mozambique to its ancient position of crossroads between expansionists of East and West with all the problems that it could bring.

Mozambique before the Europeans was not in a state of aboriginal primitivism so often suggested by Lusitanian writers who brightened the glories of the Portuguese noonday by making the night that preceded it darker than it really was. Each intruder contributed to the richness of Mozambique's unique past, and each fell short of establishing a permanent rule. Now an independent Mozambique stands with the future against the past.

CHAPTER 1: EARLY INHABITANTS AND EMPIRES

1. Allen F. Isaacman, *Mozambique: The Africanization of a European Institution; The Zambezi Prazos, 1750-1902*, (Madison: University of Wisconsin Press, 1972), p. 4.

2. One scholar, T. N. Huffman, suggested that the evolution of Zimbabwe was due more to 'surplus wealth from the East African gold trade' than to 'migrants with a special religious superiority', 'The Rise and Fall of Zimbabwe', *Journal of African History*, Vol. XIII, No. 3 (1972), pp. 353-366.

3. See Roger Summers, *Zimbabwe: A Rhodesian Mystery*. Johannesburg: Nelson 1963, and Peter Garlake, *Great Zimbabwe*. London: Thames and Hudson, 1973.

4. Brian M. Fagan, *Southern Africa During the Iron Age* (New York: Praeger, 1965), 100-19.

5. João dos Santos, 'Ethiopia Oriental' in *Records of South-Eastern Africa (RSEA)*, ed. G. M. Theal, 9 vols. (Capetown: Government of the Cape Colony, 1901), Vol. 7, pp. 218-19.

6. There is some doubt among scholars that the Mwende Mutapa empire was as extensive as claimed. Theal maintained that it existed only in the mind of the Portuguese, *RSEA*, Vol. 2, p. 9. For a recent doubter, see Richard Gray's review of Eric Axelson's *Portuguese in South-east Africa, 1488-1600* in *Journal of African History*, Vol. XVI, No. 1 (1975), p. 148.

7. 'Summary . . . of Letters by Antonio de Saldanha'; *Documentos sobre os Portugueses em Moçambique e na Africa Central-Documents on the Portuguese in Mozambique and Central Africa 1497-1840*, 6 vols. (Lisbon: Centro de Estudos Históricos Ultramarinos, 1962), Vol. III, p. 17.

8. D. P. Abraham, 'Maramuca: An Exercise in the Combined Use of Portuguese Records and Oral Tradition', *Journal of African History*, Vol. II, No. 2 (1961), p. 212.

9. Edward Alpers, 'The Mutapa and Malawi political systems to the time of the Ngoni invasions', *Aspects of Central African History*, ed. T. O. Ranger (Evanston: Northwestern University Press, 1968), pp. 9-10.

10. Dionízio de Mello e Castro, 'Notícia do Império Marave e dos Rios de Sena, 20 de Janeiro de 1763', *Anais da Junta de Investigações do Ultramar 9*, tomo 1 (1954), pp. 132-5.

11. D. P. Abraham, 'The Roles of "Chaminuka" and the Mhondoro-Cults in Shona Political History', *The Zambesian Past: Studies in Central African History*, ed. Eric Stokes and Richard Brown (Manchester: Manchester University Press, 1966), pp. 29-31.

12. 'Letter from Diogo de Alcacova to the King, Cochin, 1506 November 20', *Documentos sobre os Portugueses em Moçambique*, Vol. I, pp. 393-5.

13. Abraham, 'Maramuca', 214.

14. *Ibid.*, 215.

15. Manuel Barreto, 'Report upon the State and Conquest of the Rivers of Cuama, 1667', *RSEA*, Vol. 3, p. 480.

16. *Ibid.*, 476; Manuel Godinho, *Relação Do Novo Caminho que fez por Terra e Mar Vindo da India para Portugal no Anno de 1633* (Lisbon, 1842), p. 200-1.

17. Quoted in M. G. Marwick, 'History and Tradition in East Central Africa Through the Eyes of the Northern Rhodesian Cewa', *Journal of African History*, Vol. IV, No. 3 (1963), p. 379.

18. Harry Langworthy, *Zambia Before 1890: Aspects of Precolonial History* (London: Longman Group, 1972), pp. 30-5.

19. Francisco de Aragão e Mello, *Memória e Documentos Acêrca dos Direitos de Portugal Aos Territórios de Machona e Nyasa* (Lisbon, 1890), p. 125.

20. A. Y. Mazula, 'História dos Nianjas', *Portugal em África* 19 (1962), pp. 164-5.

21. Alpers, 'The Mutapa and Malawi political systems', 23-6.

22. Langworthy, *Zambia Before 1890*, 34.

CHAPTER 2: MUSLIM AND PORTUGUESE SEABORNE EXPANSION

1. António da Silva Rego, *Portuguese Colonisation in the Sixteenth Century: A Study of the Royal Ordinances* (Johannesburg: Witwatersrand University Press, 1959), pp. 14-18.

2. Walter Rodney, *A History of the Upper Guinea Coast, 1545-1800* (Oxord: Clarendon Press, 1970), p. 81.

3. James Duffy, *Porguguese Africa* (Cambridge: Harvard University Press, 1959), pp. 2-23.

4. Conde de Ficalho, *Viagems de Pedro de Covilhã* (Lisbon, 1898), pp. 58-60.

5. Charles R. Boxer, *The Portuguese Seaborne Empire: 1415-1825* (New York: Alfred A. Knopf, 1969), p. 36.

6. 'Account of the Voyage of Vasco da Gama Along the Coast of Mozambique', *Documentos sobre os Portugueses em Moçambique*, Vol. I, p. 19.

7. Allison Butler Herrick et al., *Area Handbook for Mozambique* (Washington: US Government Printing Office, 1969), p. 110.

8. For a still very useful account of the Portuguese on the east African coast to 1727 and Portugal's final loss of Mombasa, see Justus Strandes, *The Portuguese Period in East Africa* (originally published in German in Berlin, 1899). The 1968 edition, printed by the East African Literature Bureau in Nairobi, contains many supplemental and corrective notes that update the original.

9. 'Letter of Diogo de Alcaçova to the King Dom Manuel concerning Sofala . . .' *RESA*, Vol. I, p. 66.

10. Alexandre Lobato, *A Expansão Portuguesa em Moçambique 1498 a 1530*, 3 vols. (Lisbon: Agencia Geral do Ultramar, 1954), Vol. II, p. 22.

11. João de Barros, *Decadas da Asia*, (Coimbra, 1930; originally published in Lisbon, 1552), Vol. 5, p. 88.

12. Lobato, *A Expansão Portuguesa em Moçambique*, Vol. II, p. 23.

13. Father Monclaro, 'Account of the Journey made by Fathers of the Company of Jesus with Francisco Barreto in the Conquest of Monomotapa in 1569', *RSEA*, Vol. 3, p. 235.

14. Boxer, *The Portuguese Seaborne Empire*, 48.

15. J. H. Parry, *The Age of Reconnaissance* (New York: New American Library, 1964), pp. 154-5.

16. David Birmingham, 'Early African Trade in Angola and its Hinterland', *Pre-Colonial African Trade*, Richard Gray and David Birmingham (London: Oxford University Press, 1970), p. 164.

17. 'Instructions to the Captain-Major D. Francisco de Almeida, Lisbon, 1505 March 5', *Documentos sobre os Portugueses em Moçambique*, Vol. I, p. 185.

18. F. Lopes de Castanheda, *História de Descobrimento e Conquista da India pelos Portuguezes*, 4 vols. (Coimbra, 1924-33), Vol. I, p. 274.

19. Eric Axelson, *Portuguese in South-east Africa, 1488-1600* (Capteown: C. Struik, 1973), pp. 75-7.

20. Castanheda, *História de Descobrimento e Conquista*, I, 305.

21. Edward A. Alpers, 'Ethnicity, Politics, and History in Mozambique', *Africa Today*, Vol. 21, No. 4 (Fall, 1974), pp. 45.

22. For a listing of Portuguese top officials in Mozambique, see David P. Henige, *Colonial Governors from the Fifteenth Century to the Present: A Comprehensive List* (Madison: University of Wisconsin Press, 1970), pp. 303-5.

23. Fritz Hoppe, *A África Oriental Portuguesa no tempo do Marquês de Pombal* (Lisbon, 1970; first published in Berlin, 1965), pp. 24-5.

24. *Frei* Francisco de Santa Caterinha, 'A Dominican Account of Zambesia in 1744', ed. C. R. Boxer, *Boletim da Sociedade de Estudos de Moçambique*, Vol. 29 (1960), p. 3.

25. Axelson, *Portuguese in South-east Africa 1488-1600*, pp. 53-5.

26. Lobato, *A Expansão Portuguesa em Moçambique*, Vol. II, p. 62-3.

27. M. D. D. Newitt, 'The Early History of the Sultanate of Angoche', *Journal of African History*, Vol. XIII, No. 3 (1972), p. 402.

28. Duarte de Lemos, 'Extracts from a Letter from Duarte de Lemos to the King Dom

Manuel', *RSEA*, I, 73.

29. 'Letter from Pero Vaz Soares, Factor of Sofala, to the King, Sofala, 1513 June 30', *Documentos sobre os Portugueses*, Vol. III, pp. 459-69.
30. Lobato, *A Expansão Portuguesa em Moçambique*, Vol. II, pp. 121-2.
33. *Ibid.*, 162-3.
32. Charles R. Boxer, *Race Relations in the Portuguese Colonial Empire, 1415-1825* (Oxford: Clarendon Press, 1963), p. 44.

CHAPTER 3: PORTUGUESE PENETRATION AND DEFEAT

1. Hugh Tracey, *António Fernandes Descobridor do Monomotapa, 1514-1515*, translated and annotated by Caetano Montez (Lourenço Marques: Impresna Nacional, 1940), pp. 17-19.
2. Dos Santos, *Ethiopia Oriental, RSEA*, Vol. III, p. 271.
3. Ronald E. Gregson, 'Trade and Politics in South-East Africa: The Moors, the Portuguese and the Kingdom of Mwenemutapa', *African Social Research*, 16, (December 1973), p. 432.
4. Richard Gray, 'Portuguese Musketeers on the Zambezi', *Journal of African History*, Vol. XII, No. 4 (1971), p. 533.
5. António Bocarro, 'Extracts from Decade written by António Bocarro of the Performances of the Portuguese in the East', *RSEA*, Vol. III, pp. 308-20.
6. Eric Axelson, *Portuguese in South-East Africa, 1600-1700* (Johannesburg: Witwatersrand University Press, 1964), pp. 40-53.
7. *Ibid.*, pp. 69-70.
8. 'Copy of the treaty made by the Portuguese with the Monomotapa', *RSEA*, Vol. 5, pp. 290-2.
9. Axelson, *Portuguese in South-East Africa, 1600-1700*, pp. 72-6.
10. Manuel Barreto, 'Report upon the State and Conquest of the Rivers of Cuama', *RSEA*, Vol. 3, p. 483.
11. D. P. Abraham, 'Ethno-history of the Empire of Mutapa. Problems and Methods', *The Historian in Tropical Africa*, ed. J. Vansina, R. Mauny and L. V. Thomas (2nd ed. rev.; London: Oxford University Press, 1969), p. 109.
12. Axelson, *Portuguese in South-East Africa, 1600-1700*, p. 154.
13. D. P. Abraham, 'The Monomotapa Dynasy', *Nada*, Vol. 36 (1959), p. 69.
14. Abraham, 'Maramuca', 215-16.
15. Nicola Sutherland-Harris, 'Trade and the Rozwi Mambo', *Pre-Colonial African Trade*, ed. Richard Gray and David Birmingham (London: Oxford University Press, 1970), pp. 261-2.
16. Inacio Caetano Xavier, 'Notícias dos Dominos Portugueses na Costa de Africa Oriental 1758', in *Relações de Moçambique Setecentista*, António Alberto de Andrade (Lisbon: Agencia Geral do Ultramar, 1955), pp. 35-9.
17. António Bocarro, 'Extracts from the Decade . . . of the Portuguese in the East', *RSEA*, Vol. 3, p. 389.
18. M. D. D. Newitt, *Portuguese Settlement on the Zambesi: Exploration, Land Tenure and Colonial Rule in East Africa* (New York: Africana Publishing Company, 1973), p. 227.
19. Francisco Santana (ed.) *Documentação Avulsa Mocambicana do Arquivo Histórico Ultramarino* (Lisbon: Centro de Estudos Históricos Ultramarinos, 1967), Vol. II, pp. 329, 346.
20. Diogo do Couto, 'Narrative of the Shipwreck of the Great Ship *Sao Thomé* in the land of the Fumos, in the year 1589', *The Tragic History of the Sea*, ed. Charles R. Boxer (Cambridge: Hakluyt Society, 1959), p. 82.
21. Alan Smith, 'Delagoa Bay and the Trade of South Eastern Africa', *Pre-Colonial African Trade*, 270, 280.
22. Mabel V. Jackson, *European Powers and South-East Africa* (London: Longmans Green, 1942), p. 126.

23. Smith, 'Delagoa Bay', 281, 284.
24. Alpers, 'The Mutapa and Malawi political systems', pp. 21-2. Professor Joseph C. Miller disagrees with Alper's account of the Zimba also raiding Kilwa, Malindi and Mombasa, see 'Requiem for the "Jaga" ', *Cahiers d'Etudes Africaines*, Vol. XIII, No. 1 (1973), p. 124-5.
25. Barreto, 'Report upon the State and Conquest', *RSEA*, III, 472-8.
26. Alpers, 'The Mutapa and Malawi political systems', 22-4.
27. Dionizio de Mello e Castro, 'Notíca do Imperio Marave e dos Rios de Sena, mandada pelo coronel Dionizio de Mello e Castro ao governador Pedro de Saldanha de Alberquerque', in *Fontes para a História, Georgrafia e Commercia de Moçambique* (Sec. XVIII), *Anais da Junta de Investigações do Ultramar*, Luis Fernando de Carvalho Dias (Lisbon: Centro de Estudos Históricos Ultramarinos, 1954), Vol. IX, p. 123.
28. Alpers, 'The Mutapa and Malawi political systems', 24-5; Edouard Foa, *Du Cap au Lac Nyassa* (Paris, 1901), pp. 10-12.
29. Francisco Maria de Lacerda e Almeida, 'Notícias dadas por Manuel Caetano Pereira', *Travessia de Africa*, ed. M. Murias (Lisbon, 1936), pp. 384-95.
30. Filipe Gastão de Almeida de Eça, *Lacerda e Almeida Escravo do Dever e Martir de Sciencia 1753-1798* (Lisbon, 1951), pp. 25-36, *passim*.

CHAPTER 4: THE PRAZOS: AFRICAN AND PORTUGUESE SOCIETY

1. M. D. D. Newitt, 'The Portuguese on the Zambesi from the Seventeenth to the Nineteenth Centuries', *Race*, Vol. IX, No. 4 (April 1968), pp. 480, 488.
2. 'Letter from the King to the Vicroy of India, 28 March 1613', *RSEA*, IV, 108-9.
3. Bocarro, 'Extracts from the Decades . . . of the Portuguese in the East', *RSEA*, III, 423.
4. Giuseppe Papagno. *Colonialismo e feudalismo: La questione dei Prazos da Coroa nel Mozambico alla fine del secolo XIX* (Torino: Piccola Biblioteca Einaudi, 1972), p. 37.
5. M. D. D. Newitt, 'The Portuguese on the Zambezi: An Historical Interpretation of the Prazo System', *Journal of African History*, Vol. X, No. 1 (1969), pp. 74-5.
6. Barreto, 'Report upon the State and Conquest', *RSEA*, III, 440. This translation differs slightly from that of Theal.
7. Isaacman, *Mozambique*, 34-5.
8. *Ibid.*, 30.
9. 'Edital da Inquisição de Goa contra certos costumes e ritos da Africa Oriental, January 21, 1771', *O Chronista de Tissuary*, ed. J. H. Cunha Rivara, 4 vols. (Nova Goa, 1866-9), Vol. II, pp. 273-5.
10. Gilberto Freyre, *The Portuguese and the Tropics* (Lisbon: Gráfica Santelmo, 1961), pp. 14-19, 45-51.
11. Newitt, *Portuguese Settlement on the Zambezi*, 180-1.
12. António Pinto de Miranda, 'Memoria sobre a Costa de Africa', *Relações de Moçambique Setecentista*, 231-2.
13. Jeronimo José Nogueira de Andrade, 'Descrição em que ficaram os Negocios de Capitania de Moçambique em Fins de 1789 e considerações sobre e decadencia do seu Commercio', *Archivo das Colónias* (Lisbon, 1917-18), Vol. I, pp. 87-8.
14. Allen Isaacman, 'The Origin, Formation and Early History of the Chikunda of South Central Africa', *Journal of African History*, Vol. XIII, No. 3 (1972), pp. 452-4.
15. Barreto, 'Report upon the State and Conquest', *RSEA*, III, 477.
16. Isaacman, 'The Origin, Formation and Early History of the Chikunda', 458.
17. Newitt, *Portuguese Settlement on the Zambesi*, 195-7.
18. Francisco de Mello e Castro, *Descrição dos Rios de Senna, Anno de 1750* (Lisbon, 1861), p. 21.
19. Isaacman, *Mozambique*, 68.
20. E. A. Alpers, *The East African Slave Trade* (Nairobi: East African Publishing House, 1967), p. 9.

21. Henrique Galvão and Carlos Selvagem, *O Império Ultramarino Português*, 4 vols. (Lisbon: Empresa Nacional de Publicidade, 1953), Vol. IV, pp. 52-3.

22. Archivo Histórico Ultramarino (Lisbon), Papeis Avulsos, Moçambique Maço 13, Sheik of Quitangonha Suleiman Bwana Hajj to Governor Paulo José Miguel de Brito, December 29, 1830; cited in Nancy J. Hafkin, 'Resistance in Nineteenth Century Northern Mozambique: Results of Metropolitan-Local Conflict', paper read before African Studies Association, Syracuse, New York, 1 November 1973, p. 6.

23. James Duffy, *A Question of Slavery* (Cambridge: Harvard University Press, 1967), pp. 47-50.

24. Mello e Castro, *Descrição dos Rios de Senna*, 14; João Pedro Baptista and José Amaro, 'Journey of the Pombeiros from Angola to the Rios de Sena', *The Lands of Cazembe: Lacerda's Journey to Cazembe in 1798*, trans. Richard Burton (London, 1873), p. 237-9.

25. Mello e Castro, *Descrição dos rios de Senna*, 10-35; António Candido Pedroso Gamitto, 'Escravatura na Africa Oriental', *Archivo Pittoresco* (1859), Vol. 2, p. 369-70.

26. Alexandre Lobato, *Evolucão Administrative e Economica de Moçambique 1752-63* (Lisbon: Agencia Geral do Ultramar, 1957), p. 251.

27. Newitt, *Portuguese Settlement on the Zambesi*, 144.

28. *Ibid.*, 142.

29. Isaacman, *Mozambique*, 60.

30. A. C. P. Gamitto, *O Muata Cazembe* (Lisbon, 1854), p. 25.

31. Barreto, 'Supplement to the Report upon the State and Conquest', *RSEA*, III, 506.

32. *Ibid.*

33. Aliva de Azevedo, *Política de Ensino em Africa* (Lisbon: Junta de Investigações do Ultrama, 1958), p. 122.

34. Barreto, 'Report upon the State and Conquest', *RSEA*, III, 468.

35. Gamitto, *O Muata Cazembe*, 389.

36. W. F. W. Owen, 'Particulars of an Expedition up the Zambesi to Senna, performed by three officers of His Majesty's Ship Leven, when surveying the East Coast of Africa in 1823', *Royal Geographical Society*, Vol. 2 (1832), pp. 140-4.

37. Newitt, 'The Portuguese on the Zambesi', *Race*, 495.

CHAPTER 5: INVASIONS: NGONI AND PORTUGUESE

1. Gerhard Liesegang, 'Dingane's Attack on Lourenço Marques in 1833', *Journal of African History*, Vol. X, No. 4 (1969), pp. 577-9.

2. Sousa Ribeiro, ed., *Regimen dos Prazos da Corôa, 1832-1906* (Lourenço Marques, 1907), p. 33.

3. Until recently the Zambezi wars have not been the concern of English-speaking historians. Now the most thorough study is Newitt's *Portuguese Settlement on the Zambesi*. Some of the following account comes from chapters 14 through 18 of that work. Fundamental Portuguese books on the Zambezi wars are Filipe Gastão de Almeida de Eça's *História das Guerras no Zambesi* (Lisbon, 1953) and Teixeira Botelho's *História Militar e Política dos Portugueses em Moçambique* (Lisbon, 1934 and 1936), which have also been used.

4. M. D. D. Newitt, 'The Massingire Rising of 1884', *Journal of African History*, Vol. XI, No. 1 (1970), p. 102.

5. A. da E. Santos Vieira, *História da expansão do domínio português* (Lourenço Marques: Imprensa Nacional, 1934), pp. 44-5.

6. Allen Isaacman, 'Mozambique: The Tradition of Resistance', *Southern Africa*, Vol. 8, No. 6 (June 1975), p. 13.

7. R. J. Hammond, *Portugal and Africa 1815-1910: A Study in Uneconomic Imperialism* (Stanford: Stanford University Press, 1966), p. 293.

8. T. O. Ranger, 'Connexions Between "Primary Resistance" Movements and Modern Mass Nationalism in East and Central Africa, II', *Journal of African History*, Vol. IX, No. 4 (1968), p. 639.

9. This disparaging reference was made to African history in general. For further elaboration of this Eurocentric viewpoint, see Hugh Trevor-Roper, *The Rise of Christian Europe* (New York: Harcourt, Brace & World, 1970), p. 9.

10. Eduardo do Couto Lupi, *Angoche* (Lisbon, 1907), pp. 184; 204-6.

11. João de Azevedo Coutinho, *As Duas Conquistas de Angoche* (Lisbon, 1935), pp. 9-12; 45-53.

12. M. D. D. Newitt, 'Angoche, The Slave Trade and the Portuguese c. 1844-1910', *Journal of African History*, Vol. XIII, No. 4 (1972), pp. 669-70.

13. José Júlio Gonçalves, *O Mundo Árabo-Islâmico e o Ultramar Português* (2nd ed. Lisbon: Agencia Geral do Ultramar, 1962), pp. 272-5.

14. José Justino Teixeira Botelho, *História Militar e Política dos Portugueses em Moçambique de 1833 aos Nossos Dias* (2nd ed. rev.; Lisbon, 1934), pp. 564-72.

15. There is little written on Gungunyane in English or Portuguese. Two worthwhile contributions by Douglas L. Wheeler help to shed light on his life and career, see 'Gungunhana', *Leadership in Eastern Africa: Six Political Biographies*, ed. Norman R. Bennett (Boston: Boston University Press, 1968), pp. 167-220; and 'Gungunyane The Negotiator: A Study in African Diplomacy', *Journal of African History*, Vol. IX, No. 4 (1968), pp. 585-602.

16. António Enes, *Moçambique: Relatório Apresentado ao Governo* (3rd ed. Lisbon: Agência Geral das Colónias, 1945), 176.

17. Wheeler, 'Gungunyane The Negotiator', 602.

18. António Ennes, *A Guerra d'Africa em 1895* (Lisbon, 1898), pp. 311-15; 438-60.

19. *Ibid.*, 543-72.

20. Philip R. Warhurst, *Anglo-Portuguese Relations in South-Central Africa, 1890-1900* (London: Longmans, 1962), p. 107.

21. P. R. Warhurst, 'The Scramble and African Politics in Gazaland', *The Zambesian Past: Studies in Central African History*, ed. Eric Stokes and Richard Brown, (Manchester: Manchester University Press, 1966), p. 61.

22. Duffy, *Portuguese Africa*, 225.

23. Amadeu Cunha, *Mousinho*, 5 vols. (Lisbon, 1935-6), Vol. I, p. 29.

24. Eduardo Lupi, ed. *Aires de Ornelas* , 3 vols. (Lisbon, 1936), Vol. I, p. 72.

25. For detailed studies of Portugal's actions during the international disputes, see in addition to the above cited works of Hammond and Warhurst, Eric Axelson, *Portugal and the Scramble for Africa, 1875-1891* (Johannesburg: Witwatersrand University Press, 1967) and A. H. Hanna, *The Beginnings of Nyasaland and North-Eastern Rhodesia* (London: Oxford University Press, 1956).

26. For recent and extended treatment of the activities of the Geographical Society, see Papagno. *Colonialismo e feudalismo*, 88-150.

27. For a brief and favourable account in English of Portuguese exertions during the scramble, see Charles E. Nowell, 'Portugal and the Partition of Africa', *Journal of Modern History*, Vol. XIX, No. 1 (March, 1947), pp. 1-17.

28. F. C. C. Egerton, *Angola In Perspective* (London: Routledge and Kegan Paul, 1957), pp. 27-8.

CHAPTER 6: THE IMPOSITION OF ALIEN RULE: PORTUGUESE COLONIALISM TO WORLD WAR II

1. António Leite de Magalhães, 'Raízes de Portugal', *O Mundo Português*, IV (Lisbon, 1937), p. 363.

2. João Villas-Boas Carneiro de Moura, *Os Últimos Anos da Monarquia e os Primeiros da República em Moçambique* (Lourenço Marques: Imprensa Nacional, 1965), pp. 12-13.

3. E. A. (Colonel) Azambuja Martins, *O Soldado Africano de Moçambique* (Lisbon: Agencia Geral das Colonias, 1936), pp. 10-11.

4. *Anuário do Estado de Moçambique, 1972-1973* (Lourenço Marques: Oficinas Gráficas da Minerva Central, 1937), pp. viii-xviii.

5. A decree in 1973 divided Mozambique into the following districts and district capitals:

    Beira (port of Beira)   Nampula (city of Nampula)
    Cabo Delgado (Porto Amélia)   Niassa (Vila Cabral)
    Gaza (João Belo)   Tete (city of Tete)
    Inhambane (city of Inhambane)   Vila Pery (city of Vila Pery)
    Ilha (city of Mozambique)   Zambézia (Quelimane)
    Lourenço Marques (city of Lourenço Marques)

    To date, the independent government has incorporated Ilha district into Nampula
    district and changed the district name of Lourenço Marques to Maputo, Vila Pery to
    Manica and Beira to Sofala. The towns of Porto Amélia, João Belo and Lourenço
    Marques have been changed respectively to Pemba, Xai Xai and Maputo.

6. Norman A. Bailey, 'Government and Administration', *Portuguese Africa: A
    Handbook*, ed. David M. Abshire and Michael A. Samuels (New York: Praeger, 1969),
    p. 134.

7. British Admiralty, *A Manual of Portuguese East Africa* (London: His Majesty's
    Stationery Office, 1920), pp. 135, 163, 503-10, *passim*. This remains the best source of
    information on the chartered companies.

8. *Alfredo Freire de Andrade, Relatórios de Moçambique*, 4 vols. (Lourenço Marques,
    Imprensa Nacional, 1909), Vol. III, p. 5.

9. Quoted in Américo Chaves de Almeida, *O Problema da Africa Oriental Protuguesa*, 2
    vols. (Lisbon, 1932), Vol. I, p. 261.

10. Manuel de Brito Camacho, *Pretos e Brancos* (Lisbon: Guimaraes, 1926), p. 116.
    Although Brito Camacho justified government 'facilities' for recruiting on the need for
    development, he also championed education for Africans. In this, his views were very
    much out of tune which most settlers who believed that Africans should be taught to
    work for Europeans. Such policies made him controversial.

11. A. Duarte de Almeida, *História Colonial de Portugal* (Lisbon, n.d.), p. 228.

12. Paul (General) von Lettow-Vorbeck, *My Reminiscences of East Africa* (London, Hurst
    and Blackett, 1920), p. 232.

13. Allen Isaacman, 'Madzi-Manga, Mhondoro and the Use of Oral Traditions — A Chapter
    in Barue Religious and Political History', *Journal of African History*, Vol. XIV, No. 3(
    1973), pp. 406-408.

14. For an authoritative sketch of the rising, see Terrence O. Ranger, 'Revolt in Portuguese
    East Africa: The Makombe Rising of 1917', *St. Antony's Papers*, No. 15, ed. Kenneth
    Kirkwood (Carbondale: Southern Illinois University Press, 1963), 54-80.

15. Quoted in *New York Times*, 28 July 1970.

16. Douglas L. Wheeler, 'Thaw in Portugal', *Foreign Affairs*, Vol. 48, No. 4 (July, 1970), p.
    771.

17. For a very useful discussion of the New State's hyperbole and policies to the 1950s, see
    Duffy, *Portuguese Africa*, pages 268-88; see Professor Wheeler's penetrating analysis of
    the Portuguese character and its relationship to the African colonies in Douglas L.
    Wheeler and René Pélissier, *Angola* (New York: Praeger, 1971), pp. 10-19.

18. Marcelo Caetano, *Tradições, Princípios e Métodos da Colonização Portuguêsa* (Lisbon:
    Agencia Geral do Ultramar, 1951), pp. 275-6.

19. Wheeler and Pélissier, *Angola*, 131.

20. Charles and David Livingstone, *Narrative of an Expedition to the Zambezi and its
    Tributaries* (New York, 1886), p. 259.

21. Duffy, *Portuguese Africa*, 157.

22. Quoted in J. M. da Silva Cunha, *O Tralbalho Indígena* (Lisbon: Agência Geral das
    Colónias, 1949), p. 151.

23. Thomaz de Almeida Garrett, *Um Governo em Africa* (Lisbon: 1907), pp. 217-20.

24. *Portaria 917, Official Boletim*, No. 49, 8 December 1906.

25. Edward Alsworth Ross, *Report on Employment of Native Labor in Portuguese Africa*
    (New York: Abbott Press, 1925), pp. 58, 60.

26. J. P. Moffitt, Consul, to Assistant Secretary of State, Political Situation, 19 October
    1927, 853N.00/7, National Archives, Washington, D.C.

27. *Notícias* (Lourenço Marques), 3 August 1927.

28. José Tristão de Bettencourt, *Relatório do Governador Geral* (Lisbon: Agência Geral das

Colónias, 1945), pp. 75-81.

29. António Rita Ferreira, *O Movimento Migratório de Trabalhadores entre Moçambique e a África do Sul* (Lisbon: Estudos de Ciencias Políticas e Sociais, 1963), pp. 101-2 and 129-34.

30. António de Figueiredo, *Portugal and Its Empire: The Truth* (London: Victor Gollancz, 1961), p. 112.

31. A. Rita-Ferreira, 'Labor Emigration Among the Mocambique Thonga — Comments on a Study by Marvin Harris', *Africa*, Vol. XX (1960), p. 144.

32. For example, see *As Notícias de Lourenço Marques*, 20 August 1926 and 27 October 1926.

33. Marvin Harris, 'Labour Emigration among the Mocambique Thonga: Cultural and Political Factors', *Africa*, Vol. XXIV (1959), pp. 57.

34. 'Instructions to the Captain-Major D. Francisco de Almeida', *Documentos sobre os Portuguese em Moçambique*, I, 181.

35. António Enes, *Moçambique: Relatório apresentado ao Governo*, 193.

36. Jorge Dias, 'Contactos de Cultura', *Cóloquios de Política Ultramarina Internacionalmente Relevante* (Junta de Investigações do Ultramar, Estudos de Ciências Politicas e Sociais, No. VII, Lisbon, 1958), pp. 74-7.

37. Magnus Mörner, *Race Mixture in the History of Latin America* (Boston: Little, Brown, 1967), p. 14.

38. Boxer, *Race Relations*, 53.

39. W. F. W. Owen, RN, *Narrative of Voyages to Explore the Shores of Africa, Arabia, and Madagascas*, 2 vols. (London, 1833), Vol. II, pp. 191-2.

40. Sá da Bandeira, *O Trabalho Rural Africana e a Administração Colonial* (Lisbon, 1873), pp. 13-14; quoted in Richard J. Hammond, 'Race Attitudes and Policies in Portuguese Africa in the Nineteenth and Twentieth Centuries', *Race*, Vol. IX, No. 2 (1967), p. 207.

41. *Ibid.*

42. Cited in Alfredo Hector Wilensky, *Trends in Portuguese Overseas Legislation for Africa* (Braga: Pax, 1971), p. 159.

43. David M. Abshire and Norman A. Bailey, 'Current Racial Character', *Portuguese Africa: A Handbook*, 212.

44. C. R. Boxer, *Four Centuries of Portuguese Expansion, 1415-1825* (Berkeley: University of California Press, 1969), p. 42.

CHAPTER 7: RIDING OUT THE WINDS OF CHANGE

1. 'Indians in Mozambique', *Africa Today*, Vol. 10 (February 1963), pp. 12-13.

2. For excerpts of the report, see Henrique Galvão, *Santa Maria: My Crusade for Portugal* (New York: World Publishing Company, 1961), pp. 57-71.

3. UNESCO *Bulletin*, E/CN 14/LU/ECOP/2 (20 July 1965), p. 3.

4. British Admiralty, *A Manual of Portuguese East Africa*, 132, 463.

5. E. W. van Opzeeland, 'Rift in Mozambique Church', *Tijd* (Netherlands), 2 September 1972; reprinted and translated in *Facts and Reports*, Vol. 2, No. 20 (20 September 1972), p. 12.

6. Sebastian Soares de Resende, *Ordem Anticomunists* (Lourenço Marques, 1950), pp. 141-2.

7. Eduardo de Sousa Ferreira, 'The Present Role of the Portuguese Resettlement Policy', *Africa Today*, Vol. 21, No. 1 (Winter 1974), p. 50. It was reported that only 718 new colonists arrived in Mozambique during 1970 by the Província de Moçambique, see *Boletim Mensal de Estatistica*, Ano XII (May 1971), p. 13.

8. 'News Review', *Bank of London & South American Review*, Vol. 6, No. 72 (December 1972), p. 666.

9. 'Mozambique', *Africa Contemporary Record: Annual Survey and Documents, 1970-71*, ed. Colin Legum (London: Rex Collings, 1971), p. B 590.

10. Eduardo Mondlane, *The Struggle for Mozambique* (Baltimore: Penguin, 1969), p. 20.
11. 'Cabora Bassa — Why We Say No', *Mozambique Liberation* (Dar es Salaam), No. 45 (October–December 1970), p. 2.
12. C. F. Spence, *Moçambique* (London: Bailey Bros. & Swinfen, 1963), p. 78. There is much useful information in this economic and geographic survey.
13. Marvin Harris, *Portugal's African 'Wards'* (New York: American Committee on Africa, 1958), p. 31.
14. Mondlane, *Struggle for Mozambique*, 86.
15. Marvin Harris, 'Race, Conflict, and Reform in Mozambique', *The Transformation of East Africa*, ed. Stanley Diamond and Fred G. Burke (New York: Basic Books, 1962), pp. 164, 166.
16. Quoted in Wilensky, *Trends in Portuguese Overseas Legislation*, 206.
17. Caetano, *Tradições, Princípios e Métodos*, 41.
18. Joaquim Mousinho de Albuquerque, *Moçambique*, 2 vols. (Lisbon, 1934), Vol. I, p. 139.
19. Portuguese Colonial Policy, 20 November 1942, F.O.371/3115, PRO.
20. Thomas Jesse Jones, *Education in East Africa* (New York: Phelps-Stokes Fund, 1925), p. 312.
21. Adrian Hastings, *Wiriyamu* (London: Search Press, 1974), p. 151; Father Hastings has also reprinted the Concordat and the Missionary Agreement in the appendixes.
22. *Area Handbook for Mozambique*, 93, 95.
23. *Boletim Geral do Ultramar* (Lisbon), No. 49 (May 1966), table facing 232.
24. Eugenio Lisboa, 'Education in Angola and Mozambique', *Education in Southern Africa*, ed. Brian Rose (London: Collier-Macmillan, 1970), p. 283.
25. For an example of Portuguese exuberance on the topic of medicine, see F. J. C. Cambournac, 'Portuguese Activities in Public Health in Tropics', *Portugal and Brazil in Transition*, ed. Raymond S. Sayers (Minneapolis: University of Minnesota, 1968), pp. 328–336.
26. Wheeler and Pélissier, *Angola*, 248.
27. Galvão, *Império Ultramarino Português*, 52.
28. Rual Neves Dias, *An Imprensa Periódica em Moçambique, 1854–1954* (Lourenço Marques: Imprensa Nacional de Moçambique, 1956), pp. 66–7.
29. Brito Camacho, *Pretos e Brancos*, 219.
30. Dias, *A Imprensa Periódica*, 85.
31. Sir Claude Russell to Sir John Simon, Portugal Annual Report, 1931, Confidential, F.O.371/19496, PRO.
32. After the army *coup*, it was reported that Delgado had made a secret visit to Mozambique to contact the anti-Salazarist underground in 1960. *Notícias da Beira*, 5 May 1974.
33. Chikomuami Mahala, 'The Horror of Moçambique', *Africa South in Exile*, Vol. 5 (October–December 1960), p. 59. Mahala maintains that the PIDE were in Mozambique from the early 1950s.
34. Figueiredo, *Portugal and Its Empire: The Truth*, pp. 117–19.
35. 'Manifesto dos democratas de Moçambique dirigido a população', *Portugal Democrático* (São Paulo), IV (November 1960), p. 8; cited in Ronald H. Chilote, *Emerging Nationalism in Portuguese Africa: Documents* (Standford, California: Hoover Institution Press, 1972), pp. 401–2.
36. *New York Times*, 7 April 1961.
37. John Marcum, *The Angolan Revolution, Vol. I: The Anatomy of an Explosion, 1950–1962* (Cambridge, Massachusetts: MIT Press, 1969), p. 199.

CHAPTER 8: NATIONALISM: PROTEST AND PARTIES

1. T. O. Ranger, 'Connexions Between "Primary Resistance" Movements and Modern Mass Nationalism in East and Central Africa: II', *Journal of African History*, Vol. IX, No. 4 (1968), pp. 636–7. Although Ranger establishes a continuum in the evolution of nationalism, he remains sceptical of 'nationalist historiography which sees an exclusive line of ancestry running from one episode of violent resistance to another. . . .' He does acknowledge the impact of such 'historiography' on today's nationalist politics.

2. Dias, *Imprensa Periódica em Moçambique*, 73.

3. Alfredo Margarido, 'The Social and Economic Background of Portuguese Negro Poetry', *Diogenes*, No. 37 (1962), p. 71.

4. Eduardo dos Santos, *Pan-Africanismo de Ontem e de Hoje* (Lisbon: By the author, 1968), p. 131.

5. *O Brado Africano*, 27 February 1932.

6. Eduardo dos Santos, *Ideológias Políticas Africanas* (Lisbon: Centro de Estudos Politico, 1968), pp. 64–9.

7. At the previous London session of the conference, DuBois reported that Kamba Simango, an American-educated African from Portuguese East Africa, attended, but he provided no additional information. W. E. B. DuBois, 'The Pan-African Movement', *History of the Pan-African Congress*, ed. George Padmore (London, 1963), pp. 22.

8. Wheeler and Pélissier, *Angola*, 119–20.

9. Quoted and translated in Gerald M. Moser, 'African Literature in the Portuguese Language', *Journal of General Education*, Vol. 13 (1961), pp. 289–90.

10. Richard A. Preto-Rodas, *Negritude as a Theme in the Poetry of the Portuguese-Speaking World* (Gainesville, Florida: University of Florida Press, 1970), p. 71.

11. Gerald M. Moser, 'African Literature in Portuguese: The First Written the Last Discovered', *African Forum*, Vol. 2, No. 4 (Spring 1967), p. 94; For examples of Honwana's writing translated into English, see *New York Times*, 30 April 1967, section VI, pp. 26–7; and Ezekiel Mphahlele, ed., *African Writing Today* (Baltimore: Penguin, 1967), pp. 317–34.

12. Mondlane, *Struggle for Mozambique*, 111.

13. 'The Role of Poetry in the Mozambican Revolution', *Mozambique Revolution* (Dar es Salaam), Vol. 37 (January–February 1969), pp. 30–1.

14. A. T. Steele, 'On the Edge of Africa's Racial Troubles', *New York Herald-Tribune*, 26 November 1952. Details of riots and small organizations are hard to come by since censorship excluded reportage in the local press. Only infrequently did foreign journalists note such activities. FRELIMO has published some accounts, but until the PIDE files are released our knowledge will remain fragmentary.

15. A very brief sketch of the events in Lourenço Marques can be read in 'The Stevedores Strike: Paulo Baloi murdered by Portuguese colonialists, 64 Stevedores in Machava Prison', *Mozambique Revolution* (Dar es Salaam), No. 1 (December 1963), p. 9.

16. David J. M. Mabunda and John Sakupwanya, 'Brief History of Mocambique', *Emerging Nationalism*, 388.

17. Mondlane, *Struggle for Mozambique*, 114.

18. Paulo Gumane interviewed by the writer in Syracuse, New York, 2 November 1973.

19. Mondlane, 'The Development of Nationalism in Mocambique', *Emerging Nationalism*, 399.

20. *Ibid.*, 396.

21. Gumane interview.

22. Mondlane, *Struggle for Mozambique*, 117–18. Mondlane quotes eyewitness accounts.

23. Marcum, *The Angolan Revolution*, Vol. I, pp. 196–7.

24. Richard Gibson, *African Liberation Movements: Contemporary Struggles Against White Minority Rule* (New York: Oxford University Press, 1972), p. 277.

25. Quoted in Marcum, 'A Martyr for Mozambique', *Africa Report*, Vol. 14, No. 3 and 4 (March–April 1969), p. 7.

26. FRELIMO's programme has been circulated by it and its sympathizers in various

pamphlets and handbills. The most readily accessible source is in Mondlane's *Struggle for Mozambique*, 122-3, 189-98.

27. Helen Kitchen, 'Conversation with Eduardo Mondlane', *Africa Report*, Vol. 12, No. 8 (November 1967), p. 50. Mondlane in this interview stated that over two-thirds of FRELIMO's aid came from African sources. The widespread use of sophisticated weapons and military techniques and the nonpayment of funds to the OAU by many African countries makes this claim doubtful in the last stages of the war.

28. Thomas H. Henriksen, 'The Revolutionary Thought of Eduardo Mondlane', *Genève-Afrique*, Vol. XII, No. 1 (1973), pp. 37-52.

29. George Thayer, *The War Business* (London: Paladin, 1969), p. 138.

30. For a sampling of Machel's political ideas, see Maria Isabel Pinto Ventura, ed., *A Frelimo e a Revolução em Moçambique* (Lisbon: Maria da Fonte, 1975).

31. 'Expulsion of Leo Milas from FRELIMO', *Mozambique Revolution* (Dar es Salaam), No. 9 (August 1964), pp. 4-5.

32. Helio Felgas, *Os Movimentos Terroristas de Angola, Guiné, Moçambique* (Lisbon, 1966), p. 70.

33   Paulo Gumane, 'Failure of Unity Talks', *Emerging nationalism*, 479.

34. *Times of Zambia*, 4 March 1972; and 27 April 1972.

35. Stanley Meisler, a correspondent, published an analysis of Father Gwenjere's role in FRELIMO's internal difficulties, *Los Angeles Times*, 30 June 1968.

36. The complete answer to his detractors has been translated and annotated by Douglas L. Wheeler, 'A Document for the History of African Nationalism: A FRELIMO "White Paper" by Eduardo C. Mondlane', *African Historical Studies*, Vol. II, No. 2 (1969), pp. 319-33. Mozambican students in the United States reacted by mimeographing and distributing a reply in May 1968, see Professor Wheeler's 'A Document for the History of African Nationalism: The UNEMO "White Paper" of 1968: A Student Reply to Eduardo Mondlane's 1967 Paper', *African Historical Studies*, Vol. III, No. 1 (1970), pp. 169-79.

37. Basil Davidson, *In the Eye of the Storm: Angola's People* (New York: Doubleday, 1973), pp. 227-31.

38. *The Observer* (London), 6 February 1972.

39. *The Times of Zambia*, 18 March 1975.

40. *Daily News* (Tanzania), 17 November 1969.

41. Among the prominent defectors who left soon after Kavandame were: Alexandre Magno, former member of the Central Committee; Verónica Namiva, onetime chairperson of the Women's League; and João José Graveirinha, former deputy chief of propaganda. 'Terrorism in Southern Africa', *Africa Institute Bulletin*, Vol. XI, No. 5 (1973), p. 175.

42. *New York Times*, 28 February 1971.

43. *Voz Africana* had been the organ of the Centro Africano de Manica e Sofala but printed on presses of *Notícias da Beira*.

44. 'The War Wears a Face', *Portugal: An Informative Review*, No. 19 (January 1972), p. 10.

45. *Africa Research Bulletin* (1-31 August 1970), p. 1846.

46. Machel stated that the Portuguese Minister of Defence, General Sá Viana Rebelo declared in 1970: 'the only way of destroying FRELIMO was to use subversion'. 'The Enemy's New Methods', *Mozambique Revolution* (Dar es Salaam), No. 57 (October-December 1973), p. 4.

47. Machel stressed this point during his independence-day speech. *Notícias* (Lourenço Marques), 26 June 1975; *New York Times*, 2 July 1975.

48. For an example of the hostile reviews for Gibson's treatment of the splits within nationalist movements, see Alan Brook's review in *Anti-Apartheid News* (United Kingdom), July-August 1972, p. 11.

CHAPTER 9: THE WAR FOR NATIONAL LIBERATION

1. Hlomulo Chitofo Gwambe, 'Facts About Moçambique', *Emerging nationalism*, 425.
2. *New York Times*, 6 September 1960.
3. *Marchés Tropicaux* (Genève), No. 1268 (16 October 1971), p. 2925.
4. *Rand Daily Mail* (South Africa), 27 February 1973.
5. Quoted in the *New York Times*, 20 August 1964.
6. One Portuguese reporter made the assertion that Israel also trained FRELIMO recruits before the war. Felgas, *Os Movimentos Terroristas*, pp. 71, 73.
7. Alberto-Joaquim Chipande's statement quoted in Mondlane, *Struggle for Mozambique*, 137.
8. There are a number of reports and documents examining Western and NATO aid to Portugal. Among the most recent, critical and obtainable is: William Minter, *Portuguese Africa and the West*, New York: Monthly Review Press, 1972.
9. During the war Banda's policy— a product of his precarious position in southern Africa — vacillated between FRELIMO and the Portuguese. FRELIMO was only prohibited from sending armed men through Malawi territory. Banda allowed the Portuguese to transport oil brought by rail from Beira through its Chipoka port where it was shipped across the lake to the Mozambique town of Mepona. By this route the army could avoid road mines and ambushes in the north-east.
10. *The Times* (United Kingdom), 17 March 1971 and *The Nationalist* (Tanzania), 14 April 1971.
11. United Nations, General Assembly, Special Committee on the situation with Regard to the Implementation of the Declaration on the Granting of Independence to Colonial Countries and Peoples, Territories Under Portuguese Administration, *Working Paper Prepared by the Secretariat*, Document A/AC.109/1.538/Add. 2, April 1969, pp. 2-6; *Sunday Times* (United Kingdom), 9 July 1972; and *Sunday Tribune* (South Africa), 16 July 1972.
12. 'War Communiqué', *Mozambique Revolution* (Dar es Salaam), No. 34 (June–September 1968), p. 12.
13. *Rand Daily Mail* (South Africa), 3 February 1974.
14. Helen Kitchen, 'Conversations with Eduardo Mondlane', *Africa Report*, Vol. 12, No. 8 (November 1967), p. 51.
15. 'Editorial', *Mozambique Revolution* (Dar es Salaam), No. 38 (March–April 1969), p. 2.
16. Brendan F. Jundanian, 'Resettlement Programs: Counterinsurgency in Mozambique', *Comparative Politics*, Vol. 6, No. 4 (July 1974), p. 523.
17. *Expresso* (Portugal), 27 October 1973.
18. Published material on Angola's fortified villages indicates that life in them was far from pleasant. For an authoritative study, see Gerald J. Bender, 'The Limits of Counterinsurgency', *Comparative Poliics*, Vol. 4, No. 3 (April 1972), pp. 331-60.
19. 'A New World on the Rovuma Frontier', *Portugal: An Informative Review* (Lisbon), No. 27 (October 1972), pp. 20-1.
20. *Expresso* (Portugal), 9 October 1973.
21. *Rand Daily Mail* (South Africa), 9 October 1973.
22. Nuno Rocha, *Guerra em Moçambique* (Lisbon: Ulisseia, 1969), p. 28.
23. One observer in 1973 put the Portuguese air force in Mozambique at 5 Nore-Atlas and 5 DC-3 transports, 15 Harvard T6 prop-driven fighter-bombers, 8 Fiat jets, 14 Alouette helicopters and an undetermined number of spotter planes. Boeing 737 jets and other charter planes were used to evacuate the wounded. Michael Degnan, 'The "Three Wars" of Mozambique', *Africa Report*, Vol. 18, No. 5 (September–October 1973), pp. 12-13.
24. *A Voz da Revolução*, No. 7 (January 1967), p. 8.
25. Samora Machel, 'The Enemy's New Methods', *Mozambique Revolution*, No. 57 (October–December 1973), p. 4.
26. *Los Angeles Times*, 4 April 1969.
27. F. X. Maier, *Revolution and Terrorism in Mozambique* (New York: American African Affairs Association, 1974), p. 28.

28. 'Editorial', *Mozambique Revolution* (Dar es Salaam), No. 51 (April-June 1972), p. 2.

29. Reports have surfaced that FRELIMO actually used shoulder-held ground-to-air missiles against aircraft on at least one occasion. *The Observer* (United Kingdom), 12 May 1974; and *The Star* (South Africa), 25 May 1974. Reporter James MacManus wrote that at war's end the guerrillas had undeployed heat-seeking missiles. *Washington Post* (United States), 13 October 1974.

30. FRELIMO argued that assaults on white farms were carried out by the Portuguese posing as guerrillas so as to discredit them and provoke settler retaliation. *Washington Post*, 4 June 1974.

31. FRELIMO's president admitted that focus on the war effort and lack of commitment among the nursing students had caused a neglect of health services, see 'Our Hospitals' Role in the Revolution', *Mozambique Revolution* (Dar es Salaam), No. 58 (January-March 1974), p. 12.

32. Barbara Cornwall, *The Bush Rebels: A Personal Account of Black Revolt in Africa* (New York: Holt, Rinehart and Winston, 1972), p. 37.

33. Letter to the editor by João Hall Themido, Ambassador to the United States, *Newsweek*, Vol. 81, No. 4 (22 January 1973), p. 5. The Ambassador's letter was provoked by Andrew Jaffee's article, 'A March in Mozambique', *Newsweek*, Vol. 80, No. 22 (27 November 1972), pp. 46-7.

34. Many journalists, camera teams, delegates and sympathetic observers journeyed in FRELIMO zones and gave accounts of nationalist activities. For a listing of these visitors, see Richard W. Leonard, 'FRELIMO's Victories in Mozambique', *Issue: A Quarterly Journal of Africanist Opinion* (United States), Vol. IV, No. 2 (Summer 1974), pp. 38-40.

35. *United Nations Statistical Yearbook 1973*, s.v. 'Average Annual Rates of Gross Domestic Product at Constant Prices', and 'National Income and Gross Domestic Product'.

36. *The Star* (South Africa), 12 June 1971.

37. Eduardo de Sousa Ferreira, 'Education and Discrimination in Portuguese Territories of Africa', *UNESCO Courier*, Vol. 26, No. 11 (November 1973), p. 26.

38. *Notícias* (Lourenço Marques), 29 March 1972.

39. United Nations, General Assembly, Report on the Special Committee on the Situation with Regard to the Implementation of the Declaration or the Granting of Independence to Colonial Countries and Peoples (A/9023, Part IV), 8 October 1973, p. 9.

40. For a report by an Anglican clergyman in the northwest from 1957 to 1970 of PIDE arrests and torture of prisoners, most of whom were simple villagers, see John Paul, *Mozambique: Memoirs of a Revolution* (Harmondsworth: Penguin, 1975), pp. 124-47, *passim*.

41. Amnesty International (Dutch Branch), 'Portugal, 25,000 Political Prisoners'; translated and reprinted in *Facts and Reports* (Netherlands), Vol. 20, No. 23 (1 November 1972), p. 15.

42. *The Financial Times* (United Kingdom), 17 March 1972.

43. 'Statement by Father William Burridge on behalf of the White Fathers, May 1971', *Africa Contemporary Record: Annual Survey and Documents, 1971-1972*, ed. Colin Legum (New York: Africana Publishing Corporation, 1972), Vol. 4, pp. C 244-C 245.

44. 'Further Evidence Presented to the Decolonization Committee', *Objective: Justice*, Special Supplement No. 1 (September 1973), p. 8.

45. *Daily Telegraph* (United Kingdom), 14 December 1972.

46. E. W. van Opzeeland, 'Rift in Mozambique Church', *Tijd* (Netherlands), 27 September 1972; translated and reprinted in *Facts and Reports* (Netherlands), Vol. 2, No. 20 (30 September 1972), p. 12.

47. Adrian Hastings, *Wiriyamu* (London: Search Press, 1974), pp. 84-6.

48. 'African Massacres and "Massacres" ', *Portugal: An Informative Review* (Lisbon), No. 37 (1973), p. 9.

49. *Daily Telegraph* (United Kingdom), 20 August 1973.

50. For example, see Hastings's article in *The Times*, 10 July 1973 and a report from the Burgos Order reprinted in *The Times*, 13 July 1973; Mondlane recounts the execution of a chief for collaboration with the Portuguese, *Struggle for Mozambique*, 165.

51. For the soundest analysis of the *coup* to date and the influence of nationalist ideology on members of the Armed Forces Movement, see Kenneth Maxwell, 'The Hidden

Revolution in Portugal', *New York Review of Books*, Vol. XXII, No. 6 (17 April 1975), pp. 29-34; 'Portugal Under Pressure', *New York Review of Books*, Vol. XXII, No. 9 (29 May 1975), pp. 20-30.

52. *Notícias e Factos* (New York), No. 78 (29 april 1974), p. 1.
53. Not surprisingly FRELIMO holds this position, see 'Editorial', *Mozambique Revolution* (Dar es Salaam), No. 59 (April-June 1974), p. 2.
54. Radio Report recorded in *Facts and Reports* (Netherlands), Vol. 4, No. 15 and 16 (3 August 1974), p. 19.
55. *Expresso* (Portugal), 18 May 1974.
56. Partido de Coligação Nacional de Moçambique, Communiqué No. 1, 23 August 1974. The writer is indebted to Winifred Armstrong for sending him this material.
57. *The Observer* (United Kingdom), 4 August 1974; there were some allegations in east African newspapers that American consulate officials in Lusaka attempted to block FRELIMO from taking power by supporting and financing COREMO. Spokesmen for the United States denied such a plot. *Zambia Daily News*, 10 April 1975.
58. *Notícias da Beira*, 9 September 1974.

CHAPTER 10: THE FUTURE AGAINST THE PAST

1. A. J. Venter, 'Mozambique—One Month to Uhuru', *Scope* (South Africa), 23 May 1975, p. 30; *Christian Science Monitor* (United States), 5 May 1975.
2. *Notícias da Beira*, 2 December 1974.
3. Figures based on those given in an interview with Portugal's High Commissioner in Mozambique, Rear Admiral Vitor Crespo. *Times of Zambia*, 22 April 1975.
4. *New York Times*, 15 January 1976.
5. A plenary session of FRELIMO in Mocuba during February established party goals and procedures for politicization. *Notícias da Beira*, 17-22 February 1975.
6. *Notícias* (Lourenço Marques), 6 March 1975.
7. At the formation of the transition government, Machel broadcasted a speech to the Mozambican people. It was printed in its entirety in the *Daily News* (Tanzania), 23 September 1975.
8. For views of the Women's Detachment in the war, see *The Mozambican Woman in the Revolution*. A pamphlet published by the Liberation Support Movement. Richmond, BC Canada, 1974; and 'Our Role in the Struggle', *Mozambique Revolution* (Dar es Salaam), No. 52 (July-September 1972), pp. 7-8.
9. *Daily News* (Tanzania), 23 April 1973; and *The Observer* (United Kingdom), 23 April 1975.
10. For a source that argues that FRELIMO has backed down on initial efforts at ending prostitution, see *CFM News & Notes* (New York), No. 32 (September 1975), p. 9. The Committee for a Free Mozambique reported that prostitution, like the migratory mine labourers, is a legacy of colonialism and will be gradually phased out.
11. *Notícias* (Lourenço Marques), 21 July 1975.
12. *Notícias* (Lourenço Marques), 21 September 1975.
13. *Notícias* (Lourenço Marques), 24 December 1975; and *Daily News* (Tanzania), 2 January 1976.
14. For an optimistic assessment of Mozambique's future economic independence, see Robin B. Wright, 'Mozambique: Short Term Problems, Long Term Hope', *Africa Today*, Vol. 22, No. 3 (July-September 1975), pp. 15-19.
15. *Financial Times* (London), 9 September 1975.
16. *Notícias da Beira*, 3 March 1975.
17. *Daily Report* (Foreign Broadcasting Information Service), Vol. III, No. 134 (11 July 1975), p. 5.
18. *The Star* (South Africa), 11 October 1975.
19. *Notícias* (Lourenço Marques), 19 June 1975.
20. *Notícias* (Lourenço Marques), 25 June 1975.
21. People's Republic of Mozambique, *Constitution*, Art. 24.

APPENDIX I

MOZAMBIQUE'S PEOPLE

Mozambique's African population is ethnically diverse. This pluralism stems from numerous immigrations and invasions of Bantu-speaking peoples over the centuries. The last significant African invasion took place in the wake of a Zulu uprising in Natal, South Africa during the early nineteenth century. Estimates from the 1970 census place the African population at slightly over eight million. African population density is heaviest in the northern coastal regions, and African and non-African peoples are densest in Maputo district with 111.6 persons per square mile in 1960.

Intermarriage among sub-groups and even some main groups as well as racial inter-relatedness, common cultures and values, lessens some of the ideas of rigid separation to which strict classification perhaps gives rise. The various ethnic groups in fact share important customs. For example, peoples north of the Zambezi generally trace descent by a matrilinear system and those in the south use a patrilinear method. Around the river some groups incorporate both practices. Most of the main groups extend into neighbouring countries, and over some borders there is considerable crossing back and forth, an important factor during the guerrilla war of the 1960s and 1970s.

With estimates from the 1970 census,[1] the largest enthnolinguistic groups are:

Makonde	175,000
Yao	170,000
Makua-Lomwe	3,000,000
Ngoni	35,000
Malawi	250,000
Lower Zambezi peoples	900,000
Shona	765,000
Thonga	1,850,000
Chopi and Tonga	450,000

Up in the northeast of the country the Makonde inhabit a plateau of the same name in Cabo Delgado district. They were possibly part of the migration from the lands south of Lake Malawi centuries ago. Known for their wood carvings, the Makonde like the Makua practice scarification of the body and face in elaborate patterns. Traditionally they have cultivated the soil as the tsetse-fly prohibited cattle raising, and lived in small family groupings, recognizing only the authority of the village headman. Despite this absence of central authority, the Makonde have not only ably defended themselves in their highground sanctuary but also proved in the past aggressive toward their neighbours the Makua who they captured, selling some to Arab slavers on the coast. A constant defence posture against slavers has been offered as the chief explanation for the Makonde bellicosity, deep cultural homogeneity and resistance to Islam. The fact they kept free of Islam encouraged Christian missionaries to seek converts until the nationalist war in 1964 required their evacuation.

To the west of the Makonde are the Yao who live in the Niassa district, primarily between the Lugenda and Rovuma rivers. For hundreds of years they have inhabited this location, but after 1850 some groups moved to Tanzania and Malawi, possibly to escape internal squabbles, attacks by the Ngoni or locust plagues. In the past the Yao acted as middlemen for Arab traders, exchanging ivory, iron and finally slaves at the coast for cloth, ornaments and eventually firearms to acquire more slaves. Their long contact with Muslim traders influenced them to profess Islam and adopt Arab dress and social customs in forms compatible with Bantu culture. Long Arab robes and rectangular houses (traditional African huts are round) attest to the long Arab relationship, but traditional religious practices continue to exist alongside Islam. The Yao are intermixed with the Nyanja and Ngoni as well as Arab stock, and this hetero-genetrous composition contributes to friendly relations with these neigh-bouring groups despite earlier Yao slave raids. Today the Yao till the soil.

Encircled on three sides by the Yao are a group of Nyanjas who live along Lake Malawi. Since the late nineteenth century they had come under the influence of two Anglican missions—one at Massumba in Niassa district and the other on Malawi's Licoma Island, near the Mozambique shoreline. These Nyanja are fluent and some literate in English rather than Portuguese, which points up the weakness of Portuguese influence in the extreme north.

Below the Yao and Makonde and stretching from the coast across the country are the Makua-Lomwe peoples, the largest and possibly least known of the indigenous inhabitants. The Makua outnumber the culturally similar Lomwe by more than three to one. The linguistic and cultural differences between the two have been sharpened by the stronger pulls of Arab customs and Islam on the Makua than the Lomwe. The coastal Makua speak a Swahili dialect and live a decidedly Arab-influenced life typical of the east African littoral to the north. Their language, life-style and beliefs have led them to be categorized as a distinct group.[2] In 1967 an estimated 900,000 Muslims lived in the coastal zones of Cabo Delgado, Mozambique and Zambézia districts.[3] After 1900 many Lowme, who occupied the lands immediately to the south of Makua, moved to Malawi where they now constitute the second largest ethnic group. They are related to the Nyanja in Tete district and to the Chuabo on the coast.

The Makua, one of the few groups not to spill greatly into bordering states, are believed to have been the first Bantu immigrants to reach the Indian Ocean. Organized into small sub-groups, they are without a central authority. Like other northern peoples they are agriculturists, and like the Makonde they cicatrize intricate designs on their faces and bodies. A religious affinity with the Yao help make for friendly relations with them, but Islamic ties have added to the enmity between them and the Makonde.

Another principal group in the north are the Malawi (Marave) who inhabit Tete district north of the Zambezi. Malawi is a blanket term for there are no people calling themselves by it. As most other Mozambique peoples, the Malawi are found across the frontiers in the countries of Zambia and Malawi. The borders are scenes of much to-ing and fro-ing in search of jobs and educational opportunities in neighbouring states. The Malawi have been studied extensively by a comparatively large number of English-speaking scholars. On the basis of these studies and Portuguese investigations, the Malawi have been classified into three principal sub-groups: the Nyanja, the Chewas and the Nsenga. Branches of the Chewa in Mozambique are the Chipeta and Zimba. The Nyassa are a mini-group of the Nyanja. Most of them except the Nsenga speak the Bantu language of Nyanja. During the mid-nineteenth century the invading Ngoni displaced the Nyanja from the Angonia plateau. Ngoni tradition and altitude of the plateau made the new inhabitants the only cattle-raising people in the region. Isolated pockets of Ngoni — a small ethnic group in Mozambique but important historically — are also found in Cabo Delgado district and the extreme south.

The varied peoples of the lower Zambezi cannot be easily included within the large ethnic groups above and below the River. For thousands of years the Zambezi valley route furthered a rich cultural diffusion by African and non-African immigrants, traders and conquerors, and consequently an intense acculturation was fostered among the inhabitants. But although they have been intermarried and connected for scores of generations, the lower Zambezi peoples speak distinct dialects and hold to separate identities.

Back from the mouth of the Zambezi and along the left bank live the Chuabo people (known also as the Manganja). They were a branch of the Malawi expansion. The Podzo inhabit the opposite side of the river. Also on the south bank but up river from the Podzo dwell the Sena whose origins probably derive from the Shona but they show many heterogeneous traits. Further westward and on both sides of the river are located the Tawara and Tonga. They manifest characteristics of the Shona to the south, which prompts some scholars to exclude them from classification with the peoples of the lower Zambezi and to place them with the Shona. Finally, the Chikunda, who are scattered today in Malawi and on the lower Zambezi valley have evolved from the private armies and wars of the Portuguese estate owners along the river. Culturally similar are the Nyungwe (Nhungues) who more likely came to Mozambique from the north. Their language is widely spoken on the Zambezi.

South of the Zambezi the peoples have been better studied than many of the north because of greater Portuguese interest and the observations by South Africans and Rhodesians of those groups extending into their respective territories. The Shona groups occupy the country to the south of Zambezi in much of Rhodesia and below the Save River in Mozambique. Their ancestors were responsible for establishing great kingdoms, stone structures and a complex religion. Among the most important Shona sub-groups are the Karanga, Manyka, Teve, Barue and Ndau. The name of the sub-group Karanga (Caranga), who inhabit the Mashonaland plateau region, was applied by the early Portuguese observers to all Shona. Showing common cultural and linguistic origins, the Tawara and especially the Tonga have been recently classified as members of the Shona.

Southern Mozambique is inhabited by three distinct groups: the Tonga, Chopi and Thonga.[4] The Thonga occupy most of the lands from just north of the Save to the Maputo River on the South African frontier. They get on well with the Shona to the north. These patrilineal people are members of sub-groups and clans whose hereditary chiefs have had wide political, religious and military powers. Second largest group in Mozambique, the Thonga are in turn divided into the following sub-groups: Rhonga, Shangana, Hlengwe and Tswa. The Rhonga, who live in the area encircling the city of Lourenço Marques, have been best situated to take advantage of education and urban employment in the capital. Along the axis of the Limpopo dwell the Shangana. Named for a nineteenth-century Ngoni chief,they were formed from nearby Thonga peoples incorporated into the military organization, and stubbornly resisted the Portuguese advances under their last ruler, Gungunyane, to the end of the nineteenth century. Inhabiting the region along the Save are the Hlengwe who have experienced little outside influence and have retained many ancient practices. They live almost entirely from hunting and foraging. The Tswa, who live south of the Save and behind the coastal area, have absorbed many of the Ngoni customs. The Ngoni, whose northern counterparts have been noted above, also exist in small numbers on the Swaziland and South African borders and retain their separate identity.

Until Frelimo took control about 40 per cent of Thonga males legally and illegally journeyed to South Africa and even some to Rhodesia to work in mines. The governments in the concerned countries and Thonga society intself encouraged this for the financial rewards each received. This labour exodus drew sharp criticism due to the agricultural underdevelopment of the southern sector of the country as well as the hardships imposed on the workers and their fatherless families. As one consequence of their stay in foreign lands, some migrants have acquired literacy in English, and brought back independent African religions such as the Ethiopian movements found in South Africa.

There are two other main ethnic groups of southern Mozambique—Chopi and Tonga. Both groups also sent male workers outside the country and both sexes moved to urban life in Mozambique. Located on the coast of Inhambane and Gaza districts they have had close exposure to Methodist and Catholic teachings and education in their home territory. The Tonga are not the same as those in Tete district. Of Shona origin the Chopi are also accomplished musicians of the *mbila*, a type of xylophone, and users of the bow. Neither instrument is used by their neighbours.

The multiplicity of African ethnic groups should not obscure their many shared customs and historical experiences. Co-operation, mixing and intermarriage have been more the rule than the exception among most groups even before their colonial rulers disarmed them. Before the full tide of the overseas slave trade, defeat of an African people usually involved a loose suzerainty as long as tribute and symbolic allegiance were paid to the conqueror. War and conquest were often due more to the ambitions of individual leaders, the slave trade and the Portuguese exploiting divisions than the animosity of whole groups. The plurality of the groups helped to check the domination of one group over others. Whether the pressure for jobs, education and privileges of modern society will exacerbate ethnic distinctions as elsewhere in Africa remains to be seen.

The Indians, Chinese and Europeans make up the non-African population of Mozambique. The Indians originated from Pakistan, India and the former Portuguese enclaves of Goa, Diu and Damão in India and have immigrated to Mozambique for generations. Census statistics of 1960 reported 17,243 persons of Indian appearance, but their influence in government and small business, particularly upcountry, far outweighed their small numbers. The Goans have been proud of their adopted Catholic faith and diluted Portuguese parentage, and often loyally served the faraway Lisbon government. Other Indian groups adhered either to Hindu or Islam and, when clustered together in communities, strengthened their ethnicity by conducting classes in Urdu and Gujarati. Their economic competition and profits sent to India have been resented by Europeans and Africans.

The Chinese, of whom there were listed only 2,098 in 1960, have continued a sense of community through schools and associations. Most are self-employed in agriculture, fishing, or commerce. Africans have not regarded them with the same dislike as they have manifested toward Indian peddlers and and shopkeepers.

The Portuguese are the largest non-African group in the country. Only 3,000 British and Germans lived in Mozambique before independence. They were involved in business and large-scale sugar and sisal production. But, estimates of the Portuguese in 1974 place their numbers at some 230,000; more than two-thirds were born in Portugal. At the time of writing about 200,000 had fled with the southerly progress of the war in 1974 and independence in 1975. Most lived in the south or urban centres on the coast where they predominated in commerce, industry, civil service and the military. Their history, activities and beliefs, as those of many of the African peoples so briefly sketched above, form much of the story in this study.

APPENDIX

NOTES

1. After 1961 the Portuguese officially considered all inhabitants of Mozambique as Portuguese citizens and made no distinction in census figures between ethnic groups. The published censuses since then listed only the numbers of people living in the districts of the country. The estimates in the text come from a manuscript prepared by Antonio Rita-Ferreira, head of the Department of Information and Tourism in Lourenço Marques. It was published as 'The Ethno-History and Ethnic Grouping of the Peoples of Moçambique', in *South African Journal of African Affairs*, Vol. 3, No. 1 (1973), pp. 56-76, but with several errors in translation. Rita-Ferreira lists only 25,000 Makonde but this apparently excluded those living in exile. The 1950 census showed 136,225 Makonde in Mozambique. The returning refugees will also enlarge the numbers of other groups in the north and north-west.
2. *Anuario do Estado de Moçambique, 1972-1973* (Lourenço Marques: Oficinas Gráficas da Minerva Central, 1973), p. 14.
3. Allison Butler Herrick et al., *Area Handbook for Mozambique* (Washington: US Government Printing Office, 1969), p. 110.
4. For a recent and an authoritative discussion of the three major groups in southern Mozambique, see Alan K. Smith, 'The Peoples of Southern Mozambique: An Historical Survey', *Journal of African History*, Vol. XIV, No. 4 (1973), pp. 563-80.

APPENDIX II

President Samora Moises Machel's Message at the Investiture of the Transitional Government, 20 September 1974.

Mozambican Women and Men,
FRELIMO militants and
combatants,

The investiture of the Trasitional Government opens a new phase in our history, the phase of the final march towards independence.

Today we are assuming leadership in the government of our country in a period of transition which will lead to the proclamation of Mozambique's total and complete independence on 25 June 1975, the anniversary of the founding of FRELIMO.

We have inherited a difficult and serious social, economic, financial and cultural situation resulting from centuries of oppression and colonial plunder, aggravated by decades of colonial-fascist domination and repression and further exacerbated by the recent criminal adventure of a small band of racists and reactionaries in the city of Lourenço Marques.

We are faced with a heritage of widespread illiteracy, disease, poverty and hunger. We see our people, and particularly the people in the countryside, living in subhuman conditions of poverty and exploitation. We see destruction, resentment, and hatred created by centuries of oppression and instigated by the colonial war of aggression the reactionaries, colonialists and fascists launched in order to divide and confuse us.

It is thus a complex situation that the Transitional Government has before it, and the tasks it faces, therefore, are difficult. However, the difficulties were even greater a little over a decade ago, when we started our thrust towards national liberation. We do not hide the difficulties, nor do we shut our eyes to them. But nothing can make us forget that we are today entering upon an exalting phase in our history: for the first time the Mozambican people have a Government of their own, a Government of their representatives, a Government to serve them.

Thus the Mozambican people have an instrument both able and prepared to face the serious problems of the present phase: a Government led by FRELIMO and which has within it militants seasoned in the tough struggle for national liberation, in political and armed struggle, in clandestine struggle.

VICTORY

Our people's experience of a State and Government, the experience of all
workers has been that State and Government are oppressive structures,
hostile forces compelling us to submit and resign ourselves to foreign
domination, to the domination of big financial interests.

Under FRELIMO's leadership, the Transitional Government has the
fundamental task of creating the conditions for People's Democratic Power
to be extended to areas which up to now are still under colonial
domination. Whereas for the millions of Mozambicans who have
established their power in the liberated zones this is already a reality and a
practical experience, the same is not true for the remainder of the country.

This means that we all need to learn what our power is and how to
exercise it. We shall all need to know what distinguishes our power from
colonial power.

Power belongs to the people. It has been won by the people and it must
be exercised and defended by the people.

Before the people's victory, power belonged to colonialism and was the
expression of the domination of our countries by companies.

Who ruled? The rulers were those who served the interests of a handful
of big exploiters.

Years of rule enabled them to accumulate fortunes through the abuse of
power, by theft, large sums given in exchange for favours granted to the
companies, rewards for ceding the country's resources and even for selling
human beings.

After serving their term as governors they immediately joined the boards
of directors of large enterprises where they received inflated salaries as
payment for services rendered.

The government of the exploiter was characterized by privilege, despotic
arrogance, favouritism, nepotism and lawlessness. Problems were solved
through the system of string pulling, and such basic rights as the right to
work were made to seem like favours from the rulers. Even a woman's
dignity had exchanged value for obtaining employment.

Today, for the first time in Mozambique's history, comrades are being
appointed to government posts.

When we say comrades we are using a word bathed in· blood and
sacrifices. Comrades are those who have fought in clandestinity, those who
suffered torture and death in the prisons, those who gave of their bodies
and intellect on the battlefield, those who built freedom, those who made
us what we are, those capable of translating their aspirations into action,
who have devoted their lives to the service of our people.

The comrades who are today being given the difficult task of conducting
the State machinery until the proclamation of independence are precisely
the representatives of the people in the leadership of the State.

This representativeness has been earned in the varied and hard tasks of the politico-military struggle for national liberation. They are all veterans of the people's struggle, seasoned in the toughest school of government: the struggle for national liberation and national reconstruction in the liberated zones.

No one can claim that they are representatives of a race, ethnic group, region or religious belief. They represent the working people, their sacrifices and aspirations, the whole people from the Rovuma to the Maputo, without distinction as to race, ethnic group or religion. No one fought for a region, race, tribe or religion. We all fought and are still fighting for the same nation, for the single ideal of liberating our people.

The authenticity of the people's representatives in the leadership of the State is more than just an assertion: it must be manifested in the content of government action and in the method of work.

LEADERSHIP AND GOVERNMENT

To govern is not to issue laws and decres which the masses do not understand the reasons for but which everyone must comply with for fear of being punished.

To govern one needs to know exactly the interests of the working masses, formulated and discussed with them and not merely on their behalf. To govern is to be able to fulfill those interests in the decision taking.

To govern is always to be closely linked with the masses in order to sound out their preoccupations and discuss with them so as to come to a correct decision together not disregarding the details of everyday matters on the pretext that they are minor problems. A decision taken in this way mobilizes people and any difficulties or obstacles which crop up will be overcome because the people understand the decision and see it as their own.

Conversely, the Government will be unable to solve any problem if it remains enclosed in a building, governing by bureaucratic and administrative methods. The solution of the problems of the masses and of the country is more political than administrative. Therefore it is FRELIMO's political line, forged in the intransigent struggle to defend the interests of the masses, that must guide Government action; it is FRELIMO that must orientate the Government and the masses.

In every factory, every department, every service, every commercial establishment, in every agricultural enterprise, Party Committees must be formed to implement the watchwords of FRELIMO and the Transitional Government, thus releasing the people's initiative and setting in motion the masses' creative ability.

We will thus establish true democracy throughout the country, which is the essential principle of FRELIMO which has guided political life within the organization and in national reconstruction in the liberated areas.

FRELIMO's People's Democratic Government is also distinguished from the colonialist government by its collective working style, joint discussions and analysis of problems, mutual co-operation and the elimination of the compartmentalization of work sectors. Thus and only thus can government actions be harmonious and efficient.

Our Government's action must be guided first and foremost by our political line. The political must never be subordinated to the technical. In practice this means that in each productive unit, in each Ministry, in each public service throughout the whole of our nation, our main effort must be to develop people's consciousness of their destiny, their awareness that to build Mozambique, to build freedom, means work, doing away with laziness and poverty.

We also want to call attention to a key factor: the need for leaders to live according to FRELIMO's political line, the need for them to represent the sacrifices made by the masses in their behaviour. Power and the facilities which surround rulers can easily corrupt the firmest man.

We therefore want them to live modestly and with the people, not turning the task entrusted to them into a privilege, a means of accumulating property or handing out favours.

Material, moral and ideological corruption, bribery, seeking comforts, string pulling, nepotism, that is favours based on friendship, and especially giving preferential employment to relatives, friends or people from one's own region, all this is characteristic of the system which we are destroying. Tribalism, regionalism, racism and unprincipled alliances are serious onslaughts on our political line and divide the masses. Because power belongs to the people those who exercise it are servants of the people.

Anyone who thus deforms our line can expect no tolerance from us. We shall be intransigent on this, as we were during the hard war years. We shall never have any hesitation in exposing to the masses crimes committed against them. Deviations from our line breed contradictions, cracks through which the enemy, imperialism and the reactionary forces can enter.

To maintain the austerity required for our life as militants and thus preserve the meaning of the sacrifices of our people, all FRELIMO militants with government tasks must now as in the past shun material preoccupations, particularly regarding salaries. What is more, we cannot tolerate one of our representatives owning means of production or exploiting the labour of others.

SALARIES

For 10 years we fought without any concern of an individual financial nature, involved only in devoting all our energy to serving the people. This is the characteristic of FRELIMO's militants, cadres and leaders.

As we have always done and in accordance with our means, we try to ensure that each militant who carries out a task has the minimum material conditions required for his work, his sustenance and that of his family. But we must also not forget that we have often fought and won with bare feet, dressed in rags and hungry.

It must also be stressed that just as we fought a war without a timetable, without vacations, without days of rest, we must engage in the battle for national reconstruction in the same spirit.

This means that as always, the decisive factor for our victory is identifying with our line and implementing it, rejecting luxuries, fighting corruption to practise austerity, and fighting extravagance.

The watchword is work and self-sacrifice.

If the Government is to be really capable of making the interests of the working masses its own and never deviating from serving the people, it is essential that it remains constantly under FRELIMO's leadership.

Within FRELIMO are the organized masses, conscious of their true interests. Within FRELIMO are the militants forged and seasoned in the people's struggle, guaranteeing the intransigent defence of the interests of the workers and the Revolution. Hence, only FRELIMO is capable of organizing, guiding, orientating and leading the millions of Mozambican women and men in the present battle to build People's Democratic Power and for national reconstruction.

The Government is FRELIMO's instrument at the State level, the executive arm of the people's will. If the arm is amputated from the body it will rapidly decay and decompose.

State power has been won through the struggle of our people, united by our correct line, under FRELIMO's leadership. At the start the broad masses were not organized, we had neither weapons nor State power. Colonialism had the subjugated masses, economic and military strength and the State apparatus. Colonialism lost everything because the people were not with it and it had neither a correct political line nor just leadership.

This means that a Government which deviates from the people's interests, from FRELIMO's political line and leadership, is like the colonial-fascist regime, bound to be overthrown.

Led by FRELIMO, the Transitional Government begins its action today.

Although it is not for us to spell out the Transitional Government's programme, since this is its own task, it is nevertheless necessary to define, as from now, the tasks which must be undertaken by FRELIMO, the Government and the masses at this decisive moment in our country's reconstruction.

These have to do with mobilizing and organizing the masses, with institutions of government and national reconstruction, and finally with the People's Forces for the Liberation of Mozambique, the armed wing of our working people.

As regards the State and its institutions, it is first necessary to decolonize and, secondly, to build the appropriate structures for People's Democratic Power.

DECOLONIZATION

Decolonization does not mean the geographical transfer of the decision-making centres from Lisbon to Lourenço Marques, which the deposed regime was in fact already proposing to do, and neither it is the continuation of the oppressive regime, this time with black-skinned rulers, which is the neo-colonial pattern.

To decolonize the State means essentially to dismantle the political, administrative, cultural, financial, economic, educational, juridical and other systems which as an integral part of the colonial State, were solely designed to impose foreign domination and the will of the exploiters on the masses.

In this, although we can seek inspiration and stimulation from the revolutionary experience of other peoples, we shall build in the foundation of our own originality, basing ourselves on the specific conditions of our country. We shall thus also enrich the revolutionary heritage of humanity, a duty we have been fulfilling over these hard years of struggle.

The decisive factor for our success is the unity of our people from the Rovuma to the Maputo. The enemy rose and will always rise against this unity: yesterday's colonialism and today's reactionaries and imperialists, exploiters from every race.

As in the past, they will try to use everything. Overt or covert appeals to racism, tribalism and regionalism will be intensified. We will make relentless use of the same liberating fire that wiped out colonialism in opposing racism, tribalism and regionalism, because these are the commanders-in-chief of the enemy's forces which attack and destroy our people's unity, the main weapon in our struggle. These are the essential instruments which weakened our people in the past and allowed them to be dominated.

As regards our action in the field of socio-economic development, it is necessary right away to lay down a number of priorities, so as to know how to orientate our efforts.

We inherited a colonial economic structure in which the productive factors did not serve our country or our people, but foreign domination. We must combat this situation by laying the foundations of an independent economy to serve the working masses.

The Transitional Government must try as rapidly as possible to solve the serious financial problems, in particular the monetary situation and the establishment of a Mozambican Bank of Issue, and make a frontal attack on the most pressing problems of the broad masses in our country: hunger and lack of clothing and housing.

These ills were not an act of fate, but a result of the system of exploitation. If the productive efforts of the working masses are made within a system of social organization which fights exploitation, these problems will be gradually eliminated, as the evidence of our liberated areas shows.

Faced with the present economic and financial situation, characterized by a balance of payments deficit and a rapidly rising cost of living, especially as regards essential goods, our economic strategy must be based on the principle of relying on our own efforts, with emphasis on the following watchwords: austerity and work.

The present situation demands, on the one hand, that we fight against superfluous and luxury consumption, avoid wastage and accept sacrifices. On the other hand, we must throw ourselves fully into the economic development of our country, which means stepping up production and raising productivity.

Indeed, economic development is essentially the result of work. More work means higher production, which in turn enables us to raise our standard of living.

With the conquest of political power by the people, the foundations are laid for solving the problems of the working masses in accordance with their interests.

Adequate structures will be established for the correct solution of problems which crop up in labour relations.

Mere wage increases will not solve the problems facing the working masses especially since in the present situation they would inevitably be transferred to price increases which would automatically cancel out the higher purchasing power.

Under these conditions, at this stage in the life of our country, there is no more reason for strikes because our main concern should be to restructure and relaunch our economy.

Another defect which is characteristic of the structure we have inherited is the tremendous imbalance in regional development, particularly the imbalance between town and countryside.

The overwhelming majority of our people live in the countryside, and it is in the countryside that are to be found the natural resources which must be developed so as to make our country prosper. It was the countryside that most suffered from the destructive effects of war and it is in the countryside that the clearest signs of hunger can be seen. It is therefore towards the countryside that our main efforts to improve the living conditions of the masses will be directed. Priority must be given to the development of our agriculture, animal husbandry and the most effective use of our sub-soil resources.

Agriculture will therefore be the base of our development and industry its galvanizing factor.

Industrial development must be based on the processing of our natural resources, which will make it possible for diversity and increase the value of exports.

EDUCATION

We must launch an unyielding struggle against the vestiges of colonialism, decadent values, erroneous ideas, the attitude of uncritically imitating foreigners, and against immorality. We must affirm and develop our Mozambican personality by strengthening our unity, constantly exchanging experiences and merging the contributions made by all of us. In this respect we must bear in mind that the city is one of the centres of vice and corruption and of alienating foreign influences.

We will place training, education and culture primarily, at the service of the broad masses oppressed and humiliated by the system of colonialist and capitalist exploitation. The blood of our people was not shed only to free the land from foreign domination, but also to reconquer our Mozambican personality to bring about the resurgence of our culture and to create a new mentality, a new society. The priority aim of education will be to wage a vigorous battle against illiteracy, a product of colonialism which today affects the overwhelming majority of our people. This effort must be centred especially on rural areas, where schools are practically non-existent.

The schools must be fronts in our vigorous and conscious battle against illiteracy, ignorance and obscurantism. They must be centres for wiping out the colonial-capitalist mentality and the negative aspects of the traditional mentality: superstition, individualism, selfishness, elitism and ambition must be fought in them. There should be no place in them for social, racial or sexual discrimination. Above all, the masses must have both access to and power in the schools, universities and culture.

We are engaged in a Revolution whose advance depends on the creation of the new man, with a new mentality. We are engaged in a Revolution aimed at the establishment of People's Democratic Power. Therefore at school level we must be able to introduce collective work and create an open climate of criticism and self-criticism. Teachers and pupils must learn from one another in a climate of mutual trust and harmonious comradely relations in which it will be possible to release the initiative of each and develop the talents of all, so that all grow together in the great task of national reconstruction.

Our schools must truly be centres for the propagation of national culture and political, technical and scientific knowledge. The propaganda of knowledge must be aimed at mobilizing nature and human potentialities for development and progress of society.

DEMOCRATIZATION

It is therefore necessary to democratize teaching methods. Pupils and trainees must play a responsible part in creating a school of a new type in which manual labour is accorded its due value as one of the sources of knowledge, closely related to practice, drawing inspiration from it and serving the people.

Raising the living conditions of the masses demands fighting disease by improving health conditions. We have inherited a situation in which the vast majority of medical personnel and equipment is concentrated in the towns to serve the minority which can pay, and what is more this takes the form of intense racial and social discrimination in hospitals.

As from now, we must throw ourselves enthusiastically into health work among the broad masses, so as to wipe out the causes of disease, improve eating habits by enriching the diet and eliminating unhygienic traditions. In this field priority must be given to preventive medicine, which is in line with our present capacity and faciliies.

This work is not simply a bureaucratic or technical task, but above all a political battle, demanding the mobilization of the people which is now possible on a national scale because the people are in power.

The judiciary must be reorganized so as to make justice accessible and comprehensible to the ordinary citizen of our land. The bourgeois system surrounded the administration of justice with unnecessary complexity, with legalism which made it inaccessible to the masses, with deliberately confusing and misleading jargon, and with such slow proceedings, and high costs as to create a barrier between the people and justice. In short, the existing legal system in our country serves the rich and is accessible only to them. The path we want to follow is that of simplifying and speeding up the application of justice, within the framework of new laws and rules which the Transitional Government must begin to study immediately, bearing in mind the existing situation and the gradual transformation which must be effected.

The basic policy in the field of justice should be inspired by our experience in the liberated areas, where crimes and offences have been almost completely eliminated owing to two combined factors: the improvement of the people's living conditions and the heightening of their political consciousness by thorough and constant political work. This means that it must be our concern to prevent crime by eliminating its causes.

It is the duty of the People's Forces for the Liberation of Mozambique, FRELIMO's army, the people in arms, an army of peasants and workers, to consolidate the people's victory and defend the Revolution.

FRELIMO's army is not a barracks army. It is an army which studies, produces and fights. This means that the army must have a study centre so that its members, especially veteran militants of the national liberation struggle, have the possibility of continuing to raise their political, educational, cultural and technical level. It will thus be possible further to develop our army's operational and organizational capacity, and it will be able fully to assume the defence of the nation.

At the same time we find in the army people who come from every region of our country, bringing with them the rich and varied traditions of our people. In the army these traditions are harmoniously merged, ceasing to be regional and local culture to become national culture. So, being a centre of cultural fusion, our army also is a centre for the propagation of national culture among the broad masses. We must never forget that an army without culture is an army without national personality, with no popularly based motivation, and hence it is a weak army.

Now as in the past, every unit of the People's Forces for the Liberation of Mozambique must continue to be a production centre. FRELIMO's army is not an army of parasites; it is an army with a tradition of productive labour, an army which produces for its own subsistence, which helps the people to improve their living conditions and learn about new production methods and new crops. This work must be continued.

At the same time the PFLM must remain actively vigilant and in a state of constant preparedness, so as to put down any attempt at external aggression as well as any attempt by reactionaries aimed at jeopardizing independence, sabotaging national reconstruction and destroying the Revolution.

The PFLM also have the task of mobilizing and organizing the broad masses. Since the start of the struggle, our combatants have been actively carrying out political work among the masses which contributed decisively to our victory over colonialism. This work must continue and even more vigorously, guided by the objectives which correspond to the new phase.

At this hour of struggle and also of happiness, we must not allow ourselves to be carried away by feelings of victory and excessive euphoria. The PFLM must be well aware that they come from the people, that it was the people who built our victory, and that they are our only heroes. It is therefore by remaining closely linked with the people, by still organizing the masses, that we will be able to win the new battle in which we are now engaged.

One of the major fronts in the struggle for the genuine liberation of our people is the liberation of women.

Mozambican women are still weighed down by two burdens: on the one hand reactionary traditions which deprive them of initiative in society and reduce them to mere instruments of men, and on the other, the colonial-capitalist system which regards them as objects of exploitation and a means of production. We must wage a close struggle for the emancipation of women and the restoration of their dignity.

We must, in particular, but an immediate end to that supremely degrading expression of the colonial-capitalist system, prostitution, the sale of the body as though it were a mobile shop. The Transitional Government has the task of reintegrating these elements in society through productive labour.

Finally we wish to address ourselves to Mozambique's white population whether Portuguese or foreign nationals in general. The first words we wish to convey to them are words of calm and trust. FRELIMO has never fought against the Portuguese people or against the white race. FRELIMO is an organization for all Mozambicans without distinction as to race, colour, ethnic group or religion. Our struggle has always been against the colonial system of oppression and exploitation. Therefore all those who live off their honest labour, whom we know to be the overwhelming majority of the white population, have a positive contribution to make to our country's national reconstruction together with the entire Mozambican people.

At the same time, we wish to remind the whole people that, with this phase, we are not entering upon a new era of race relations in Mozambique: all superiority and inferiority complexes created and reinforced by centuries of colonialism must be completely eliminated. The white population must wage a profound internal struggle and eliminate the attitudes of superiority and paternalism towards blacks and other racial groups which still influence the minds of many, so as to blend in with the Mozambican people as a whole.

This watchword is also valid for many people in the Asian community and many mulattoes, who still regard themselves as superior or different to the black population.

The black population must also wage internal struggle against the inferiority complexes instilled in it by centuries of colonialism, and which fascism rendered particularly acute. These are the complexes behind the reactions of individual revenge and hatred which are contrary to our policy.

FRELIMO fought for the people's interest and can never allow the sacrifices made to be used as an instrument of personal revenge and hatred, however great the burden of suffering and humiliation under colonialism.

There are no superior and inferior races. But it is not enough to talk about racial harmony for everyone to get on well together from one day to the next. What is needed is the political work of constant explanation, a conscious effort to change attitudes and habits, a deliberate effort to make people of the different races which go to make up our people live together in harmony. The togetherness which must be established must be full and real, and not just superficial togetherness during hours of work and in professional relations. Most especially, clubs and associations based on racial, ethnic or regional origins must be transformed into associations for all Mozambicans, into centres of Mozambican culture where all can meet in a healthy spirit of true fraternity, and with a clearly defined political line on the building of a new society. We should like especially to draw attention to the fact that since the fact of being Mozambican is not determined by skin colour, language, religious belief, social origin or sex, we must vigorously combat the minority concept which some people are trying to instill in the minds of especially white Mozambicans.

There are no minorities, there are no special rights or duties for any sector of the Mozambican people: we are all Mozambicans with the rights that work gives us, and with the identical duty of building a united, prosperous, just, harmonious, peaceful and democratic nation.

In all we have said we have kept the dominant idea that politics must guide Government action, and that this action will not succeed unless it is fully understood by the masses.

Hence the chief task of all FRELIMO militants is to further the work of organizing the masses and guiding them in each factory, each agricultural unit, each PFLM detachment, each co-operative, each neighbourhood, each department, so that the government is constantly aware of the people's feelings and thoughts. In other words the FRELIMO militant's work is to create the conditions to release the creative initiative of the masses, to free them from passive obedience and to create structures and channels through which the will of the masses can determine government action.

This also means that they should not passively wait for solutions sent down from on high by the minister in his office, but, on the contrary, what can be done immediately by relying on one's own efforts should be analysed in every productive unit, village, neighbourhood, and family cell. At the same time, and guided by FRELIMO's political line, suggestions on organization and improvement which contribute to progress and increase productivity in each sector must be studied and formulated.

For this purpose, in each place of work or residence a Party Committee should be set up, comprising the militants who are most dedicated and most committed to the cause of independence, progress, democracy and the Mozambican Revolution.

Another task of these Committees and of all the people is active and constant vigilance against open or disguised sabotage attempts by agents of colonialist reaction who, although they have lost the decisive battle have not yet laid down their arms and still have accomplices at various levels.

All those attepts must be publicly exposed in order to neutralize those responsible. Yet we shall never allow this task to be used for settling personal scores, attempts at personal advancement for selfish ends or any kind of manifestation of racism.

We can therefore see that the action of racist and colonialist forces will sometimes take the form of overt or covert sabotage, that is, of typical reactionary activities.

Such action is doomed to fail because one will be dealing with a clearly defined enemy. Therefore, reactionary action will also take other more insidious forms which, assuming a revolutionary appearance, will in fact be aimed at creating chaos and divisions among our forces. This means that we shall find reactionaries disguised as ultra-revolutionaries, who will demand of the Government drastic and extremist measures, seeking to present them as immediate revolutionary necessities. These elements, as such, are weak, but their action will be aimed at manipulating certain sectors of our population, selfless and militant but politically uneducated sectors which are likely to be used by the enemy.

Ultra-leftism is thus a weapon of reaction.

We should like, on this occasion, to address ourselves to the High Commissioner of the Portuguese Republic in Mozambique, in whom we see a representative of the new leaders of the Portuguese people and Armed Forces Movement.

We wish to reaffirm the friendship which unites us with the Portuguese people, and in particular with the Portuguese democratic forces, a friendship forged in the common struggle against the colonial-fascist regime.

That common struggle continues.

Colonialism has already been buried, Mozambique's independence will be a fact within a few months. Let us therefore definitely turn towards the future. What matters now is to build the future relations between our peoples, between the democratic forces of our countries. And the future relations between our peoples largely depend on the actions of the High Commissioner and on frank and sincere co-operation between the High Commissioner and the Transitional Government.

CO-OPERATION

Together with the High Commissioner, the Transitional Government will build, stone by stone, the edifice of friendship and co-operation which we hope will be a historical example. We are faced with the tremendous challenge of a unique historical situation — the simultaneous liberation of two peoples through a common victory against fascism and colonialism. Neither of us liberated the other, it was mutual liberation through a parallel struggle which must take on new scope in the future.

Even now in the co-operation established between our forces in the struggle against the death throes of colonial-fascist reaction, we presented to the world a singular demonstration of the fact that the identification of peoples in the struggle against a common enemy is not an empty word, but it is possible, open and fruitful, even between yesterday's colonized and those who were forced to be instruments of that colonization.

We therefore expect the High Commissioner, in the spirit of the Lusaka Agreement, to carry out to the full what we regard his most inspiring duties, which are to give impetus to the process of decolonization, eliminate the vestiges of colonialism and lay the foundations for a new type of relations between our peoples.

In line with its political principles, and remaining true to the commitments it has undertaken, FRELIMO will co-operate sincerely with the High Commissioner of the Portuguese Republic and with the Portuguese Armed Forces; so as to fulfil together the tasks of the present phase and build the future.

At this moment, we wish to pay heartfelt and stirring tribute to the memory of all our heroes, to all those who made both us and our country what we are today. Among them all and to remind us of them all, we wish to evoke the unforgettable memory of Comrade Eduardo Chivambo Mondlane, founder member and first President of FRELIMO, the true inspirer and driving force of our struggle, who fell in the national liberation struggle. May his example of heroism and sacrifice be a source of inspiration and encouragement to enable us to fulfil the new tasks.

At a time when the city of Lourenço Marques, and with it the whole of Mozambique, is in mourning because of a fascist adventure, let us be able to transform our sorrow into new strength to galvanize us to continue on the road of building independence, freedom and democracy in our country.

If the destruction of Portuguese colonialism in Mozambique was brought about primarily by sacrifice and efforts of the Mozambican people, it is nevertheless important to emphasize at this time the great contribution united Africa made to this victory, which is the common victory of the liberation movements in the Portuguese colonies and of the entire African liberation movement.

We therefore wish to hail the representatives of the Organization of African Unity who are here to show by their presence their consistent solidarity with our struggle. We particularly wish to hail the representatives of Tanzania and Zambia, great brother peoples who, with heroism and determination were able to assume the role of strategic rear and therefore made our victory possible. Here we honour the memory of the Tanzanian and Zambian brothers who fell victim to colonialist aggression, consolidating through their sacrifices friendship and solidarity which, forged in the hard years of war, will be strengthened and consolidated in peace. Through them we send our greetings to our brothers in all countries bordering on the fighting territories, in Guinea, Senegal, the People's Republic of the Congo and Zaire.

We salute the valuable and decisive contribution made by the generous political, moral and material help given to us by the socialist countries in the highest internationalist spirit.

Through the Assistant Secretary-General of the United Nations, we greet the United Nations Organization and the international community in general, whose growing moral, diplomatic and material support was a powerful factor in encouraging our struggle and isolating the colonial-fascist regime.

We wish to hail especially the support given by the democratic forces throughout the world, by progressive international organizations and revolutionary and anti-colonialist forces in western countries.

In conclusion, we wish to greet the Portuguese people, through the Portuguese democratic forces with whom we forged bonds of militant fraternity during the difficult years of common struggle, bonds which, more than the written words of treaties, are the guarantee of our future friendship and co-operation.

As we engage in this new struggle, we call upon our entire people to remain united, firm and vigilant under the banner of FRELIMO, embarking with enthusiasm, discipline and hard work on the building of a free, developed and democratic Mozambique, under the watchwords: UNITY, WORK, VIGILANCE.

INDEX